# OUR
# SISTER
# EDITORS

# OUR
# SISTER
# EDITORS

## Sarah J. Hale
## and the Tradition of
## Nineteenth-Century American
## Women Editors

### PATRICIA OKKER

The University of Georgia Press
ATHENS & LONDON

Published by the University of Georgia Press
Athens, Georgia 30602
© 1995 by Patricia Okker
Designed by Kathi L. Dailey
Set in Walbaum by Tseng Information Systems, Inc.
Printed and bound by Thomson-Shore, Inc.
The paper in this book meets the guidelines for permanence and
durability of the Committee on Production Guidelines for Book
Longevity of the Council on Library Resources.

Printed in the United States of America

99  98  97  96  95   C  5  4  3  2  1

Quotation of a letter from Sarah Josepha Hale to Kennedy Furlong,
17 February 1855, appears by courtesy of the Yale Collection of American
Literature, Beinecke Rare Book and Manuscript Library, Yale University.
Quotation of a letter from Sarah Josepha Hale to Harpers, 24 July 1850,
appears by courtesy of The Pierpont Morgan Library,
New York (MA 1950).

Library of Congress Cataloging in Publication Data
Okker, Patricia.
Our sister editors : Sarah J. Hale and the tradition of nineteenth-century
American women editors / Patricia Okker.
p.  cm.
Includes bibliographical references and index.
ISBN 0-8203-1686-5 (alk. paper)
1. Hale, Sarah Josepha Buell, 1788–1879—Knowledge—
Communications.   2. Periodicals, Publishing of—United States—
History—19th century.   3. Women in journalism—United States—
History—19th century.   4. Women periodical editors—United States—
Biography.   5. Women authors, American—19th century—Biography.
6. Women publishers—United States—Biography.
PS1774.H2Z83   1995
070.4'8347'092—dc20
[B]      94-15269

British Library Cataloging in Publication Data available

# CONTENTS

# ACKNOWLEDGMENTS

Throughout my work on this project, I have been fortunate to have wonderful readers who have challenged, questioned, and encouraged my thinking on Sarah Hale and women editors. In particular, I thank Nina Baym, Robert Dale Parker, Emily Stipes Watts, and Lauren Onkey for their insightful comments and suggestions.

For assistance with the appendix of women editors, I am grateful to the Research Council and the English Department at the University of Missouri, Columbia, for their generous support, and to Timothy Sougstad for his efficient and diligent work.

I would also like to thank the Beinecke Rare Book and Manuscript Library, Yale University, and the Pierpont Morgan Library for permission to quote from Hale's private letters, and the libraries of the University of Illinois at Urbana-Champaign, the Historical Society of Pennsylvania, and the State Historical Society of Missouri for permission to reproduce illustrations. A section of chapter 6 previously appeared in somewhat different form as "Sarah Josepha Hale, Lydia Sigourney, and the Poetic Tradition in Two Nineteenth-Century Women's Magazines," *American Periodicals* 3 (1993): 32–42.

Finally, I would like to thank my friends and family, especially Richard Edging, for offering the encouragement and support that have nurtured me and this project.

# INTRODUCTION

When Sarah Josepha Hale died in 1879 at the age of ninety, the *Philadelphia Evening Bulletin* devoted a long obituary to reviewing her fifty years as magazine editor, the various women's issues she supported, and her authorship of more than twenty separate publications. Hale was, the *Bulletin* declared in its opening line, a "venerable authoress and editress" (1 May 1879). In many ways this phrase serves as an apt representation of Hale's literary career. At the same time that she was seen as "venerable"—associated with the power usually reserved for an aging patriarch or church official—Hale was also defined as feminine—an "editress," never an editor. Though late twentieth-century readers are likely to see *editress* and *authoress* as derogatory diminutives, Hale, like many women editors of her time, accepted and even championed such designations. Indeed, as the phrase "venerable authoress and editress" suggests, many women editors like Hale envisioned their gendered identity as the source of their power and authority.

*Power* and *authority* are terms clearly appropriate to describe Hale's literary career. As editor of two magazines—first the *Ladies' Magazine* of Boston from 1828 until 1836 and then *Godey's Lady's Book* of Philadelphia from 1837 until 1877—she reviewed thousands of books, regularly contributed fiction and poetry to the magazines, wrote monthly editorials, and published the work of such writers as Nathaniel Hawthorne, Harriet Beecher Stowe, Edgar Allan Poe, and Lydia Sigourney. By all accounts Hale's editorial career was a huge success. Boasting over 150,000 subscribers on the eve of the Civil War, the *Lady's Book* was the most widely read periodical in the United States at the time. Hale's work, though, was not confined to periodicals: she proved equally productive in the book industry. She wrote seven volumes of poetry (two for children), six volumes of fiction, several popular books on cooking and housekeeping, and an ambitious nine-hundred-page reference work about women in history. In addition, she edited more than two dozen books, ranging from poetry anthologies to collections of letters. The quality and quantity of Hale's literary productions earned her the respect of many of her peers, and she was included in the most important literature anthologies of her day.[1]

Although Hale was recognized in her own time as an influential woman of letters, by the early twentieth century her reputation had declined dramatically. She was remembered—if at all—as the woman responsible for establishing Thanksgiving as a national holiday or, even more commonly, simply as the author of "Mary's Lamb," later known as "Mary Had a Little Lamb."[2] One study in 1916, for example, described Hale as a writer "of plays and cook-books; mother alike of Thanksgiving Day and Mary's Little Lamb." Another, in 1961, portrayed her as a writer "of children's verse" and the "author of several cook books, some volumes on family hygiene and an encyclopedia of famous women in history." Still others have minimized her importance by focusing on her appearance rather than her literary accomplishments. Thus she was described in 1969 as looking "like everybody's mother—an ample, full-bosomed, pleasant lady who yet had a no-nonsense air of efficiency about her."[3]

Like many other nineteenth-century women writers, Hale has been criticized by scholars for being "sentimental." Though such attacks generally began early in the twentieth century, as critics attempted to define modernism in opposition to popular literature, the tradition of using *sentimentalism* as a derogatory rather than a descriptive term has continued. Many scholars have resorted to images of decay and disease to emphasize their disdain of Hale's supposed sentimentality. Hale's magazines have repeatedly been described as "reeking" or "infected" with sentimentality or as being little more than "sentimental trash."[4]

Unfortunately, the general condescension toward Hale's literary pursuits has affected the five book-length studies of her life and career.

The earliest and longest such study is Ruth E. Finley's *Lady of Godey's* (1931). Although Finley provides valuable information, she places little emphasis on Hale's literary accomplishments. Finley devotes entire chapters to Hale's efforts to make Thanksgiving a national holiday, to her support of the Bunker Hill Monument, to her involvement with the founding of Vassar College, and to the fashion plates in her magazines, but she summarizes the bulk of Hale's writing career in one chapter: "A Female Writer." The only other chapter that emphasizes Hale's writing focuses on "Mary's Lamb." Finley certainly gives deserved credit to Hale's social activism, but she separates such work from the literary career that made it possible.[5]

Isabelle Webb Entrikin's dissertation on Hale, published in 1946, is more scholarly than Finley's study, and it too offers valuable information about Hale's career. Still, Entrikin's work suffers from many of the same limitations as Finley's. Covering all of Hale's career as well as considerable biographical material in only 136 pages, Entrikin treats Hale's literary pursuits in a manner that is often sketchy and sometimes condescending. Entrikin acknowledges, for example, Hale's "considerable literary reputation" in her own day, but she argues that such a reputation "does not hold up very well today." According to Entrikin, Hale's work can best be summed up by its "timidity" and by the "lack of perception" in her "critical pronouncements."[6]

None of the three more recent books on Hale rectifies these problems. Olive Burt's 1960 biography of Hale, written for juveniles and inaccurately titled *First Woman Editor,* is a semifictional account published as part of a series that includes biographies of the first American cowgirl and Annie Oakley. Norma R. Fryatt's 1975 work stays closer to actual sources than does Burt's book, but it too is aimed at young readers and, like Finley's text, presents Hale as an emblem of quaint Victorian culture rather than as an accomplished writer and editor. The most recent full-length book on Hale, by Sherbrooke Rogers, published in 1985, is the most serious of these three studies, but its primary audience is again older adolescents, and most of the chapters focus on Hale's social rather than literary interests.[7]

The tremendously productive efforts by feminist critics during the past fifteen years to recover nineteenth-century American women's writings have provided an important revision of Hale's literary career. Recent studies by Nicole Tonkovich Hoffman, Barbara Bardes and Suzanne Gossett, and Nina Baym have challenged the assumptions earlier scholars made about Hale and have, in their own ways, reexamined her place in nineteenth-century literary and political culture.[8] Still, much work is needed. Indeed, what is arguably Hale's most important contribution—her editorship of the *Ladies' Magazine* and the *Lady's Book*—has remained until now largely unexamined.

As the first book-length work on Hale's editorial career, this study explores the enormous influence she exerted on nineteenth-century literary culture. Focusing specifically on her theories of the author, the reader, and the text, I examine the ways Hale revised earlier notions about the function and nature of literature. At the base of many of these literary formulations was Hale's understanding of sexual difference and her version of the so-called ideology of separate spheres, which associated men with the competitive world of commerce and public politics and women with morality and domesticity. Hale's particular conception of this ideology suggests its flexibility. While many of her contemporaries employed a separatist rhetoric that depended on a strict and gendered distinction between public and private, Hale manipulated the idea of a women's culture to argue for a separate public space for women—a space, not coincidentally, occupied by women's periodicals.

Although I began this project assuming—as had many previous scholars—that Hale was, like Margaret Fuller, to a great extent an anomaly in the male-dominated periodical industry, I gradually realized that many other nineteenth-century American women carved out a space for themselves as editors of magazines and newspapers. Thus, while Hale's career is certainly unique in its length and influence, it can only be fully understood in the context of the far more comprehensive developments within the periodical industry—including the rise of women's magazines and women editors. Although many nineteenth-century women editors will never be known, if only because their periodicals no longer exist, I have identified more than six hundred American women who edited nineteenth-century periodicals, and it is within this larger context that I begin my study of Hale. Like Hale, many of these women edited periodicals for women and thus worked in a highly gendered—and inherently public—space. Rhetorics of sexual difference and separate spheres were by no means uncontested among these women, and women in the periodical industry—as readers, writers, or editors—frequently challenged each other's assumptions about the nature of womanhood. But whether they were endorsing the idea that women are inherently more moral than men or, conversely, that the mind has "no sex," women editors were more often than not self-conscious about their status as women within the industry. Though their political and ideological perspectives differed considerably, these women editors insisted on the right of women to participate in the public world of the periodical industry and to accept positions of authority within it.

# 1

## Women Periodical Editors in the Nineteenth-Century United States

According to one definition, a magazine is a warehouse, often of ammunition. Given that nineteenth-century periodicals edited by women, such as *Godey's Lady's Book* and the *Ladies' Home Journal,* are more likely to bring to mind fashion plates or doily patterns than explosions and revolutions, such a definition hardly seems fitting here. Still, regardless of the intentions of editors and publishers, magazines edited by women did, at least in some senses, serve explosive functions. Whatever the ideologies they propounded, these periodicals insisted on the right of women to speak in a public forum. In doing so, they challenged a popular nineteenth-century rhetoric—the so-called ideology of separate spheres—that was often interpreted as associating men with the public worlds of politics and commerce and women with private domestic space. By establishing a market for periodicals by and for women, nineteenth-century women rejected the gendered public-private dichotomy and created the idea of a public space for women. I have identified more than six hundred nineteenth-century American women periodical editors (see appendix). Theirs is a rich and varied tradition, which can tell us much about how women—mostly, though not exclusively, white and middle class—used ideologies of gender to establish their place in the periodical marketplace. In constructing an overview of this tradition, I hope to suggest the explosive nature of the public women's space they created and maintained. Though the women editors frequently relied on domestic paradigms, the public space they established inevitably challenged ideologies that defined women's role solely within a domestic space.

The tradition of women editors that thrived in the nineteenth century actually began much earlier with the printers and journalists of colonial America. As Marion Marzolf has explained in her history of women journalists, aptly titled *Up from the Footnote*, at least fourteen women worked as printers before the American Revolution. The earliest was Dinah Nuthead, who began printing in Maryland in 1696. Like many other colonial printers, women printers, including the four women who published weekly newspapers, often assumed editing and publishing duties as well. Legally, of course, they could own no property, so most of these women began their printing careers because of husbands or fathers who taught them the trade or who died and left them the business. Such was the case with Elizabeth Timothy, who edited the *South Carolina Gazette* for seven years after her husband died in 1738. As editor, Timothy published news from the colonies and abroad, reprinted drama and poetry, and published some original contributions of southern writers—all while improving the financial condition of her paper.[1] The ability of women like Timothy to take over their "husbands' " businesses and to do so successfully suggests that many of these papers may have earlier been joint ventures.

The number of women to hold editorial positions remained small in the beginning of the nineteenth century, but women's editorial options were certainly increasing. Some women, like Sarah Hillhouse, continued in the tradition of their colonial predecessors. In 1803, after the death of her husband, Hillhouse began to publish and edit the Washington, Georgia, *Monitor*, a paper whose circulation at the time was eight hundred.[2] Others, however, embarked on editorial careers independent of male family members. After a successful career as a novelist and actress, Susanna Haswell Rowson began writing for and may have begun editing the *Boston Weekly Magazine* in 1802, although it is unclear whether she had any editorial responsibilities. If it was not Rowson, the first woman to edit a magazine in the United States was probably Mary Clarke Carr, who began editing Philadelphia's *Intellectual Regale; or, Ladies' Tea-Tray* in 1814.[3]

Carr and possibly Rowson mark the beginning of a strong trend in nineteenth-century women's editorships: women often edited periodicals intended for women readers. American women's magazines had certainly existed much earlier—the earliest known one was Philadelphia's *Lady's Magazine, and Repository of Entertaining Knowledge,* begun in 1792—but these earlier periodicals were edited by men and consisted to a great extent of paternalistic advice for women. With Rowson's *Boston Weekly* and Carr's *Intellectual Regale,* however, magazines began appearing that were both for women and by women. In the 1820s a number of women began editing periodicals whose titles often proclaimed their appeal to a specifically and exclusively female audience. Editors of the 1820s to seek such an audience included Mrs. Colvin, who began her own *Mrs. A. S. Colvin's Weekly Messenger* from Washington, D.C., in 1822; an anonymous "Lady of Providence," with the *Ladies' Magazine* in 1823; a "Lady," with Indiana's *Western Ladies' Casket* in 1823; another "Lady," with Philadelphia's *Minerva* in 1827; and Rebecca Bates, with Ohio's *Social Circle* in 1827. Harriet Muzzy also found an editorial position focusing on women readers in her work with Thomas C. Clarke's Philadelphia magazines. In 1827 she served as a department editor for *Album and Ladies' Weekly Gazette,* and in 1828 she accepted an assistant editorship with the *Ladies' Literary Port Folio.*

With the rapid growth of American magazines in the late 1820s, women found even more editing opportunities.[4] In 1828 alone, six women began editing American magazines: a "Lady of Providence" at the *Toilet; or, Ladies Cabinet of Literature,* Sarah J. Hale at the *Ladies' Magazine,* Katherine Ware at the *Bower of Taste,* Eliza L. Follen at the *Christian Teacher's Manual,* Julia L. Dumont at the *Chrystal and Ladies' Magazine,* and Frances Wright at the *New-Harmony Gazette.*

In significant ways, this group of editors from 1828 suggests the range of women's editing opportunities throughout the century. Though most women would edit periodicals for other women or for children, Frances Wright's editorship of the *New-Harmony Gazette,* a periodical begun in 1825 that was associated with the socialist community in Indiana, demonstrates that some women could find an audience of both women and men. Wright would be followed later in the century by women like

Jeanette Gilder, who in 1881 co-founded and then edited the *Critic*, New York's journal of literary criticism. Mary Baker Eddy founded the *Christian Science Journal* in 1883. A few women, moreover, edited periodicals intended for a predominantly male audience. In 1868 Myra Bradwell founded and then edited an influential weekly legal newspaper called *Chicago Legal News*.[5]

In addition to suggesting the readership that nineteenth-century women editors would reach, this group of early editors signals the geographic range of their peers throughout the century. Of the six women who began editing in 1828, three worked in Boston, one in Providence, another in Pittsburgh, and one in New Harmony, Indiana. By the 1850s women were editing periodicals in the East (e.g., Boston, New York, Philadelphia, and Washington, D.C.), in what is now the Midwest (Milwaukee, Cincinnati, and Columbus), and to a lesser extent in the South (Madison, Georgia; Greensboro, North Carolina; and Petersburg, Virginia) and in the West (San Francisco). By the post–Civil War years, women editors worked in cities in virtually every part of the country, including Atlanta, Boston, Chicago, Denver, Hartford, Houston, Kansas City, Louisville, Nashville, New Orleans, New York, Philadelphia, Portland (Oregon and Maine), Rochester, St. Louis, Salt Lake City, San Francisco, Syracuse, and Washington, D.C. While many editors did live in or near large cities, many others did not; throughout the century women edited from such places as Zanesville, Ohio; Brunswick, Maine; Seneca Falls, New York; Milton, Wisconsin; Penfield, Georgia; and Muskogee, Creek Nation. This geographic diversity suggests that the Northeast did not dominate nineteenth-century literary culture nearly as much as some literary historians have claimed.

Topically, women editors showed considerable diversity as well. As one might expect, given both nineteenth-century ideologies of gender and the history of American women, periodicals focusing on family and domestic issues, religion, social reform (including suffrage), and literature were the most popular kinds of periodicals for nineteenth-century American women to edit. While these topics remained popular to various degrees throughout the century, patterns of periodical content do emerge that reflect the enormous changes that nineteenth-century American women experienced. During the antebellum period, for instance, when Victorian womanhood was often defined primarily in relation to morality and domesticity, women were more likely to edit periodicals associated with the home and the family than other kinds. Similarly, suffrage papers, though they existed as early as the 1850s, became increasingly common in the 1860s and 1870s, as the women's rights movement gained strength. Again reflecting historical change, women editors frequently focused on temperance in the 1870s and on women's clubs in the 1890s.

While these historical differences represent important changes in the tradition of women's editorships, characterizing women's editing by type of periodical masks the enormous diversity found within categories. Consider, for instance, just four magazines with titles suggesting a domestic subject: the *Mother's Magazine* (1833–88), the *Home Guardian* (1838–92), the *Home* (1856–60), and *Hearth and Home* (1868–75). Despite the similarities in the titles, these four periodicals differed considerably. Abigail Goodrich Whittelsey's *Mother's Magazine* featured material on child care and children's education, and Martha Violet Ball's *Home Guardian* was aimed at helping "fallen" women. In contrast to this emphasis on social reform, Erastus F. Beadle's *Home*, edited by Harriet Ellen Grannis Arey and later Metta V. Victor, consisted of serialized fiction, recipes, biographical and historical sketches, steel engravings, poetry, and book reviews. *Hearth and Home*, whose editors included Harriet Beecher Stowe and Mary Mapes Dodge, began as an agricultural and literary publication but turned increasingly to literature, publishing such writers as Rebecca Harding Davis, Rose Terry Cook, Harriet Spofford, Louisa May Alcott, and Elizabeth Stuart Phelps. To characterize all these periodicals as "domestic" or "family" publications not only hides their variety but also ignores the extent to which their editors resisted narrow definitions of domesticity. Rather than promoting a circumscribed notion of the home, the periodical industry encouraged a broad and diverse paradigm of domesticity.

The diversity that marks domestic publications also appears in other types of periodicals. The social reform periodicals, for instance, treated a wide range of issues, including water cures, suffrage, abolition of slavery, sanitation, Native American rights, temperance, and dress reform.[6] Similarly, the periodicals with either a nominal or substantive religious affiliation included Universalist, Baptist, Catholic, Jewish, Shaker, Mormon, and Christian Scientist papers. A considerable number of spiritualist periodicals were also published, such as the Reverend Mrs. Adeline Buffum's *News from the Spirit World*.[7]

The number of women who edited periodicals not associated with the most common subjects—domestic life, social reform, religion, and literature—also suggests the broad range of women's editorships. Consider a few memorable examples: Ellen S. Tupper, for instance, edited a beekeeping magazine, Mary Sargent Hopkins managed *Wheelwoman*, a bicycle magazine for women, and Theresa A. Nirdlinger edited the *Casket*, a journal for professional undertakers.

The diversity of periodicals edited by women also extended to matters of ethnicity and race. At midcentury Mathilde Franziska Giesler Anneke founded and edited a radical prosuffrage journal for women written in German and published in Milwaukee and later Newark, New Jersey. Similarly, Ida Hansen and Mina Jensen, sisters born in Norway who lived in Iowa in the 1880s, published a magazine for Scandinavian women. Titled *Kvinden og Hjemmet* (The Woman and the Home), their magazine was published in two separate editions—one in Dano-Norwegian, the other in Swedish.

Other women editors, especially those working after the Civil War, turned their attention to Native American peoples and issues. Some of these periodicals were edited by white women and intended for a white audience. While demonstrating the editors' concern about Native Americans, these publications often exhibited considerable ethnocentrism.[8] Similar to these papers for white audiences were those intended for Native Americans but published by the now infamous Indian schools and missions. Like the periodicals directed to whites, these magazines and newspapers generally advocated assimilation. The *Indian's Friend*, for example, boasted the motto "To Aid Civilization, Teach Industry, and Give Religious Instruction to the Indians of Our Country." Some of the school papers, however, especially those published from reservations rather than eastern schools, recognized the values of tribal cultures. The *Hallequah*, for example, was a school monthly founded in 1879 and edited by three women students at the Seneca, Shawnee, and Wyandotte Industrial Boarding School. On the one hand, its emphasis on religion and mission news suggests that it promoted, like other school papers, a policy of assimilation that devalued traditional tribal life. On the other hand, the apparent independence of its editors from school administration, its declared mission to serve not only as a school paper but also as a "newsletter to the neighboring people," and its inclusion of tribal history, some in the Shawnee and Wyandot languages, suggest that this magazine may well have helped its readership sustain tribal identity.[9] Another important periodical that presented tribal culture positively was *Twin Territories: The Indian Magazine,* founded in 1898 and edited by Ora Eddleman (later Ora Eddleman Reed), who was part Cherokee.

A number of African American women also obtained editorial positions during the nineteenth century. Though published in Canada, not the United States, the first periodical edited by an African American woman was likely Mary Ann Shadd Cary's *Provincial Freeman,* a newspaper for freed American blacks issued in the 1850s. Many other African American women assumed editorial positions in the 1880s and 1890s. Some served as department editors for periodicals edited primarily by men, while others undertook primary editing responsibilities.[10] Ida B. Wells Barnett was part owner and editor of the *Memphis Free Speech;* Amelia L. Tilghman edited an African American music magazine, the *Musical Messenger,* in the 1880s; and Amelia E. Johnson edited two African American periodicals, a journal for children and a literary monthly. In the 1890s two important African American periodicals were produced by women. Both Julia Ringwood Coston and Josephine St. Pierre Ruffin hired large staffs of women to help them edit, respectively, *Ringwood's Afro-American Journal of Fashion,* published in Cleveland, and the *Woman's Era,* a Boston journal associated with African American women's clubs.[11]

The diversity of these editorships—in readership, geography, and contents—does not necessarily suggest any literary importance. One could argue, as scholars have long assumed, that periodicals that focus on fashion, like Coston's, or others that feature domestic life or politics have no place in literary history. Still, most women editors did demonstrate some interest in fiction and poetry, and many magazines edited by and for women concentrated on literature, including Sarah J.

Hale's *Godey's Lady's Book*, Louisa Knapp's *Ladies' Home Journal*, Ann Stephens's *Portland Magazine*, and Harriet Farley and Harriot Curtis's *Lowell Offering*, a magazine for the young women factory workers in Lowell, Massachusetts. Other less specifically literary periodicals also included poetry and fiction amid their other contents. Ida Hansen and Mina Jensen's *Kvinden og Hjemmet* featured two literary supplements, and fiction appeared in *Ringwood's Afro-American Journal of Fashion*. Similarly, Anne Royall's *Huntress*, which focused on congressional events, included some tales, and Ora Eddleman's *Twin Territories: The Indian Magazine* published poetry, fiction, essays on Native American history and culture, and reports on local and regional politics.

To suggest the possible importance of this material to the study of American literature, I would like to compare some circulation figures. The transcendentalist periodical the *Dial*, well established in literary history and the canon, had an estimated circulation of no more than three hundred, slightly fewer, that is, than the *Hallequah*, the school paper edited by women students at the Seneca, Shawnee, and Wyandotte Industrial Boarding School in Indian Territory. Many other publications edited by women boasted much higher subscription rates. The Swedish and Dano-Norwegian publications produced by the Hansen-Jensen sisters eventually reached a combined circulation of 80,000, and in 1860 *Godey's Lady's Book* claimed 150,000 readers—five hundred times more readers than the *Dial*.[12] My point here is not to dismiss the *Dial* as insignificant because of its small circulation but to argue that we must expand our understanding of the important literary documents of the nineteenth century. For the 80,000 readers that Ida Hansen and Mina Jensen reached, most of whom, presumably, were women in the process of becoming "American," *Kvinden og Hjemmet* may well have contributed to an understanding of American literature and America itself. Careful study of such periodicals will most certainly provide us new texts for our classrooms and libraries.

As this overview demonstrates, most nineteenth-century women editors managed periodicals, however diverse, that were intended primarily for women, and their magazines and newspapers frequently proclaimed a gendered, separatist identity in titles such as *Ladies'*

*Wreath, Woman's Era*, and *Ladies' Friend*. In working with such gendered periodicals, women editors inevitably employed various rhetorics of separate spheres, which assumed men and women to be so
essentially different that they lived in separate worlds. I use the term
*rhetorics* to describe this ideology in order to emphasize that "separate spheres" constituted neither a monolithic ideology nor necessarily
any reflection of "reality." Certainly, the allusions to separatism within
just the titles of nineteenth-century women's magazines suggest the
extent to which the meaning of *separate spheres* was deeply contested.
Some of the periodicals with gendered separatist titles, like Charlotte E. McKay's *True Woman*, supported those values—piety, purity,
domesticity, and submissiveness—that Barbara Welter has associated
with the "cult of true womanhood."[13] Many others, however, like the
*Woman's Campaign*, the *Woman's Chronicle*, the *Woman's Journal*,
and the *Woman's Standard*, used an almost identical rhetoric within
the suffrage movement. Generally, of course, periodicals used different
terms—most notably *ladies* or *woman*—to signal their political orientation, but neither marker was stable. Both the *Ladies' Own Magazine*
(published from 1869 until 1874) and *Moore's Western Ladies' Book*
(published in the late 1840s and 1850s) used the more conservative (and
more class-oriented) term *ladies*, but these magazines also supported
women's rights. The metaphoric nature of such separatist identifications is also demonstrated by the many periodicals, such as *Godey's
Lady's Book*, that were read by both women and men.[14]

Although the ideology of separate spheres is most often identified with the antebellum period, editors drew on separatist rhetorics
throughout the century. Some periodicals did change names late in the
century to become less gendered—the term *Lady's* was dropped from
*Godey's Lady's Book* in 1892, for example—but many new magazines
appeared with the same separatist markers employed decades before.
The *Woman's Home Companion* was first published in 1874, and the
*Ladies' Home Journal* began in 1883. While specifically gendered periodicals for women remained popular throughout the century, very few
periodicals of the time identified themselves as being written exclusively for men. Periodicals did exist, of course, that were read almost
entirely by men, but they tended to identify their audience by occu-

pation or political affiliation, not by gender. The ideology of separate spheres, then, was an inherent part of the periodical industry only for women, and this rhetoric survived long after the antebellum years.

The obvious question to ask is why these separatist rhetorics appealed to so many women editors. That is, whom did these rhetorics empower, and how were they employed within the nineteenth-century periodical industry?

The emergence of women editors in the 1820s provides a good starting point for examining the power of these separatist rhetorics. Although the dramatic increase of women editors in the late 1820s resulted in part from the rapid growth in the entire periodical industry, another important factor was the development of Victorian notions of sexual difference, specifically the belief in essential differences between men and women. Implicit in such ideologies was the notion of a separate women's culture, and periodicals edited by and for women promoted and depended on this idea. In relying on notions of separate spheres in their periodicals, however, women editors did more than accept cultural definitions imposed upon them. While they often endorsed the Victorian notion of women as essentially different and usually more moral than men, they generally did not accept the gendered public-private dichotomy on which some interpretations of separate spheres depended. Indeed, regardless of their own ideologies, women editors worked within a *public* feminine space. Whatever their intentions, women editors employed a version of separate spheres that challenged the association of men with public life and women with private life. In so doing, they exploded limiting definitions of what they— and other women—could do and be.[15]

But the separatist rhetoric was appealing not only for its challenge to Victorian associations of women with private domesticity. As the association of the term *magazine* with ammunition suggests, a periodical defined by a separatist rhetoric served a defensive as well as an offensive function. The defensive potential of this rhetoric is most clearly suggested by the contemporary responses to nineteenth-century women editors. When women worked within a separatist space—or one that was at least nominally separatist on the basis of gender— women editors were generally well accepted and even promoted. In fact, male publishers often boasted of having a woman editor, and male publishers of women's magazines sometimes paid women for the privilege of listing them as editors, even when the women did no editorial work. (Such is the case, definitely, with Lydia Sigourney, probably with Emma Embury, and, at times, with Ann Stephens.)

In contrast to the social acceptance these women editors experienced, those women who spoke to (or were perceived to speak to) audiences other than women and children at times illicited harsh rebukes. Consider, for instance, this caustic complaint: "Verily, verily, if our sister-editors get along so merrily, merrily—they will soon be obliged to kill their own mutton. What need have they of our guardianship, the guardianship of he-editors, now they are able not only to mend their own pens, but to mend our manners along with them? not only to sharpen their own instruments, but to bleed *us* with them after they *are* sharpened?" (*Yankee and Boston Literary Gazette*, Oct. 1829, 218). Suggesting the limitations placed upon women editors, this writer primarily objected that the women dared to speak to men, to "he-editors." It was not so bad, he suggested, that women editors might want "to mend their own pens." What was unacceptable was that women editors might want to "mend our [that is, men's] manners along with them . . . to bleed *us.*" At the point this writer perceived that women editors were dropping the separatist rhetoric, in other words, they came under attack.

Jane Grey Swisshelm's description of the reaction she received when she began editing and publishing the antislavery *Pittsburgh Saturday Visiter* in 1848 suggests, as well, the danger of women editors' not using a separatist rhetoric. As Swisshelm's account in her autobiography makes clear, she was attacked not so much because she was an editor but because she dared to comment directly on politics, a topic perceived to be the domain of men only. The *Visiter*, she wrote,

> was quite an insignificant looking sheet, but no sooner did the American eagle catch sight of it, than he swooned and fell off his perch. Democratic roosters straightened out their necks and ran screaming with terror. Whig coons scampered up trees and barked furiously. The world was falling and every one had "heard it, saw it, and felt it."

It appeared that on some inauspicious morning each one of three-fourths of the secular editors from Maine to Georgia had gone to his office suspecting nothing, when from some corner of his exchange list there sprang upon him such a horror as he had little thought to see.

A woman had started a political paper! A woman! Could he believe his eyes! A woman! Instantly he sprang to his feet and clutched his pantaloons, shouted to the assistant editor, when he, too, read and grasped frantically at his cassimeres, called to the reporters, pressmen and typos and devils, who all rushed in, heard the news, seized their nether garments and joined the general chorus, "My breeches! oh, my breeches!" Here was a woman resolved to steal their pantaloons, their trousers, and when these were gone they might cry "Ye have taken away my gods, and what have I more?" The imminence of the peril called for prompt action, and with one accord they shouted, "On to the breach, in defense of our breeches! Repel the invader or fill the trenches with our noble dead."[16]

Swisshelm's sarcastic account here reveals the dangers she felt in abandoning a strictly separatist editorship. Portraying herself as an "invader," Swisshelm relied on the spatial and martial image of "trenches" to suggest the separation between herself and men expected by her critics. Her repeated references to the threat of stolen "pantaloons," moreover, suggest that she assumed that men associated her speaking on politics with her wanting to be—or to be equal to—a man. By implication, the only safe way of being a woman editor was to insist on one's womanhood and to defend rather than challenge a gendered separatism. Only with that separatist claim could women hope to gain entry into the periodical industry.

The dual role of a gendered separatism as both a challenge to the gendered public-private dichotomy and a defense against personal attacks is demonstrated by the number of women editors who relied on gendered identifications not only for their periodicals but for themselves as well. The most common marker was the term *editress*, which many editors used, including Anne Royall, Sarah J. Hale, Lois Bryan Adams, Miriam Squier Leslie ("Frank Leslie"), and Louisa Knapp. Other editors found other ways to mark their gendered status. When in 1850 Caroline Kirkland was identified in *Sartain's Union Magazine of Literature and Art* simply as C. M. Kirkland, she ordered the magazine to add the title "Mrs.," as she had "no desire to appear before the public in any unusual form."[17] To appear identical—or equal—to male editors was "unusual" and unacceptable.

Like many other editors, Ann Stephens asserted the difference between "sister" and "brother" editors.[18] In response to criticism about her editorial efforts, for example, Stephens characterized herself as inherently different from her male colleagues and her publication as inherently different from theirs:

> The editor earnestly deprecates the unfair criticisms and ill will of sterner reapers in the field. Let them go on in the strength of giant intellects, measuring pens in political strife. Their's [sic] it is to dig the bosom of the earth, to scour the mountains, to draw the lightning from the clouds, and pore with keen eye over the starry heavens, in their search for philosophical knowledge. Earth, ocean, air and sky, we willingly yield to them. The privilege of deep research is man's right; with it we have no wish to interfere. All we ask is permission to use the knowledge he has scattered over the enlightened world. But poetry, fiction, and the lighter branches of the sciences are woman's appropriate sphere, as much as the flower-garden, the drawing-room, and the nursery. (*Portland Magazine*, Oct. 1834, 1)

Stephens's account reveals the delicate balance between the defensive and potentially explosive modes of a separatist identity. On the one hand, Stephens's reference to "woman's appropriate sphere" and her request for "permission" imply that she accepted limitations on her editorial authority. On the other hand, Stephens's rhetoric is hardly that of a self-effacing woman grateful for the limited allowances granted by men. She expressed no discomfort in criticizing their attacks on her, and her description of her male colleagues and their "giant intellects" seems almost a caricature. Moreover, she did not assume they had any natural authority over her. While she did "ask" permission, she did so only after choosing, "willingly," to "yield" their interests to them, while insisting on her own interests. Using the gendered rhetoric of separate spheres, then, Stephens marked her territory as her own, female space.

Even when women editors did not use the spatial image of spheres, the separatist identity of their periodicals often suggested a physical, female space. Not surprising, this physical separatism was especially apparent in periodicals edited and published by women. Eliminating the presence of the male publisher who sometimes acted as intermediary between reader and editor, many periodicals of the nineteenth century were run entirely by women. Some, like Abigail Goodrich Whittelsey's *Mrs. Whittelsey's Magazine for Mothers* (1850–52), advocated conservative notions of womanhood. Many other women-owned periodicals, however, relied on a separatist rhetoric to challenge restrictive constructions of women's role. Anne Royall insisted on her right to engage in political debate by publishing two newspapers—*Paul Pry* (1831–36) and the *Huntress* (1836–54)—from her kitchen in Washington, D.C., and Anne Elizabeth McDowell published her own women's rights paper in the late 1850s, titled *Woman's Advocate*. Other women-owned periodicals include Jane Grey Swisshelm's *Pittsburgh Saturday Visiter* (1848–57), M. Cora Bland's *Ladies' Own Magazine* (1869–74), Paulina Wright Davis's *Una* (1853–55), Susan B. Anthony and Elizabeth Cady Stanton's *Revolution* (1868–72), and Emily Pitts Stevens's *Pioneer* (1869–73). At least one periodical boasted that all of the members of its production team were women. In 1873 Mary Nolan's *Central Magazine* announced that the printing was being done exclusively by women, making the magazine "altogether woman's work." Continuing to congratulate itself for being an all-women's publication, *Central Magazine* later published a picture of its composing room (figure 1). An article described the magazine as having the "first printing office established in the United States, where the various duties of authorship, editing, proof reading, composition and imposition of matter is performed solely by woman's labor" (*Central Magazine*, May 1873, 336; Oct. 1874, 139).

Matilda Bradley Carse's work with women's publishing shows even more clearly the value many women placed on having a separate physical space in which to produce their texts. In 1880 Carse founded and then served as president of the Woman's Temperance Publishing Association, an Illinois stock company owned entirely by women that, at its peak, had more than one hundred employees. In addition to books and tracts, the association published several periodicals of the Woman's Christian Temperance Union (WCTU), including the *Signal*, the *Union Signal*, the *Young Crusader*, and the *Oak and Ivy Leaf*. In 1887 Carse

Figure 1. The composing room of *Central Magazine*.
From *Central Magazine*, Oct. 1874. Courtesy of the
State Historical Society of Missouri, Columbia.

expanded her efforts by founding the Woman's Temperance Building Association, with the hopes of constructing a Chicago office building that would house the WCTU, with other portions of the building being rented for profit. Although not intended to be used exclusively by women, the building was promoted as a public female space. Called the Woman's Temple, this office building was created using the same separatist rhetoric found in the periodicals. Carse's full plan for the Woman's Temple was never realized, but her attempts to create a physical space for women to produce a variety of texts, including periodicals, demonstrate the important connections between women's periodicals and what Estelle Freedman has described as "female institution building." As Freedman explains, the public organizations and institutions created by American women in the late nineteenth and early twentieth centuries—specifically women's clubs, women's colleges, and actual buildings such as the Woman's Pavilion at the 1876 Centennial Exposition in Philadelphia and the Woman's Building at the 1893 World Columbian Exposition in Chicago—encouraged women's increased status in society without abandoning the supportive networks of women's culture.[19]

Much the same can be said of the periodicals of the previous decades that were truly women-identified, that is, edited by and for women. Like the later women's buildings and organizations, women-identified periodicals provided an opportunity for like-minded women to come together in a public forum. The connections between these women-identified periodicals and the separate female organizations are especially evident in the case of Sorosis, the women's club begun in 1868 and often credited with pioneering the women's club movement. Sorosis was founded when women reporters were banned from the New York Press Club. These women—many of them periodical editors, including Jane Cunningham Croly ("Jennie June") and Kate Field—responded by forming their own public female institution, just as women editors decades earlier had established periodicals by and for women.

While Sorosis is a powerful example of the strength of a separate women's culture within periodicals, similar cases occurred throughout the century. Not all nineteenth-century women editors supported one another, of course, and some defined themselves in direct opposition to each other. Nevertheless, many nineteenth-century women editors relied on each other for assistance and mentorship. Frances Gage, who would eventually become associate editor of two Ohio periodicals, built her literary reputation by contributing to periodicals edited by women, including the *Ohio Cultivator,* whose women's section was edited by Josephine C. Bateham, Amelia Bloomer's *Lily,* and Jane Grey Swiss-helm's *Pittsburgh Saturday Visiter.* Similarly, after working briefly as Oregon editor for Emily Pitts Stevens's *Pioneer,* Abigail Scott Duni-way started her own periodical, the *New Northwest,* a move that she credited Stevens with inspiring.[20]

Though Sarah J. Hale did not support the suffrage periodicals, her *Ladies' Magazine* and *Godey's Lady's Book* provided a special opportunity for building a sense of community among women editors. Hale frequently announced and supported other magazines edited by women, and many nineteenth-century women editors—including Harriet Beecher Stowe, Metta V. Victor, Virginia F. Townsend, Mary Sargeant Neal Gove Nichols, and Ann Stephens—began their literary careers with Hale's magazines or occasionally turned to them to supplement their own editorial or other literary work. As early as 1834 Ann Stephens wrote that Hale supported her own efforts with the *Portland Magazine:* "In commencing this magazine we may be deemed presumptuous; and we may be so—but not because we are a woman. . . . We mark out no new path; establish no precedent. . . . The *Ladies' Magazine,* of Boston, [edited by Hale] has succeeded well in a city where it has been surrounded by competitors . . . and from the commencement until now, the *American Ladies' Magazine* has been edited by a woman" (*Portland Magazine,* Oct. 1834, 2).[21] Although certainly less structured than the networks within turn-of-the-century women's clubs, these connections nevertheless provided many of the same professional benefits.[22]

The supportive network noted among women editors mirrored the kind of relationships that often emerged between a woman editor and her audience. Such relationships differed markedly from those found in early women's periodicals, which were edited by men. In such cases, the editorial voice reinforced the authority of men over women: men speak, and women listen. As Kathryn Shevelow has suggested in her research on the *Tatler*, this editor-reader relationship replicated father-daughter relationships, where the daughter was expected to depend upon the wisdom of the paternal voice. Because the *Tatler* assumed that women's action and even speech were impossible without the approval of the paternal editor, its message was, as Shevelow describes it, one of "female subordination in a patriarchal culture." In contrast to this paternalistic editorial voice, nineteenth-century American women editors often employed an editorial voice parallel to the kinds of relationships nineteenth-century American women formed with one another. As Carroll Smith-Rosenberg has observed, these women formed close emotional bonds with one another, creating a world of female intimacy in which men "made but a shadowy appearance."[23]

In periodicals edited by and for women, the editors often used the rhetoric of intimate female relations, creating what I call the sisterly editorial voice. This voice is characterized by a relative informality and an assumed equal and personal relationship between editor and reader. Just as some editors referred to other women editors as "sisters," so too did they invoke the informality of expressions such as "old friends" and "sisters" when referring to readers.[24] Consider, for example, the opening of an editorial titled "Ourselves," written by Lois Bryan Adams for the *Michigan Farmer* in 1856. Though the periodical itself targeted both men and women, the household department in which this editorial appeared was assumed to be for and by women: "Ourselves—permit us to drop the pompous plural for a time, and pretend to no more than we are—a single unit—I. It is well enough on ordinary occasions for a woman to adopt the custom of editors generally, and keep the potent 'we' between herself and readers; but now I wish to come a little nearer, to sit down beside you, my *Farmer* household friends, and feel free to talk with you concerning our mutual interests" (*Michigan Farmer*, Dec. 1856, 369). While male editors sometimes also chose to drop the editorial *we*, Adams's association of her choice of *I* with her identity as a woman fits well with the sisterly editorial voice generally. Here she assumes a friendly, even intimate relationship with her readers who share "mutual interests." By 1884 the sisterly editorial voice was familiar enough for Louisa Knapp's readers of the *Ladies' Home Journal* to write her about personal problems, such as alcoholic husbands. Writing a column similar to today's "Dear Abby," Knapp printed these letters along with her suggestions. Like Adams before her, Knapp assumed that she knew her readers personally.

Many editors using the sisterly editorial voice invoked a spatial metaphor that suggested the intimate relations between reader and editor. As Sarah J. Hale once wrote, "One very gratifying result of periodical literature is the relations it establishes between those who sustain it. It brings editors and readers into a closer companionship with each other than is ever felt by the authors and buyers of books. We are the confidential friends of our subscribers; we feel sure that those who, every month in the year, gather to our 'Table,' and press around our 'Arm-Chair,' would welcome us with heart and hand to their own happy homes" (*Godey's Lady's Book*, Jan. 1860, 79).[25] Similarly, when Mildred Aldrich assumed the editorship of the literary journal *Mahogany Tree*, she rejected the earlier editor's image of himself in a tree "talk[ing] down" to readers from an "elevated perch." Refusing a hierarchical interpretation of the magazine's title, Aldrich imagined herself seated at a mahogany table, promising comfort for "every guest" beside her (*Mahogany Tree*, 9 July 1892, 403; 10 Sept. 1892, 1–2).

Significantly, editors employed the sisterly editorial voice regardless of ideological lines. This editorial voice was used not only by antebellum women's magazines but by postwar suffrage papers as well. The *Woman's Journal*, for instance, affiliated with the American Woman Suffrage Association, opened in 1870, urging readers, "our friends," to "call and see us, at our new office," described as a "sort of social centre for women." Making such an invitation to intimacy even more concrete, the editors promised to announce visiting hours when "our friends may be sure to meet one, or any of the editors" (8 Jan. 1870, 4). Other periodicals also relied on the sisterly editorial voice. Rosa Sonneschein opened her *American Jewess* in 1895 by welcoming comments from "her sisters." As she explained, she was "more than willing to share [the editorial column] with all women who talk," and she invited "the co-operation of my sisters from all parts of the compass" (April 1895, 39). And the quite different *Far and Near*, associated with the Working Girls' Societies of America, described its primary aim as "bring[ing] those who are far apart near to one another" (Nov. 1890, 1).

The flexibility of the sisterly editorial voice is further demonstrated by its use within the *Woman's Era*, the African American women's club journal edited by Josephine St. Pierre Ruffin and her daughter, Florida Ruffin Ridley. Ruffin and Ridley, as well as the magazine's many department editors, employed the sisterly editorial voice to unite African American women in their fight against racial oppression. Though the *Era* consistently celebrated the power of African American women coming together, the editors also used the sisterly editorial voice to denounce the tendency of white women's groups to boast women's unity when addressing only the concerns of white women. Thus one subscriber to the *Era* criticized the *Ladies' Home Journal* for ignoring "our interests and our peculiar race wants" (*Woman's Era*, Dec. 1894, 19). Though critical of the false sense of gender unity within white women's publications, the *Era*'s editors found the sisterly editorial voice empowering. Indeed, they combined their critiques with a call for a unity that crossed racial lines. One editorial urged the Association for the Advancement of Women to "boldly face" the nation's "race question": "It is a question which they can not longer evade. We thoroughly believe that it is the women of America—black and white—who are to solve this race problem" (Nov. 1894, 8).

As the *Woman's Era* demonstrates, the sisterly editorial voice, while informal, was not without authority. In contrast to the strategies of denial and self-effacement sometimes noted in the works of nineteenth-century American women writers, confidence in their public authority as editors generally characterized the women who used the sisterly editorial voice.[26] Indeed, their authority often depended on the gendered identity of the editorial voice. Consider, for example, this statement in the *Woman's Exponent*, a Mormon magazine founded in 1872 in Salt Lake City and edited by Louisa Greene Richards:

> Who are so well able to speak for the women of Utah as the women of Utah themselves? "It is better to represent ourselves than to be misrepresented by others!"
>
> For these reasons, and that women may help each other by the diffusion of knowledge and information possessed by many and suitable to all, the publication of *Woman's Exponent*, a journal owned by, controlled by and edited by Utah ladies, has been commenced. (31 Jan. 1873, 136)

Here authority was based on the very willingness of editors to promote themselves as women.

The authority of women editors was not confined to situations in which they could hide behind the editorial *we*. On the contrary, many women editors spoke with pride of their individual accomplishments. In a letter to Phebe A. Hanaford, for example, Emma Molloy described how she "naturally fell into the routine of collecting, soliciting, writing, and type-setting, until I became indispensable to my husband." Likewise, Harriet Farley offered this confident account of her editorial duties with the *Lowell Offering:* "I do all the publishing, editing, canvassing; and, as it is bound in my office, I can, in a hurry, help fold, cut covers, stitch, &c. I have a little girl to assist me in the folding, stitching, &c.; the rest, after it comes from the printer's hand, is all my own work. I employ no agents, and depend upon no one for assistance. My edition is four thousand."[27] In a similar account of her accomplishments with the *Inland Monthly Magazine,* Charlotte Smith openly mocked the assumption that women should hide behind an editorial *we:* "First you must understand that we are a wonderful woman. We edit, solicit, correspond, we are general and traveling agent, proof reader, and housekeeper to boot. It sometimes surprises us that we are able to do it all" (*Inland Monthly Magazine,* Dec. 1873, 421).

Like many of the antebellum women writers who defended their occupation on the basis of "doing good," women editors often established their editorial authority by relying on Victorian constructions of woman as inherently moral and domestic. As late as 1884 Louisa Knapp described the *Ladies' Home Journal* as a "pure and high-toned family paper." As she explained, "We propose to make it a household necessity—so good, so pure, so true, so brave, so full, so complete, that a young couple will no more think of going to housekeeping without it than without a cook-stove" (*Ladies' Home Journal,* Jan. 1884, 4). On an even grander scale, Hulda Barker Loud explained in 1889 that she had purchased a newspaper in order to help save the world.[28] This appeal to doing good was especially common in children's periodicals. In the initial issue of the *Child's Friend,* for instance, Eliza L. Follen blended Victorian expectations of women's maternal love and moral guidance, urging her readers to "come to us, you shall find love, you shall find instruction in our pages" (Oct. 1843, 1).

Often this moral rhetoric of "doing good" was fused with patriotic appeals. In 1836 Anne Royall promoted her political newspaper, the *Huntress*, as a publication helping to sustain national liberty. Its epigraph read: "Education—'The Main pillar which sustains the Temple of Liberty,'—Johnson." Since many periodicals were distributed only locally, the patriotic rhetoric often appeared in a regional context, with editors promoting their publications as demonstrations of regional supremacy. The cover of Charlotte Smith's *Inland Monthly Magazine* (1872–78), for instance, featured a map with St. Louis as the center of the nation (and later of the world), and the magazine boasted that it would demonstrate the literary achievements of the West. Similarly, in the opening editorial of the *Portland Magazine* (1834–36), Ann Stephens projected an image of herself as one who could prove to outsiders the quality of life in Portland, Maine. After reminding readers of the city's accomplishments in "theology, in law, fiction and poetry" and in "commerce and industry," Stephens asked, "With all these advantages why should not our state be able to support a literary magazine?" (Oct. 1834, 2). As the editor promoting the region's literary accomplishments, Stephens presented herself not only as a woman doing good for her community but as an authority in literary matters as well.

Stephens's description of her role in the community demonstrates how many editors relied on the sometimes competing rhetorics of Victorian womanhood and of the sisterly editorial voice. Stephens depended on a Victorian emphasis on women's moral influence when she explained that her "object is good" and that she would "do her duty." When explaining the precise nature of her "duty," Stephens again in fairly conventional Victorian terms defined "woman" primarily in relation to her care for her family. As Stephens explained, since man trusted woman to care for the "budding intellect and unformed principles of his sons and daughters," he should also allow her "the power of contributing to the amusement of his leisure hours." Stephens's rhetoric is ultimately inconsistent, however. Although she implied that her editorial authority rested solely on the positive influence she would have on men, she had already identified the magazine as one intended for the "Ladies of Maine" (*Portland Magazine*, Oct. 1834, 1–2). In other words, Stephens seemed willing to use the rhetoric of Victorian womanhood, but she found no need to obey its call. While using a rhetoric designed to focus on women's influence on men, Stephens insisted on her right to speak to women directly, and in so doing she transformed a hierarchical structure of moral women influencing corrupt and powerful men into a sisterly structure of women speaking to each other.

The various bases of authority used by women editors can be seen even more clearly in the case of one of the most innovative editors of the century. Born in 1836, Miriam Florence Folline would later become known as Mrs. Frank Leslie and the leader of the Leslie publishing empire.[29] Her editing career began in 1863, when, as Miriam Squier, she assumed editorial duties at *Frank Leslie's Lady's Magazine*, a publication owned by her husband's employer, Frank Leslie. Initially, Miriam Squier's editorial authority rested entirely on her expertise in fashion, an authority no doubt assisted by the proclamation years earlier in *Frank Leslie's Illustrated Newspaper* that she was the "acknowledged belle" at President Lincoln's 1861 inaugural ball (23 March 1861, 285). As editor of Leslie's *Lady's Magazine*, Miriam Squier highlighted the periodical's coverage of fashion, and her reputation as an authority on fashion must have increased after she accompanied her husband on a trip to Peru, where she recorded Peruvian fashions for her New York readers.

Squier broadened her editorial authority beyond fashion in 1865, when she founded another Leslie publication, *Frank Leslie's Chimney Corner*, which she subsequently edited. As editor of a family magazine rather than one devoted to fashion, Squier presented herself as one motivated by doing good. Though always reminding the reader of the magazine's entertaining quality, she accented its wholesome effect on family members. Squier repeatedly described the magazine's contents as "healthy" and "instructive." As she explained, to "please and delight the sense of sight, while at the same time the mind is furnished with healthy and suitable nourishment, is the aim of the *Chimney Corner*" (1 June 1867, 10). Squier's appeal to family members of all ages and her combination of serialized fiction, adventure stories, biographical sketches, and household and fashion advice proved successful. The paper eventually reached a circulation of eighty thousand and lasted until 1885. Squier's persona as an entertaining and instructive editor continued with her next publications, the short-lived *Once a Week: The*

*Young Lady's Own Journal* and then the more successful *Frank Leslie's Lady's Journal.* Though far more fashion-oriented than the *Chimney Corner,* the *Lady's Journal* promised to provide essays on "EDUCATION, HOUSEHOLD MANAGEMENT, and other socially important topics," and the editor promised "vigilance" over the literary department. As Squier explained, her aim was, again, "to influence for good" (*Frank Leslie's Lady's Journal,* 18 Nov. 1871, 2; 25 Nov. 1871, 18).

Squier's persona as a wholesome editor is not without irony, for during much of her editorship of both the *Chimney Corner* and the *Lady's Journal* she was a key actor in two public and scandalous divorces. The questions about Miriam Squier's relationship with Frank Leslie—her publisher and also her husband's employer—began in the mid-1860s, leading eventually to Frank Leslie's divorce from his wife in 1872, Miriam Squier's divorce from E. G. Squier in 1873, and the subsequent marriage in 1874 of Frank Leslie and Miriam Squier. Surprisingly, during the many public accusations leading to these divorces, Miriam Squier continued to edit the "family" periodicals. Perhaps because of the scandal, however, Squier shifted her persona slightly in 1871. When *Once a Week: The Young Lady's Own Journal* failed in November 1871, Squier abandoned the image of herself as a role model specifically for young women and presented herself in the *Lady's Journal* as one who could speak directly to women of all ages, presumably those who were not particularly impressionable.

Once Miriam Squier married Frank Leslie, she began reshaping her editorial authority. Her editorials in the *Lady's Journal* continued to feature fashion, but she also assumed two new areas of expertise: literature and the business side of periodical publication. Miriam Leslie's most important literary contribution during this period began with the Leslies' rail tour of the West in 1877. In such cities as Chicago, Omaha, Sacramento, San Francisco, and Los Angeles, Miriam Leslie recorded her observations of the American people and landscape, observations presented to her readers in the book *California: A Pleasure Trip from Gotham to the Golden Gate,* with excerpts reprinted in the Leslie periodicals.

Miriam Leslie's business and technical achievements realized fulfillment several years later. When the Leslies returned from their western excursion, they met with considerable financial troubles. Amid these continuing problems, Frank Leslie died in 1880, leaving his wife a large but debt-ridden publishing empire. While careful financial dealings helped the publishing firm, real success came with Miriam Leslie's response to the shooting of President James Garfield on 2 July 1881 and Garfield's subsequent death in September. Capitalizing on the nation's demand for news about the president, Miriam Leslie published elaborate illustrations of the events, and circulation rose from thirty thousand to two hundred thousand. In the next two decades Miriam Leslie continued to strengthen the Leslie publishing business.

Miriam Leslie's ability to fuse an authority based on her fashionable life, her literary reputation, and her business expertise as a publisher is perhaps best represented in her decision in 1890 to introduce herself in public lectures as Frank Leslie, a name change later made legal. On the one hand, the name change represents her accomplishments within the business. No longer the wife of the publisher, she became the publisher—in fact and name. On the other hand, her adoption of the name Frank Leslie seems a stark contrast to her public persona, for she continued to appear publicly in the context of fashionable life and semiscandalous marriages. During an 1890 lecture tour she spoke on such topics as European royalty and love, and she married in 1891— and divorced in 1893—William Wilde, brother of Oscar Wilde.

Lest Miriam Leslie's transformation to Frank Leslie be construed as an action to distance herself from other women in the periodical industry, it is worth remembering that the name change occurred at a time when Leslie became increasingly supportive of other women journalists. Believing that women made superior interviewers, she created jobs for women in journalism and spoke out publicly in support of women journalists. In return, her colleagues recognized her as a leader in the field. The women compositors in Topeka, for example, founded a Leslie Club and featured her picture in the first issue of their magazine, the *Printer Girl* (1888–89). Nowhere is Leslie's connection to other women, especially in journalism, more apparent than in the surprising decision she made regarding her will. At her death in 1914, Leslie bequeathed the bulk of her two-million-dollar estate to Carrie Chapman Catt, a woman she knew only slightly, for the purposes of carrying on the cause of "Woman's Suffrage." Catt, formerly the editor of the *Woman's Standard* in Iowa, used the legacy to support the Leslie Bureau of Suffrage Education, responsible for the publicity and publishing of the National American Woman Suffrage Association.[30]

Leslie's career in periodicals is hardly typical, but it provides us a valuable opportunity to view women's editorships. Although her specific formulation of editorial identity—part fashion expert, part family woman, part literary figure, part financial tycoon—was uniquely hers, she, like so many women editors, did claim her right to a public authority within periodicals. Like many other women editors, moreover, Leslie claimed that authority to a great extent on the basis of her gender: as a fashionable woman, she was qualified to be a fashion editor; as a financially troubled widow, she turned to business to "save" her husband's empire. Furthermore, Leslie often relied on the sisterly editorial voice, making connections with her readers. However remote her life was from theirs, she frequently invoked the image of informal exchange between editor and reader in columns titled "Chit-Chat with the Ladies" and "Ladies' Conversazióne."

The sisterly editorial voice, with its gendered basis of authority and the informal exchange between readers and editors, often affected not only the tone of the editorial columns but the very form of the periodical as well. In contrast to those women's periodicals dominated by a patriarchal and relatively monolithic editorial voice, women's periodicals that employed the sisterly editorial voice tended to value and present readers, writers, and editors as equally important participants in a periodical conversation. Put simply, nineteenth-century periodicals by and for women were generally multivocal and dialogic. One manifestation of this dialogism was the letters to editors appearing in women's magazines. Such letters did not, of course, appear solely in periodicals edited by and for women, but within such periodicals they broke down the barrier between editor and audience to create an actual dialogue.

The diverse contents of these publications suggest another form of dialogism. Like many other magazines, *Godey's Lady's Book* consisted of an amazingly diverse collection of material, including poems, stories, serialized novels, fashion plates, sewing patterns, advertisements for sewing machines, book reviews, and even architectural designs. Throughout her career, Sarah J. Hale repeatedly celebrated the miscellaneous nature of her magazine. During the first year of her editorship she glorified the power of multiplicity in a short piece, titled "A Pic Nic Chapter," which consisted of four short tales from around the world. In the introduction to these tales, Hale characterized "long critical dissertations" as "inconsistent" with her plan for her magazine: "There is, usually, but a small portion of wisdom in a large book, as there are rarely found many choice and valuable flowers in the same bed, while a bouquet embodies, not unfrequently, the richest and rarest specimens in the whole garden." The bouquet and the picnic can well serve as metaphors of most magazines. Like a bouquet, a magazine revels in diversity; like a picnic, it spurns formality. As Hale described the chapter, a magazine celebrates "variety without formality" (*GLB*, Oct. 1837, 183).

However much diverse contents are an inherent part of all magazines, Hale's decision to describe her magazine's multiplicity using the language of a meal (a picnic) and of flowers—two discourses highly gendered in antebellum America—suggests the extent to which many women editors claimed their magazines' variety as feminine. Two other popular women's nineteenth-century art forms—the quilt and the scrapbook—reveal a similar association of multiplicity with the feminine. Like a bouquet, a quilt, or a scrapbook, periodicals edited by and for women collected different pieces and voices, without insisting on one dominant voice.[31]

In order to explore the polyphonic nature of nineteenth-century women's magazines and, at the same time, to bring Sarah J. Hale's *Godey's Lady's Book* into focus, I would like to describe the various contents of one particular issue, that of November 1846. I chose this particular issue primarily because one of its texts is a familiar one, Edgar Allan Poe's "The Cask of Amontillado." Although I do not mean to suggest that this story is the centerpiece of the issue, having one text familiar will provide an opportunity for more extensive analysis of the multivocality of the *Lady's Book*.

*Godey's Lady's Book* of November 1846 comprises an engraving by J. Gross titled "Beneficence of Washington"; an accompanying unsigned story, titled "The Prescription; or, The Beneficence of Washington"; a story, "The Batson Cottage" by Miss [Eliza] Leslie; an engraving by A. L. Dick of a painting by M. W. Sharp, depicting a Saturday evening bath; an accompanying poem by J. Ross Dix titled "Saturday Evening"; an unsigned essay, "Language"; a poem, "The Swiss Emigrant on the Western Prairies" by J. M'Lellan Jr.; chapters 5 and 6 of a serial novel by J. F. Otis, titled *Sutherland Hall*; a poem, "Absence" by E. Oakes Smith; part 4 of a series titled "Our Artists"; a poem, "Parting Lines" by the Reverend William Love; "The Cask of Amontillado" by Edgar A. Poe; a poem, "Gentle Influences" by Mrs. C. H. Esling; an essay by Sibyl Sylvester titled "A Peep at Paris," which was part 4 of "Sketches Abroad"; a poem, "The Vesper Chime" by Miss Mary Gardiner; part of the "Model Cottages" series, consisting of drawings and descriptions of a German Swiss cottage; music and lyrics for a song by Alfred H. Coon, "Love Thee, Dearest? Ever!"; the "Ladies' Work Department," featuring instructions for crocheted bags and purses; the "Editors' Table," featuring an essay on progress and on women as schoolteachers as well as short announcements; the "Editors' Book Table," including reviews or announcements of more than forty books as well as numerous brief comments by Louis Godey; and, finally, a fashion plate, featuring four women in winter cloaks. Altogether, the November 1846 issue consisted of forty-eight double-columned pages of text and three engravings.

As this overview demonstrates, the magazine had significantly diverse contents, and different voices emerge. Both men and women appeared as authors, and fiction was published alongside engravings, essays alongside songs. In addition, several of the editorial announcements suggest a dialogue between reader and editor. As she did in most issues of the magazine, Hale announced to readers articles submitted by "correspondents" that had been accepted (as well as some that had been "declined"), suggesting that readers as well as professional writers had an opportunity to submit material to the magazine. Similarly, another announcement personally addressed "H.G.J." of Springfield, Massachusetts, and yet another fulfilled a subscriber's request to print a poem. These direct communications between readers and editors reveal the magazine's dialogic nature.

Although an important feature of many periodicals edited by and for women, the dialogue between editor and reader was by no means the only, or even the most significant, form of multivocality. Indeed, the dialogue created between the various contents represents a far more complex form. The complexity arises, in part, from the degree of editorial control. While an editor could always manipulate reader-editor dialogue because she determined what was published, the dialogue between the components of the magazine inevitably resisted editorial control. Most editors certainly rejected items that directly challenged their own ideologies, but the diversity of contents and voices made it impossible for any editor to maintain an absolutely monolithic ideology. As soon as an editor allowed a variety of voices and even contents, ideological tensions emerged, however subtle, within the magazine itself.

While by no means an open warfare, ideological tensions arising from diverse contents are evident in the November 1846 issue of *Godey's Lady's Book*, specifically focusing on the topics of sexual difference and gendered separatism. On the one hand, a number of articles seem to support a fairly rigid notion of inherent sexual difference. Sibyl Sylvester's "A Peep at Paris," for instance, generally advocated the idea that men and women are so essentially different that they naturally live in different worlds or "spheres," and Sylvester expressed disapproval of Parisian women's tendency to live publicly, eating in restaurants and walking the streets. As Sylvester noted, "The sex is permitted to associate itself with everything—business, politics and intrigue included—without a proper sense of the degradation." "The sex is thrust," Sylvester continued, "entirely out of its legitimate sphere of action." Though the author recognized these behaviors as evidence of "freedom," she rejected this freedom as "fatal" to women's "mental purity" (*GLB*, Nov. 1846, 225–27). Here, as in other Victorian definitions of womanhood, the notion of separate "spheres" was based on "woman's" inherent "purity."

In an inverse way, Poe's "Cask of Amontillado" can be read as supporting this absolute distinction between men and women. One of the versions of a separate sphere ideology, after all, was that men and women must live separately because men are inherently corrupt and competitive, and the two men of this story embody precisely those features of the world of men from which women were supposedly protected by separate spheres. As many scholars have pointed out, Montresor is able to lure Fortunato into the catacombs primarily because of Fortunato's competitiveness. If Fortunato demonstrates men's supposedly inherent competitiveness, then Montresor suggests immorality and violence. Practically gleeful at the murder of Fortunato, Montresor is also, apparently, without remorse. The possibility of a gendered reading of behavior in this story is heightened by Fortunato's desperate plea to return to the palazzo, where "Lady Fortunato and the rest" are waiting. Only with the intervention of a woman, with her essential morality, can Fortunato hope to escape. In refusing Fortunato's plea, Montresor reveals his essential "manhood." In this way, Fortunato's declaration that Montresor is "not of the brotherhood" is best taken ironically. Here, in a separate space without women, men exhibit their supposedly essential competitive and immoral nature (*GLB*, Nov. 1846, 217–18). For Poe's mostly female readers of the *Lady's Book*, the implication may well have been that women can protect themselves from such corruption only by maintaining a separate space.

But while "A Peep at Paris" and "The Cask of Amontillado" together suggest that women can protect their essential moral purity by remaining separate from men's public affairs, other essays and stories in the same issue contest such a conclusion. Hale's own editorial, for instance, insists that one sign of civilization's progress is that "woman" has been "redeem[ed]" from "her inferior position" and placed "where the Creator designed she should stand—side by side with man, a help-meet for him in *all* his pursuits and improvements" (*GLB*, Nov. 1846, 235). Promoting collaborative projects between men and women, Hale rejected the image of spatial separatism. Similarly, Hale's "Editors' Book Table" undercuts a notion of absolute separatism or even inherent sexual difference. Indeed, few of the books recommended or announced—such as an engineering encyclopedia, Byron's *Childe Harold*, a biography of Oliver Cromwell, and Margaret Fuller's *Papers on Literature and Art*— seem to imply an exclusively female audience.

Even more so than Hale's editorials, Eliza Leslie's "Batson Cottage" challenges the idea of any essential difference between men and women and any corresponding belief in separate spheres. Here a snobbish Clementine Chelbourne convinces her mother to leave the fancy hotel where they are spending the summer in order to stay in a "genuine" country cottage owned by a widow. Convinced that rural life results inevitably in domestic bliss, moral idealism, and innocence, Clementine is dismayed at what she finds: the cottage is ugly, the widow's niece does housework and thus has neither "white" nor "delicate" hands, and the widow's young daughter prefers artificial flowers to real ones. In contrast to her idealized view of country life, Clementine finds nothing but harsh economic realities: the family goes to bed at sundown so as not to waste money on candles, and the daughter repeatedly responds to Clementine's halfhearted attempts at friendship with requests for money.

In part a middle-class mockery of upper-class pretensions, "The Batson Cottage" also challenges many of the middle-class assumptions about separate spheres and sexual difference. Although the Batson Cottage is an exclusively female space, it is neither particularly nurturing nor moral, and it is anything but a refuge from the public world of commerce. Quite the contrary—the Batsons' cottage and their rural poverty are their only commercial products, and the story ends as Mrs. Batson tries to bargain again for more "city people to board" (*GLB*, Nov. 1846, 200). Rather than supporting the assertions about women's purity and appropriate distance from the public world of commerce as do other portions of the magazine, "The Batson Cottage" implies that such ideologies are class-biased constructions. Lacking financial resources, the family is unable to live in a gendered separatist world, where men work publicly and women influence men's morality. Indeed, the only time that the Batsons do seem to accept gendered divisions of labor is when they hire a free black man living near their house to bring in Clementine's trunks. Only in a racially divided society, then, can the Batsons assume for even a moment the middle-class privilege of a gendered separatism.

These are by no means the only intertextual relations and tensions found within *Godey's Lady's Book* or even this particular issue. One could find similar relations and tensions concerning different topics, and individual texts can also be read in the context of material published elsewhere in the magazine.[32] Still, the tensions within this issue of the magazine on the question of sexual difference and separate spheres do suggest the extent to which periodicals that diffused editorial authority by including diverse contents presented their readers not with a totalizing ideology but with a dialogue of different and sometimes competing voices.

If tensions exist within one issue of a magazine about the employment—even viability—of an ideology of separate spheres, they are certain to emerge within an editorial career like Hale's that lasted fifty years and within *Godey's Lady's Book*, published from 1830 until 1898. Even more so, tensions are inevitable among the various women editors working with a gendered, separatist periodical. Though the women editing periodicals for other women often shared some connection with this ideology, they turned to it for different reasons and effects. Some used a gendered separatism to defend themselves against attack; some used it to challenge an ideology that associated women with private space; some, no doubt, used a similar rhetoric to support a patriarchal culture and to keep other women from speaking.

However much they were contested and despite their potential for restricting women's opportunities, notions about sexual difference and gendered separatism did ease women's entry into the periodical industry during the tumultuous days of the 1820s, and women editors continued to turn to separatist rhetorics throughout the century. If some women editors rejected the notion of "sister editors" or "editresses" and asserted equality and similarity with male editors, such a stance was made possible, at least in part, by the women who had gone before them, carrying their gendered identity as a defensive and offensive weapon. Such is certainly the case of Sarah J. Hale. While as many women editors may have scorned her as emulated her, her tenacious insistence on the value of "editresses" may well have made possible the careers of even her detractors.

# 2

## From Intellectual Equality
## to Moral Difference: Hale's Conversion
## to Separate Spheres

There is no sex in talents, in genius.
—*Ladies' Magazine*, Nov. 1828

The proposition, "Genius has no sex," is preposterous as well as false.
—*Godey's Lady's Book*, Feb. 1857

The epigraphs to this chapter, both taken from Sarah J. Hale's editorial columns, suggest that, as numerous scholars have observed, ideologies of sexual difference underwent profound transformation in the early nineteenth century. As Thomas Laqueur puts it, in European cultures before the eighteenth century, women were imagined as similar, though inferior, to men. Sometime during the eighteenth century a new model emerged, what Laqueur calls "radical dimorphism, of biological divergence," in which men and women were understood to be "different in every conceivable aspect of body and soul, in every physical and moral aspect." Within American culture, this development is best seen in the shift from postrevolutionary to Victorian notions of gender. As Nina Baym has explained, postrevolutionary Enlightenment ideologies assumed that the mind has "no sex" so as to assert women's intellectual equality with men; in contrast, Victorian notions of "woman" constructed her as essentially different from man.[1] This shift from equality to difference is key to Hale's own development as an editor. Though she would in some ways remain loyal to Enlightenment

38

philosophies, during the late 1820s and the 1830s she gradually came to promote an essential sexual difference based on Victorian notions of woman's inherent morality and the idea of a separate women's culture. These Victorian ideologies of gender, then, became the basis for her editorial career.

Born in 1788 in rural New Hampshire to a mother who stressed the importance of educating boys and girls and a father who had fought in the American Revolution, Sarah Josepha Buell was raised in the context of Enlightenment theories of sex and gender, specifically the postrevolutionary notion of the republican mother.[2] Linking womanhood directly with motherhood, late eighteenth-century supporters of improved education for women frequently defended their cause on the basis of women's role in raising the republic's next generation, specifically a woman's responsibility in raising her sons to be the nation's next leaders. Challenging the idea that women were intellectually inferior to men, these reformers insisted that women's education should focus on intellectual subjects rather than so-called ornamental arts, such as singing and dancing. Only with properly educated mothers, they reasoned, could the republic survive and prosper.[3]

Hale's own education shows the influence of such republican ideologies. Although, like most girls at the end of the eighteenth century, Hale had few opportunities for formal schooling, she, like many other women intellectuals of her time, received an excellent education by relying on her family.[4] Her mother, Martha Buell, served the role of republican mother, educating her daughters and sons. As Hale herself recalled, her mother was responsible for much of her early education as well as her love for reading: "I owe my early predilection for literary pursuits to the teaching and example of my mother. She had enjoyed uncommon advantages of education for a female of her times—possessed a mind clear as rock water, and a most happy talent of communicating knowledge. She had read many of the old black-letter chronicles and romances of the days of chivalry; and innumerable were the ballads, songs and stories with which she amused and instructed her children."[5] Hale's language here suggests the influence of Enlightenment thought. Rather than emphasizing, as she would later do, women's moral and spiritual influence, Hale highlighted her mother's intellect—her "mind clear as rock water"—and her "talent of communicating knowledge."

Hale's early reading shows the influence of Enlightenment constructions of "woman" as well, particularly the idea that the mind has "no sex." Indeed, nothing in Hale's early reading suggests that she or her family considered women intellectually inferior to, or even intellectually different from, men. Hale herself said that her early reading included Milton, Addison, Johnson, Pope, Cowper, and Burns, and she claimed to have obtained all of Shakespeare's works by age fifteen. Later in life, she recalled that the Bible and *Pilgrim's Progress* were her favorite books.[6]

Two other books to which Hale assigned particular importance were Ann Radcliffe's *Mysteries of Udolpho* (1794) and David Ramsay's *History of the American Revolution* (1789). Her description of these two books suggests that, like others influenced by Enlightenment ideologies, Hale defined gender-specific work in the context of her patriotism. Like the republican mother who teaches her children for the benefit of the nation and urges other women to educate themselves as well, Hale envisioned helping her sex as practically identical to serving her country. Recalling that little of what she read was written by Americans and "none by *women*," Hale described her subsequent discovery of Radcliffe's novel: "How happy it made me! The wish to promote the reputation of my own sex, and to do something for my own country, was among the earliest mental emotions I can recollect. This love of country was deeply engraved on my heart, by reading, when I was not more than ten years old, Ramsey's [*sic*] 'History of the American Revolution.' It made me a patriot for life. These feelings have had a salutary influence by directing my thoughts to a definite object;—my literary pursuits have had an aim beyond self-seeking of any kind."[7] Though Hale's fondness for Radcliffe's novel anticipated her later support for women writers, the fusion of gendered and patriotic rhetoric suggests Hale's engagement with Enlightenment ideologies of womanhood. Like all good republicans, Hale put her country above her own self-interests, and like a good republican woman, she defined her role in the new nation in specifically gendered terms.

Though she would later support the idea of separatist education—

with women teaching girls—Hale herself depended upon her older brother to fill the gaps of her inadequate formal schooling. As she remembered much later, Horatio, who was one year older than she, was "very unwilling that [she] should be deprived of all his collegiate advantages."[8] Horatio compensated for Hale's lack of formal training by tutoring her each summer during his vacations in Newport, New Hampshire. Thus, although she could not attend Dartmouth College with him—no college in America accepted women at this time—Hale obtained an education then impossible for even most white males, who could not afford such privileged schooling. As a result of these summer sessions and her own private work during the year, Hale studied Latin, Greek, philosophy, English grammar, rhetoric, geography, and literature. Significantly, her attention to these subjects reveals her confidence in the logic and rationality of the Enlightenment.

Hale's endorsement of republican motherhood, specifically of women's role in educating young children, is demonstrated by her occupational decisions. Like many other women who would eventually become editors—including Caroline Kirkland, Harriet Beecher Stowe, Caroline Augusta White Soule, and Lucy Stone—Hale turned to teaching as a young woman. In 1806, when she was eighteen and still studying with Horatio, Hale opened a private school for local children. Though women had not begun entering the teaching profession in great numbers, as they would later in the century, some women, especially in rural villages, did teach in what were called dame schools.[9] Her position as teacher was not itself exceptional, but her methodology and curriculum were. According to her biographer Ruth E. Finley, Hale rejected the standard idea that children learned best by rote memorization and recitation, preferring instead that students learn to think independently. In keeping with the idea that the mind has "no sex," Hale challenged traditional curricula as well, teaching the girls in her school reading, writing, and mathematics rather than sewing. According to one story of Hale's teaching, she even taught the girls Latin—a practice Finley describes as "heresy indeed if true."[10] Despite her unconventional methods and curriculum (or perhaps because of them), Hale's school survived; she remained a schoolteacher for seven years, leaving only after she married.

Hale's reliance on men for improving her education continued after her marriage in 1813 to David Hale, a lawyer who also came from New Hampshire. According to Hale's accounts of her marriage, she and her husband spent two hours each evening reading and studying. Again Hale depended on the Enlightenment principle of women's intellectual equality with men, for she showed no interest in limiting the intellectual range of her work. In addition to reading current fiction, Hale and her husband studied composition, French, and science, especially botany. Hale's study with her husband influenced her editorial career in at least two important ways. First, the nature of their readings likely helped Hale respond, years later, to the diverse topics she would encounter in her periodicals. Had she confined her study to domestic skills, she might have been unprepared to review the wide range of historical, scientific, and literary books featured in her magazines. Perhaps even more important, Hale's study with her husband helped develop her writing style, specifically the informal prose style that would mark her sisterly editorial voice. As Hale recalled, "Under his instruction and example, my prose style of writing, which the critics generally allow to be 'pure idiomatic English,' was formed; I acknowledge that my early predilection was for the pompous words and sounding periods of Johnson; and I had greatly admired the sublime flights and glittering fancies of Counsellor Phillips, the Irish orator, . . . but my husband convinced me, by analyzing his sentences, that these were, as he called them, 'sublime nonsense.'" Throughout the nine years of her marriage, during which she worked on her writing and published a few poems, Hale maintained a sense of an intimate audience. As she later explained, her "chief aim in literature" during this period was "to prepare something for the amusement" of her husband and four children.[11]

Although throughout her career Hale would often write as if for close friends and family, the shift from family-centered to public writer began with the death of her husband in September 1822, shortly before the birth of their fifth child. According to Hale, she "had never seriously contemplated becoming an authoress" before then. After an attempt at the millinery business with her sister-in-law, she turned to literature, publishing her first volume of poetry, *The Oblivion of Genius and Other Original Poems,* in 1823 and contributing to periodicals. Suggesting the limited options for middle-class women to find wage-earning work and still maintain their class standing, Hale said that writing was her "best resource" and one of the "very few employments in which females can engage with any hope of profit." When describing her literary start, Hale continually emphasized her need to support her children, especially to provide them an education: "I cared not that they should inherit wealth . . . but to be deprived the advantages of education was to make them 'poor indeed.' "[12] Like many other women editors and writers of the antebellum period, Hale defended her literary and professional ambitions on the basis of her familial responsibilities, which she defined in typically republican ways.

Hale's writings during these early years show little sign that she would eventually promote absolute notions of sexual difference and the idea of gendered separate spheres. Hale's novel *Northwood: A Tale of New England,* published in 1827, reveals her grounding in Enlightenment values. Though the novel does associate women with domesticity and men with politics, it repeatedly portrays ideal men and women as practically identical—rational, industrious, and frugal.[13] Hale's view of shared, rather than divergent, traits among men and women is particularly evident in the novel's exploration of marriage. Lydia and Horace Brainard are relatively unhappy together, precisely because Lydia's education neglected her intellectual abilities. Thus, when Horace's attempts at "rational conversation" with his new wife fail and he realizes that only "insipid, common-place chat" can entertain her, he reflects unhappily that "he must travel the journal of life with such a companion." In contrast, ideal marriages are presented as partnerships of similar individuals. Mrs. Romelee, for instance, is described as her husband's "helpmate" and "a tried and discreet friend," and the narrator later celebrates a wedding ceremony in which "two rational beings . . . voluntarily enter into a league of perpetual friendship."[14]

No doubt the rural setting of the novel contributes to the sense of men and women as more alike than different. In this world of small New England farms, men and women live and work together, not in separate worlds. While Victorian ideologies of separate spheres frequently delineated men's and women's work as properly public and private respectively, all members of Hale's ideal New England family contribute to the success of the family farm—itself inseparable from the domestic space. Several of the novel's women are noted for their abilities in running dairies, and the presentation of Mr. Romelee's cider and Mrs. Romelee's currant wine suggests that they share responsibilities for the family orchard. Just as the duties of running the farm are shared in Hale's novel, so too are responsibilities of raising children. Indeed, when Sidney Romelee first returns to his parents' home after an absence of nearly thirteen years, he finds his father—not his mother—sitting before the hearth, reading, with one of his daughters seated on his knee.

Though she would continue to rely on certain elements of Enlightenment ideologies throughout her editorial career, Hale started to shift toward Victorian notions of sexual difference soon after she turned to writing as an occupation. One sign of this change was Hale's new sense of her audience, specifically her increased submission to women's periodicals. In 1826 alone, Hale contributed twenty-one pieces to the *Boston Spectator and Ladies' Album,* and she won that magazine's literary prize for her poem "Hymn to Charity." [15]

Hale's self-definition as a woman writing for other women became even more pronounced when, based in part on the limited success of *Northwood,* publisher and clergyman John Lauris Blake offered Hale the position as editor of his new magazine.[16] The first issue of the *Ladies' Magazine* appeared in Boston in January 1828.[17] Hale edited the first few issues from her home in Newport, but she moved to Boston in April. Although the *Ladies' Magazine* was not, as some have suggested, the first women's periodical to be edited by a woman, it was the first such magazine to achieve any kind of success, surviving nine years.

During her editorship of the *Ladies' Magazine,* Hale vacillated between an Enlightenment emphasis on women's intellectual equality with men and a Victorian belief in women's moral difference from men. Initially, the magazine emphasized Enlightenment principles of women's intellectual equality and the importance of women's education. In this way, Hale's editorship of the *Ladies' Magazine* shared much with her previous work as a teacher. Just as she insisted that women's schooling be intellectually challenging rather than merely ornamental, so Hale rejected the idea that her magazine would simply entertain. Thus, in contrast to other early women's magazines—based on British models and noted for their distinctly anti-intellectual flavor and their emphasis on fashionable life—Hale's *Ladies' Magazine* focused on women's education, social reform, and American literature.[18] In the introductory issue, Hale explained that her intent was "to accelerate the progress of mental improvement," and she promised particular attention to "the cause of education" (*LM*, Jan. 1828, 1–2). In keeping with the educational tone of the magazine, its essays were generally serious and treated such topics as dueling, temperance, letter writing, suicide, and women's physical education. Essays arguing for an intellectually rigorous education for women were especially common, and Hale frequently used her editorial column to do a bit of teaching herself, often in regard to social issues, such as property rights for married women and increased work opportunities for women. She also used her editorial pages to endorse women's civic organizations, such as the Fatherless and Widows' Society and the Seaman's Aid Society, both in Boston.

Hale advocated a strong literary component as part of the intellectual and educational basis of the magazine. As she explained in her opening editorial, literature was necessary for any "mental improvement." In her support of literature, Hale abandoned the popular practices of so-called scissors editors, who reprinted material from other sources, mostly British. Hale instead insisted on original material, and the magazine's fiction and sketches emphasized American characteristics and settings. She also published book reviews and longer essays on such literary issues as novel reading, English poetry, and women writers. Biographical sketches of famous contemporary women were common.

Hale's reliance on Enlightenment rhetoric within this intellectual and educational focus is demonstrated by her introductory essay that opened the magazine in January 1828. Associating "the experiment of universal instruction" with the "perfection of our social happiness," Hale defined her own periodical project as part of that national experiment. She explained that the magazine was "designed to mark the progress of female improvement, and cherish the effusions of female intellect," and she portrayed the magazine as assisting women—specifically mothers—in fulfilling their republican duties: "It is that mothers may be competent to the task of instructing their children, training them from infancy to the contemplation and love of all that is great and good, and the practice of piety and virtue. Then the sons of the republic will become polished pillars in the temple of our national glory, and the daughters bright gems to adorn it." Hale's reliance here on republican ideology is also demonstrated by her specific addresses to men. While she did speak of women's "domestic duties" and women's "sphere," Hale did not really endorse the idea of either a physical separation or an essential difference between men and women, referring instead to woman as the "rational companion" of man. Furthermore, she insisted that although the *Ladies' Magazine* was "ostensibly designed for the ladies, [it] is not intended to be exclusively devoted to female literature." Hale "respectfully" invited the "gentlemen" to "examine its contents," and she devoted five full paragraphs to asking for their patronage. In keeping with her focus on this audience, Hale referred to women not as "our sex," as she would later do, but rather as "the sex" (*LM*, Jan. 1828, 1–3). Thus, although Hale did identify herself as a woman and did use some elements of the sisterly editorial voice in early issues of the *Ladies' Magazine* (including printing letters to the editor), she initially denied a strictly separatist identity for her magazine and avoided intimacy with her readers.

Still, the magazine was titled *Ladies' Magazine*, suggesting at least some elements of a separatist identity. Unlike later separatist rhetorics, which established women as the center of attention, however, Hale's limited use of separatism seems to have been motivated by her desire to avoid criticism. She willingly accepted a marginal position for herself and, to some extent, for other women. She credited men, after all, not women, with the "triumph" of improved education for women, and she even minimized the magazine's worth. "Competition," she insisted, "even were it *possible*, with any established literary journal, is neither wished nor intended" (*LM*, Jan. 1828, 1–4).

Hale's struggle to determine the appropriate degree of separatism is further revealed in her efforts to define her role as book reviewer. Although she published monthly book reviews, Hale repeatedly rejected the title of literary critic, which she associated with men. Instead, she identified herself as an "inspector" of literature and as a writer of "notices" (*LM*, Jan. 1828, 46; Nov. 1828, 522). Defining how such a position differed from that of a "critic," Hale explained her preference of "giving directions where the young may find what will improve their minds and confirm them in the love of virtue, rather than occupy their time with disquisitions on the structure of sentences or the rhythm of poetry" (*LM*, Jan. 1829, 38–39). Similarly, Hale informed her readers that she wrote "*notices* of books" rather than "*criticisms* in the *critical* acceptation of that learned word." As she explained, criticism noted "the faults of authors," while her "notices" identified "the beauties" (*LM*, Nov. 1828, 522).

At the basis of this distinction is gender: a "male critic," Hale wrote, was free "to criticise on style, or cut up books with the keen dissecting knife of ridicule, or triumph in the superior wit or argument, . . . or to 'deal damnation' on the dull." Such behavior did "not accord with the province of woman" (*LM*, Nov. 1828, 522). In many ways, Hale's editorial stance appears to be what Ann Douglas would call the amateurish pose of the professional.[19] When Hale insisted, for example, that a woman who practiced literary criticism had violated "propriety" and forgotten "the dignity" of her sex, she seemed to deny the possibility of a woman as critic. Similarly, by describing her judgments as especially appropriate for the "young," Hale appeared to renounce her ability to make intellectual, literary judgments. Indeed, she made such a claim quite explicit when she announced that she did "not feel qualified to perform the task" of the literary critic (*LM*, Nov. 1828; 522–23; Jan. 1829, 36–38).

Despite the appearance of self-effacement, Hale's comments indicate her positive self-identity as a woman critic. Rather than suggesting inferiority, Hale's position demonstrates the confidence necessary to condemn current practices in literary criticism. When she described how male critics practiced "the science of carping," she did not suggest that she might be incapable of such work, but rather that the male critics' attacks were inappropriate. Such behavior, according to Hale, was motivated not by love of literature but by selfishness. Suggesting that male critics found unnecessary fault only to boast of their abilities,

Hale described "the hardihood of mind, which enables the male critic to depend on himself, and command the acquiescence of the world in his sentiments, more perhaps by his own boldness, than the real justness of his opinions" (*LM*, Nov. 1828, 522–23). A female critic could certainly judge the work, as did Hale throughout her editorial reviews, but the female reviewer, according to Hale, would never celebrate in "triumph" upon finding artistic flaws, nor would she present unjust opinions simply to appear bold.

In distinguishing her work from that of the male critics, Hale also identified a positive sense of her function as editor. Hale's self-identity here suggests the beginnings of a shift toward Victorian ideologies of gender. Not willing to see all critics as identical, Hale began to articulate an essential difference between men and women editors. Significantly, Hale defined her own critical discourse in typically Victorian terms, with a special emphasis on morality. As she explained in 1829,

> It was never our design, when we undertook to conduct the *Ladies' Magazine*, to engage in those elaborate discussions, or profound researches which confer the title of scientific and learned on the work they occupy. Nor did we propose to be critical, in the sense the philologist would deem necessary, in that important department. We only intended to explain to our readers what we considered the *moral* tendency of the books we might notice, or more particularly their fitness for, and probable effect on female minds. We considered this course most appropriate for a woman, and the most likely to prove acceptable as well as beneficial to our own sex. (*LM*, June 1829, 282)

Rather than suggesting her limitations, then, Hale's testimony about not finding authors' faults is more accurately an attempt to define the kind of faults she would cite. Indeed, when describing her role as critic, Hale explained that she would criticize authors only when their "sins should be in *morals*" (*LM*, Nov. 1828, 522). Hale was not, of course, the only reviewer in the 1820s calling for moral criticism, but her version of moral criticism as gendered suggests her shift away from an Enlightenment emphasis on intellectual equality toward Victorian ideologies of essential sexual difference based on women's morality.[20]

The transition from an Enlightenment to a Victorian ideology of womanhood is evident within other features of her magazine as well. Beginning in 1830, for example, Hale's intermittent use of fashion plates—which were increasingly identified with the idea of a separate women's culture—suggests her experimentation with Victorian notions of gender.[21] Similarly, many of the magazine's essays began featuring Victorian rhetoric. Consider, for example, an 1831 essay titled "Boarding Schools," which was unsigned but in all likelihood written by Hale. The essay began in fairly conventional Enlightenment terms, arguing the necessity "to instruct equally both sexes." Though defending that argument in part on the basis of the republican mother's influence on men, the essay itself interpreted that influence in ways remarkably similar to Victorian notions of essential sexual difference. Arguing that "till women are permitted to become rational, men will continue [to be] fools," the author of the essay defined fools "in the scriptural sense, meaning ignorant, weak, wicked, unstable, perverse." Though ostensibly supporting "equal" education, the writer suggested that men and women needed different educations: while both men and women must receive intellectual stimulation, men must also experience the influence of women. Education alone was insufficient for men's proper development. The implication clearly was that men and women had very different essential natures (*LM*, April 1831, 145).

In addition to implying an essential sexual difference, the essay suggested a shift toward Victorian notions of separate spheres. While the republican image of domestic space often focused on a woman's influence on her sons (assumed to be the next leaders of the republic), this essay focused almost exclusively on women and girls.[22] The emphasis here was not on a mother's teaching of her sons and daughters but on daughters alone. Similarly, the schools and the home were depicted as multigenerational worlds of women, with mothers responsible for transmitting female culture to their daughters. Although supporting formal education for young girls, for example, the essay recommended that girls from age twelve or fourteen continue their education at home so that the "mother [may] become the preceptress and companion of her daughter." The emerging vision of women's culture is also suggested in the idea that the "useful and ornamental in education, must be made to harmonize." Rather than rejecting the so-called ornamental arts, this essay insisted upon the value of women's learning housekeeping as well as music, sewing, drawing, and painting (*LM*, April 1831, 147–49).

No doubt many factors contributed to Hale's increasing reliance on Victorian notions of womanhood and women's culture. Certainly, Victorian rhetoric and images of a separate women's culture—including fashion plates—were proving popular in other women's magazines. Still, Hale's turn to Victorian ideologies of gender was probably not based solely on market forces. As an independent, unmarried woman eager to earn a living for herself and her children, Hale would have likely found republican ideologies of gender limiting, for such rhetorics tended to define women primarily as wives and mothers and as occupying the domestic space. Unable to earn her living within that space but still insisting on her identity as a mother, Hale needed—both professionally and personally—a rhetoric that fused womanhood with the public space, which, unlike the domestic sphere, offered financial remuneration for work. To a great extent, Victorian ideologies of gender provided just what Hale needed. Indeed, without undercutting the association of women as mothers and wives, Victorian notions of sexual difference offered women both an image of a separate women's culture and, perhaps even more important, a rationale for their emergence into the public sphere.

Hale's conversion to a Victorian perspective on gender was sealed in January 1837, when she began editing Louis Godey's *Lady's Book*, later titled *Godey's Lady's Book*.[23] Before Hale's arrival, the *Lady's Book* had consisted primarily of reprints, engravings, fashion plates, recipes, and embroidery patterns and thus offered its readers a fare entirely different from that available in Hale's *Ladies' Magazine*, which focused on women's intellectual and moral strengths and original American literature. Suggesting the extent to which Hale and Godey combined their different approaches, Hale's inaugural essay for the *Lady's Book*, titled "The 'Conversazióne,'" depicted the magazine's transition as a "perfecting process" in which the two periodicals, with their "pleasant voices blended in one sweet melody," combined to create something new: "Though not a *new* work in name," Hale explained, the *Lady's Book* was "improved and beautified" (*GLB*, Jan. 1837, 1). Hale's image of two voices blending was an apt one, for the "new" *Lady's Book* continued to feature the often elaborate fashion plates, engravings, and needlework patterns—the so-called embellishments for which Louis Godey became famous. At the same time, Hale injected her own editorial interests into the new magazine. She emphasized women's education and original literature, as she had in the *Ladies' Magazine,* and she used her editorial pages to promote her patriotic and social causes, including a campaign to complete the Bunker Hill Monument, one to save Mount Vernon, and others to support such women's interests as the founding of Vassar College and the training of women as physicians.

Although some twentieth-century scholars have written that Louis Godey maintained most, if not all, editorial control of the *Lady's Book,* Godey and Hale seem to have had a clear sense of divided duties. Indeed, from the beginning of their partnership and throughout the more than forty years that they worked together, Louis Godey served primarily as publisher, and Sarah J. Hale was literary editor. In advertisements, Godey described the magazine's reading matter as "under the control" of Hale, and Hale in her closing editorial in 1877 described Godey as "the sole proprietor and business manager" and herself as "the literary editress" (*GLB,* Dec. 1877, 522).[24] The only feature that she evidently did not manage was fashion. Repeatedly reminding readers of this fact, Louis Godey instructed them to address material to the fashion editor in care of him.[25] These distinct duties are evident within the magazine columns as well. While Godey often used his column to advertise and boast the magazine's successes, Hale's "Editors' Table" generally focused on book reviews and editorial essays.

Though Louis Godey's and Sarah J. Hale's voices within the magazine did, at times, compete with one another, the magazine established by this merger did find a coherent identity, one that, significantly, celebrated Victorian ideologies of gender. Godey's expertise in the embellishments and Hale's interest in original literature and women's causes combined to create a strong sense of a separate women's culture. Hale's essay "The 'Conversazióne' " reveals her commitment to Victorian gender ideals. While in the *Ladies' Magazine* Hale focused on women's rational abilities as equal to men's, here she rigorously asserted an essential sexual difference. Arguing that there were "mental differences in the character of the sexes," Hale explained: "The strength of man's character is in his physical propensities—the strength of woman lies in her moral sentiments." In an even more detailed elaboration of her notion of essential sexual difference, Hale quoted at length a Professor Wilson, who deemed women "spiritual beings" and "pure as dew-drops, or moonbeams," but men "vile, corrupt, polluted, and self-ish." Though Hale herself avoided complete agreement, on the grounds that she had "more sons than daughters," her attention to Wilson's claims functioned as an implicit endorsement of an absolute sexual difference (*GLB*, Jan. 1837, 1–3).

Hale, though, did not completely renounce her earlier assertions about women's intellectual equality with men. Indeed, what Hale did in this essay and what she tried to do throughout her editorial career was to combine Enlightenment and Victorian ideologies of gender. When explaining the Victorian belief in "mental differences" between men and women, Hale refused to give up the principle of equality: the difference of "the minds of the sexes," she insisted, "is not in strength of intellect, but in the manner of awakening the reason and directing its power." Similarly, as much as she associated women with moral influence, Hale continued to assert the importance of education, including the rational study of "mathematics, philosophy, and rhetoric" (*GLB*, Jan. 1837, 1–2).

In Hale's writings this blend of women's intellectual equality and moral difference proved a flexible—and powerful—rhetoric, and she repeatedly moved from one ideology to the other, without any apparent sense of contradiction. In "The 'Conversazióne,'" for instance, she defended her patronage of improved women's education on the basis of "the enlightened intellect of woman." Elsewhere in the essay, however, she employed the rhetoric of difference to claim her own authority as editor and the superiority of her periodical. Immediately after explaining the "mental differences" of "the sexes," Hale argued: "It is on these principles that the claim of superior excellence for 'The Lady's Book,' is founded. If men are, by their position and knowledge of the world, better qualified to instruct men, it can hardly fail to be conceded that a woman is more susceptible of those delicate traits of feeling and sympathies of the soul which predominate in her own sex" (*GLB*, Jan. 1837,

2). The implication, of course, is that the *Lady's Book* had improved precisely because its editor was a woman.

In contrast, at the time that Hale began her editorship of the *Ladies' Magazine* she made no such claim. In her opening editorial in that publication, Hale explicitly asked for the patronage of men, and she granted men the authority to determine whether the magazine was appropriate for their wives, daughters, sisters, and lovers. Hale's opening essay in the *Lady's Book*, however, defines a space that is exclusively women's. Though she did acknowledge that "gentlemen" might be paying for the magazine, she granted women the right to "introduce" men to it. Hale's editorial voice in this *Lady's Book* essay is informal and reveals an intimacy with readers. In contrast to her earlier references to women as "the sex," here she relied on the more intimate "our own sex." Similarly, in elaborating on the essay's title, Hale relied heavily on the sisterly editorial voice, as she imagined the magazine to be equivalent to a party of women: "In short, we intend our work as a '*Conversazióne*' of the highest character, to which we invite every lady in our land—this 'Book' is the ticket of admission, and the first week-day in every month the time of attendance" (*GLB*, Jan. 1837, 1–2). As this passage suggests, Hale's "new" *Lady's Book* both depended on and helped to sustain a separate women's culture. Without an image of such a culture, Hale would have had no way of identifying an exclusively female audience. At the same time, the magazine itself was one of the elements of that culture. In the experience of receiving and presumably reading the magazine on the same day, Hale's readers would have likely had a sense of that shared culture.

The *Lady's Book*'s contributions to and dependence on a separate women's culture are also suggested in Hale's introductory essay in other ways. Again in contrast to Hale's claim in 1828 that her magazine would not be "exclusively devoted to female literature," here all the writers Hale promised her readers were women.[26] Similarly, though twentieth-century scholars have generally referred to the magazine as *Godey's* and have thus de-emphasized its separatist identity, Hale declared the title *The Lady's Book* to be "perfect." Despite the subsequent title changes, in fact, both Hale and Louis Godey continued to refer to the magazine as the *Lady's Book*, or simply the *Book*, throughout their tenures at the magazine. In keeping with the designation popular in its own day and in order to suggest the magazine's image of itself as a woman-identified periodical, I will use the title *Lady's Book*.

Hale's transition to a Victorian ideology of gender and her corresponding sense of writing to an exclusively female audience are also suggested by her publications outside the two magazines that she edited. During her editorship of the *Ladies' Magazine*, Hale's publications generally depended on an Enlightenment philosophy. Like *Northwood* that preceded them, *Sketches of American Character* (1829) and *Traits of American Life* (1835), for example, featured republican virtues and rationality.[27] Significantly, both texts also assumed a general rather than a sex-specific audience. Though originally published as series of sketches in the *Ladies' Magazine*, *Sketches* and *Traits* did not focus specifically on women's issues. Rather, as the preface to *Sketches* explained, the focus was on "Americans" and their "peculiar characteristics," on "the minds, manners, and habits of the citizens of our republic."[28]

Hale increasingly turned her attention to more specialized audiences, and by the early 1830s she was well on her way to establishing a successful career in children's literature. Her *Poems for Our Children*, in which "Mary's Lamb" appeared, was published in 1830; *Flora's Interpreter; or, The American Book of Flowers and Sentiments*, which was intended to help educate children, appeared in 1832; and *The School Song Book* was issued first in 1834 and then again in 1841 as *My Little Song Book*. Hale also edited a number of works for children, including a ten-volume series, the Little Boys' and Girls' Library, and an abridged Bible for children, and she assumed Lydia Maria Child's editorial position of the *Juvenile Miscellany* from 1834 until April 1836, when it ceased publication.[29]

Although Hale continued to write children's literature throughout her life, she turned increasingly to writing for a specifically female adult audience in her book publications at the same time that she promoted the idea of a separate women's culture in her magazines. In the first year that she edited the *Lady's Book*, she published an anthology of poetry, her first clearly separatist book, *The Ladies' Wreath: A Selection from the Female Poetic Writers of England and America* (1837).

In addition to singling out women writers, Hale defined her audience as primarily women. The title page declared that the book was "Prepared Especially for Young Ladies," and Hale explained in the preface: "I cannot but believe that this book will find favor in the eyes of my own sex. It is particularly intended for young ladies."[30] Many of her subsequent books and anthologies have a similar gender-specific orientation, including her advice books on housekeeping and cooking, two novels of domestic life, an anthology of literature for brides, and editions of the letters of Lady Mary Wortley Montagu and of Madame de Sévigné.[31]

Hale's transformation in her book publications to a woman-centered Victorian ideology is best demonstrated by her most ambitious—and most explicitly gendered—book, *Woman's Record; or, Sketches of All Distinguished Women from 'The Beginning' till A.D. 1850*, first issued in 1853. Dividing history into four eras, this nine-hundred-page work presents biographical essays on more than sixteen hundred women, ranging from Sappho and Cleopatra to Emma Willard and Hale herself. As Nina Baym has observed, *Woman's Record* reconceived history with women at its center.[32] In the sketches of the many writers featured, Hale often included samples of their work, giving *Woman's Record* some of the miscellaneous qualities of a magazine. Hale's commitment to this woman-centered book continued well past its initial publication. She continued her biographical researches and issued revised and expanded editions of the work in 1855 and 1870.

Hale's ventures into the more specialized audiences of children and women, beginning in the late 1820s and 1830s, were not unrelated. As William Charvat has suggested, American writers in the early nineteenth century struggled to find and to determine their audience. As the publishing industry grew in the 1820s and 1830s, writers had to move beyond local and familiar audiences.[33] Certainly one way of establishing a readership in the larger, often undefined public was to focus, as Hale did, on specific groups. Hale's efforts to reach the two audiences that she chose, moreover, clearly overlapped. Since women were the primary teachers of very young children—both as paid teachers and as mothers—Hale had to reach women in order to establish a market for her children's texts. By establishing a name for herself among women as an able writer of children's literature, Hale may well have increased her chances of finding a readership of adult women.

Hale's creation of a writing career aimed primarily at women and children is intimately connected with her editorship of the *Ladies' Magazine* and the *Lady's Book*. Indeed, Hale's successes in both the book and periodical industries suggest that her work in one contributed to the success of the other. Certainly, as editor and frequent contributor to the *Ladies' Magazine* and the *Lady's Book*, Hale was able to make readers familiar with her other work. That she expected her magazine readers to buy her books is evidenced by the fact that she often announced her books in the magazines, and at times readers could purchase her books through the *Lady's Book*. Similarly, Hale's efforts within the book industry likely contributed to her success as a magazine editor. When she used the popularity of Harriet Beecher Stowe's *Uncle Tom's Cabin* as an opportunity to revise and reissue her own novel about slavery, for instance, Hale was able to publicize her editorial experience as well. In the preface to the 1852 edition of *Northwood*, Hale informed readers of her editorship of both the *Lady's Book* and the *Ladies' Magazine*, the latter of which, she claimed, was "the first literary work exclusively devoted to women ever published in America."[34]

By all accounts, Hale was particularly successful in establishing a readership for her books and periodicals. Circulation for the *Lady's Book* continued to rise in the antebellum period. In 1849 the *Lady's Book* boasted 40,000 subscribers; by 1860 that number had risen to 150,000. The numbers of readers, not simply subscribers, were even higher. In his New Year's address in 1869, Louis Godey claimed to be greeting 500,000 readers (*GLB*, July 1849, 39; July 1860, 83; Jan. 1869, 99). Although self-proclaimed figures are not necessarily reliable, they do suggest the *Lady's Book*'s enormous popularity; estimates indicate that the average number of subscribers for American magazines at midcentury was roughly 7,000. A comparison with other magazines provides an even greater sense of the relative popularity of the *Lady's Book*. The *North American Review* probably never attained more than a few thousand subscribers, and the *Southern Literary Messenger* had a list of 4,000 in the early 1840s. *Graham's Magazine* and *Peterson's Magazine* seem to have come closest to the *Lady's Book*'s figures, with *Peterson's* circulation probably exceeding that of the *Lady's Book* by the Civil War. Although, like many of its competitors, the *Lady's Book* probably exaggerated its circulation figures by counting delinquent subscribers, its appeals for payment were much less common and less desperate than those in *Graham's*, for example, suggesting perhaps a higher rate of paying customers. Certainly, the *Lady's Book* did not threaten readers—as did the *Southern Literary Messenger*—with the collapse of the magazine if they did not pay.[35]

Hale did quite well in the book industry, though her success there was perhaps less spectacular than her achievements in periodicals. Her *Sketches of American Character* has been listed as a runner-up in a study of American best-sellers, and *Flora's Interpreter* apparently remained in print for nearly four decades.[36] Similarly, like *Woman's Record*, which was revised and reissued twice after its initial publication, Hale's cookbooks and housekeeping books proved popular. Her *Ladies' New Book of Cookery* (1852) was revised and reissued in 1857 as *Mrs. Hale's New Cook Book*, and her *New Household Receipt-Book*, first published in 1853, was expanded and reissued in 1857 as *Mrs. Hale's Receipts for the Million.*

Hale's success in creating an identity for herself and in finding a readership for her books and periodicals is also demonstrated by the length of her career. In 1863, at age seventy-five and suffering from poor eyesight, she began working from home rather than the magazine's office. With her grandson Richard Hunter making the necessary deliveries between home and office, Hale wrote her editorial column for fourteen more years, while continuing to publish outside the magazine as well. A highly productive writer almost until her death, Hale enjoyed an established place in Philadelphia's literary circle. Recalling the "streams of people going upstairs" to her room, Hale's grandson explained: "Everybody who came to Philadelphia must have called on her, and of course there were always her many local friends and the endless authors and artists who contributed to the magazine."[37] Hale's last editorial appeared in December 1877, when she was eighty-nine;

Louis Godey announced his retirement in the same issue. Neither editor nor publisher lived long after leaving their magazine: Godey died on 29 November 1878, and Hale died on 30 April 1879, at age ninety.

Although no single woman can represent the hundreds of nineteenth-century women who became editors, Sarah Josepha Hale's career does reflect the conditions under which many women, especially those in the antebellum period, would establish their editing careers. Like many other women born in the late eighteenth-century United States, Hale was raised in the context of Enlightenment ideologies of womanhood, which stressed women's intellectual equality with men. Though she never abandoned her emphasis on women's intellectual abilities, Hale increasingly embraced Victorian notions of gender. Specifically, she came to reject her earlier idea that the mind has "no sex," as she endorsed the idea of an essential sexual difference between men and women, based, in part, on women's supposedly innate moral sense. Such a belief became a foundational principle for many other women editors of the antebellum period, as they carved out a market for themselves in a separatist community of women.

Hale's employment of this separatist and essentialist ideology, like that of many other women editors, was neither simple nor consistent. Even in the post–Civil War years, when American women's rights activists challenged notions of sexual difference in an effort to win political equality, Hale remained loyal to the separatist vision that she came to accept in the 1820s and 1830s. For Hale and for many other women editors, the metaphor of separate spheres remained an empowering rhetoric on which to base an editorial career.

# 3

## Essentialism and Empowerment: Hale's Theory of Separate Spheres

In late twentieth-century feminist discourse, essentialism is, with few exceptions, equated with either a severe limiting of women's opportunities or, at best, a naive blindness to differences of race, class, and sexuality within the constructed category of "woman." Given Hale's own endorsements of an essential sexual difference, then, it is hardly surprising that she has been characterized as an antifeminist.[1] But to describe Hale in this way simply or even primarily because she posited an ideology of gender now often considered untenable is to assume our own constructions as "natural." With such a bias, we are likely to describe ideologies of the past as "conventional" or "radical" based only on whether they conform to current, late twentieth-century ideas. Far more useful, I would argue, are investigations that focus on how an ideology was constructed and employed within its own cultural context. Such an approach is especially warranted when examining essentialism, which, as Diana Fuss has argued, "is neither good nor bad, progressive nor reactionary, beneficial nor dangerous." According to Fuss, "The question we should be asking is not 'is this text essentialist (and therefore "bad")?' but rather, 'if this text is essentialist, *what motivates its deployment?*'"[2]

To investigate Hale's employment of an essential woman in the context of nineteenth-century theories of separate spheres, then, is my task in this chapter. However her theory of sexual difference and of separatism may initially seem like a complete surrender to a patriarchal

premise of "separate and unequal," Hale used her theory of an essential difference between men and women to raise the status of women's
work within the home and to encourage women's participation in public events, including occupations outside the home. Moreover, although
Hale endorsed the idea of a separate women's culture, she refused to
equate that culture with the so-called private sphere. Indeed, rather
than argue, as did some of her contemporaries, that women's essential nature fitted them solely for the domestic world, Hale advocated a
separate—and essential—public space for women.

An essay published in 1852 provides a useful starting point to investigate how Hale deployed an essentialist theory of womanhood that
sought, in part, to improve the status of women's domestic work. Introducing an essay by L. Aime-Martin on rural life in France, Hale
concurred with Aime-Martin about the inevitable differences between
men's and women's work and about their relative importance. Aime-
Martin wrote, "Surely the avocations of the cottage are neither less
numerous nor of less importance than those of the field. If it require[s]
a vigorous arm to handle the spade or the plough, it requires not less
careful hands to receive the crop, to gather in the fruits, to rear the
poultry, to prepare the butter and cheese, to card and spin the wool,
and to maintain everywhere order and neatness." Unlike twentieth-
century feminists, who generally reject the idea of sex-specific labor,
both Aime-Martin and Hale assumed that the differences between
women's and men's work were based on biology.[3] While men's more
physical labor requires a "vigorous arm," women need the less powerful "careful hands." The division of labor here, however, does not imply
that women's work is less important than men's. Quite the contrary—
the tasks listed for women are more complex and more numerous than
those for men. While men need only "handle the spade or the plough,"
women must harvest, cook, raise animals, make clothing, and "maintain everywhere order and neatness" (*GLB*, Jan. 1852, 89).[4]

In exploring the nature of women's work, Hale repeatedly celebrated
the idea of a separate women's culture. Although scholars often dismiss
the glorification of domestic work found throughout the *Lady's Book*
as a quaint Victorian obsession with the home, Hale, like twentieth-
century feminists who have reclaimed the quilt as a legitimate art form,

clearly placed significant artistic value on women's domestic work. In *The Ladies' New Book of Cookery* she defined cooking as "an Art belonging to woman's department of knowledge."[5] In the *Lady's Book* she argued: "*Needle-work as an Art*, in its fine specimens, similar to drawing and painting, conserves, improves, and beautifies woman, making her more fitted for all other accomplishments; this art will have, as it ever has had, a large share in the artistic designs and lessons of our Book" (*GLB*, Dec. 1860, 556). Notwithstanding our current prejudices against the beaded headpieces and pincushions of the *Lady's Book*, Hale envisioned all women's "crafts" as art—difficult, beautiful, and socially significant.

In addition to elevating domestic work to the level of art, Hale also described it as a profession, requiring significant education and training. Often credited with coining the term *domestic science*, Hale repeatedly argued that housekeeping was worthy of serious study, and she wanted domestic science included in college curricula:

> Women have never yet had any suitable means of education for their household duties. "DOMESTIC SCIENCE," far more important to the health, happiness, and moral improvement of mankind than any other sort of scientific learning, has never yet had a College, nor even a School founded to teach its arts, rules, methods of practice, and deep mysteries of knowledge. Congress has literally given millions of acres of the public lands to found Agricultural Colleges for working men; working women have no recognition in this National bounty. Is it not time to try the experiment of fitting woman for her own work? (*GLB*, March 1865, 278)

Here, as elsewhere in her descriptions of women's work and education, Hale relied on a nonhierarchical notion of difference. While she posited different forms of education for women and men, her pairing of "working men" with "working women" suggests the equal status Hale gave to the agricultural labors of men and the domestic labors of women.

Hale's approach here suggests how she manipulated and sometimes deviated from Victorian notions of sexual difference. Her assumption that women's work was domestic and her association of that work with the "moral improvement of mankind" demonstrate her clear affinity with Victorian notions of absolute sexual difference and separate spheres. But Hale undercut the Victorian idea that women were inherently more moral than men when she argued the necessity of college educations for women. If, as Hale asserted here, women needed a college education to exert their moral influence, then morality could hardly be an essential part of female nature. In focusing on women's learned, rather than innate, abilities, Hale challenged the limited association of women with morality.

The context of Hale's argument about programs of domestic science reveals an even greater challenge to a strict Victorian reverence for sexual difference. In her response to the Morrill Act passed by Congress in 1862, Hale shifted her focus, momentarily, away from difference to some kind of equality. By suggesting that the Morrill Act be extended to provide programs not only in agriculture and engineering but also in "domestic science," Hale insisted that Congress fund women's and men's education. Such a rhetorical strategy demonstrates not only Hale's flexibility in using gender ideologies but also the problems in assuming that an essential theory of sexual difference can only be employed to limit women's opportunities. Hale did not argue here, of course, that women should be engineers. Still, her argument for women's education depended on—and did not conflict with—her belief in an essential "woman." Indeed, she insisted that women needed access to higher education precisely because their education should be different from men's.

Hale's interest in women's education went far beyond advocating domestic training. Like her predecessors in the early republican period, Hale also encouraged women to study such subjects as history, mathematics, and science. But while always insisting on the benefits of such an education for a woman's family and the nation, Hale employed Victorian ideologies of gender and thus transformed the image of the republican mother. No longer assumed to influence destiny solely in the raising of good sons—or good daughters who will then raise good sons—"woman" in Hale's Victorian view emerged from the margins of a patriarchal culture to assume her place at the center of her own culture. Thus, in contrast to the intergenerational image of the republican mother with her sons, the intergenerational image in the *Lady's*

*Book* focused almost entirely on women. The magazine's engravings, for instance, frequently depicted mothers and daughters together.

Nowhere is this image of woman at the center of her own culture more evident than in the fashion plates of the *Lady's Book*. These "embellishments" repeatedly portray women in the company of other women. As Isabelle Lehuu has noted, the women in these fashion plates "did not pay attention to the spectator; they looked at each other and were involved in their closed society or separate sphere."[6] A fashion plate from February 1840, for example, shows two women sharing a settee and looking in each other's direction (figure 2). The intimacy of these women is further suggested by their clothing and their props, which mark their shared status as "ladies." Moreover, like many other fashion plates in the *Lady's Book*, this one shows women holding the material objects of women's culture, as it was defined in the magazine. One woman sits with a needlework stand resting on her lap, and the other woman holds a sealed envelope. While the envelope's seal contributes to the sense of intimacy here—presumably the woman either is about to open this personal note or has just written it—the envelope itself suggests the extent to which print culture was defined throughout the magazine as part of women's culture. As I will discuss in more detail in chapter 5, women in the *Lady's Book* were frequently depicted reading or carrying books and periodicals. The elaborate scrollwork beneath the candle on the wall, moreover, parallels the frequent appearance of artistic objects such as vases and paintings in other plates. Together, these props underscore what is implied by the images of the women themselves: that a women's culture does exist, that it allows for considerable intimacy between women, and that its fashionable, artistic, and intellectual components have a material manifestation in objects such as fancy clothing, needlework, and books.

This image of women's culture suggests one reason why a separatist and essentialist ideology of gender appealed to Hale. Certainly, if one can argue that women are essentially different from men and that they have a separate culture complete with its own material objects, then one has a basis for selling such objects, which include, not coincidentally, periodicals like the *Lady's Book*. Hale's essentialism was thus grounded in her commercial endeavor. This economic per-

Figure 2. Fashion plate.
From *Godey's Lady's Book*, Feb. 1840. Courtesy of the
University of Illinois at Urbana-Champaign.

spective on her essentialism helps explain why no women's periodical before Hale's *Ladies' Magazine* (1828–36) was able to sustain itself. Enlightenment ideologies of the sexless mind, after all, provided no philosophical underpinnings for separatist periodicals. Only with Victorian celebrations of essential sexual difference did the commercial potential of separatist women's periodicals emerge.

However much Hale's essentialism was bound up with commerce, to define it solely in these terms is to miss much of the significance of her employment of Victorian ideology. While republican ideologies assumed all women to be mothers and thus defined a woman's education solely by its effect on her family, Hale redefined a woman's education as personally beneficial. While never making the woman's individual development the only goal of improved curricula, Hale frequently presented personal growth and family service as compatible aims. She once declared that "knowledge will discipline her own mind, and make her more capable of promoting the happiness and success of those she loves" (*GLB*, Jan. 1837, 2). Hale's use of *and* here is instructive: self-fulfillment and influence on others are distinct but compatible results of improved women's education. Hale insisted, in other words, that education was a woman's *individual* right: "Every American born citizen or citizeness," she argued, "has the right of education" (*GLB*, June 1867, 557). Hale's use of the terms *citizen* and *citizeness* suggests the importance of essentialism to such pleas for education as an individual's "right." By employing Victorian essentialism, which endorsed the idea of a separate women's culture, Hale could reject the equation of womanhood with motherhood. Women could be defined independent of their husbands and brothers and sons precisely because they were perceived to be so essentially different from men. Once the equation of woman and mother was broken, Hale could—and indeed did—argue for women's education to benefit women, not just their families.

Hale's interest in defining women as more than wives and mothers is well documented in her magazines. While still with the *Ladies' Magazine*, for instance, Hale published essays faulting parents for encouraging daughters to think of marriage as their only goal. One essay published in early 1835, "The End and Aim of the Present System of Female Education," argued that parents "tremendously overrate" the importance of marriage for their daughters. The essayist insisted that young women should be prepared "for *any* lot which might befall them" (*LM*, Feb. 1835, 73, 75).

Hale made similar arguments in the *Lady's Book*, and even the magazine's fiction, which generally featured women in familial situations, occasionally portrayed single women. Edith Woodley's story "The Old Cedar Chest," for example, presents the happy life of an unmarried woman. As her niece and nephew uncover mementos of her old boyfriends, Aunt Tabitha explains that her decision not to marry was a matter of choice. When asked how many suitors she had, Aunt Tabitha insists it would "be a tedious undertakin' to give you a list of 'em all" (*GLB*, Jan. 1852, 15). In her editorial column the following month, Hale praised the story for teaching young women "that they will be happier in a single life than to marry a man they cannot *respect* as well as *love*," and in a later essay she urged people to realize that a woman might happily "remain single, if she choose, earning her own livelihood or otherwise" (*GLB*, Feb. 1852, 163; Sept. 1861, 227). While the single women in these accounts were generally defined through their familial relations—as aunts, sisters, or daughters—their worth and happiness were not determined by their roles as wives or mothers.

Hale's enthusiastic support for the sewing machine provides another example of how she used Victorian ideologies of sexual difference to defend women's personal fulfillment. Though her optimism proved unrealistic, Hale presented the sewing machine as a device that would enable women to escape the drudgery of housework.[7] Describing the sewing machine as the "Queen of Inventions," Hale praised it for "lightening the tasks of woman," and she published a manufacturer's chart that documented its supposed laborsaving implications. Hale claimed that a woman might be able to make a man's shirt in one hour and sixteen minutes with the machine, which could cover up to "a yard a minute" on long, straight seams, rather than the fourteen hours and twenty-six minutes required to accomplish the same task by hand (*GLB*, July 1860, 77; Aug. 1860, 174). Hale insisted that such benefits could reach even those families who could not afford a machine of their own. Suggesting that ten families join together to make the purchase, Hale calculated that for an investment of six or seven dollars each family could use the machine two and a half days per month (*GLB*, Sept. 1860, 271).

What is significant about Hale's support for the sewing machine is that while recognizing that a woman's family and even the "world" would benefit from her having to spend less time sewing, Hale also acknowledged that a woman might use her time for personal pursuits, "for family occupations *and* enjoyments" (*GLB*, July 1860, 77; emphasis added). Like so much of Hale's rhetoric, this recognition of women's personal fulfillment is presented in the context of Victorian essentialism. Perhaps realizing that the sewing machine represented a potential challenge to the ideology of separate spheres, in collapsing the distinction between the industrial and domestic worlds, Hale used her discussion of the device to reassert her vision of an essential sexual difference. In the essay "The Queen of Inventions," Hale denied that she was entering into "any discussion on the comparative equality of the sexes." She asserted, "As well might we compare light and gravitation—the one power never seen, the other always obtruded, and both alike indispensable to life" (*GLB*, July 1860, 77). Thus Hale reaffirmed the idea of an absolute sexual difference but rejected any implied hierarchy, and she used that essentialist ideology to defend something that she believed would provide for women's personal fulfillment.

If the ability to focus on women as individuals independent of their families was one of the benefits of Hale's essentialism and separatism, an even greater potential of this ideology was the idea of the expansion of women's sphere. In contrast to republican ideologies that defined women's power primarily by the effect on their own families, Hale's essentialist and separatist vision of gender included a much broader conception of women's sphere and power. In "The End and Aim of the Present System of Female Education," the author, probably Hale, asserted that women had a duty to define their own roles as broadly as possible and that women who confined themselves to their own domestic worlds were shirking their responsibilities: "Instead of mixing more in the world, of exerting her influence farther and wider, of setting a purer, higher, more excellent example, of extending, enlarging and adorning her sphere of usefulness, . . . as every woman *should* do,—she retires behind a curtain, shuts the world from her view, . . . shrinks into nothingness, and makes her home that sacred, that hallowed place, her sepulchre." Insisting that such a woman, "in effect, *dies* to all but her own family," the writer argued that "if the world were composed of this class of married women, it would be but one vast hermitage, one drear abode of solitude and darkness" (*LM*, Feb. 1835, 65). As the essay's rhetoric makes clear, the idea of the expansion of woman's sphere is inherently tied to the Victorian idea of an essential difference between men and women. Indeed, the phrase "farther and wider" depends upon the woman's setting a "purer, higher" moral example.

Hale continued to make such declarations throughout her editorial career at the *Lady's Book*. While some of her contemporaries used the idea that the fate of the world depended on whether women were good wives and mothers to confine women within the home and family structures, Hale used the notion of women's essential moral superiority over men to argue for expanding the sphere of women. Since women have the potential to exert a positive influence on others, she argued, society benefits when women extend their influence as far as possible.[8] In associating the domestic life with "the *sceptre* of woman's empire" (*GLB*, Jan. 1837, 5; emphasis added), Hale suggested that women's domestic roles functioned as an emblem of authority that they carried with them wherever they went in their constantly expanding sphere. Indeed, Hale often argued directly with those who sought to confine women, chastising men who attempted "to limit the sphere of woman." Conversely, Hale compared the expanding "sphere of woman" to "the moral light of the Gospel [which] is diffusing clearer and wider views of the truths it indicates" (*GLB*, Nov. 1837, 229–30). Again, the idea of an expanding sphere is tied to women's morality. In the absence of an essential sexual difference, Hale would have no reason to argue for expansion.

Though usually grounded in morality, Hale's idea of an expanding women's sphere was flexible enough to allow a number of interpretations. At times Hale defined this expanding sphere in its relation to the effects of women's domestic work. Thus, during the Civil War era, Hale encouraged her readers to recognize and act upon the political dimensions of their work. Hale identified the power of nineteenth-century women as consumers, like the women of the revolutionary period almost a century before, who participated in the war effort by purchasing American homespun rather than English cloth.[9] Twice in 1865 she published letters to the editor urging women to buy American-made goods, such as cotton, flannel, and Connecticut scissors. According to one letter, women could help American and specifically Northern manufacturing by refusing English goods. Besides demonstrating women's power as consumers, these activities would enhance women's roles as producers as well. Buying American goods would provide work for those women forced into employment when their husbands were killed or disabled in the war (*GLB*, April 1865, 371; Oct. 1865, 359). For the writer of these letters, and presumably for Hale, women who worked in the domestic sphere were hardly confined to that world. Quite the contrary—they had the power to affect national affairs. Decades before American women obtained the right to vote, then, Hale urged women to participate in political activities.

In yet another interpretation of this expanding women's sphere, Hale frequently expressed her support for women's physical education. She criticized the physical confinement of American women and attributed women's poor health to such practices. Hale's remedy was that women should go "forth into the fields and woods" or cities, letting "the minimum of these daily excursions average at least *two miles.*" English women, Hale noted, "walk ten miles without complaining of fatigue" (*GLB*, June 1841, 281). In addition to recommending walking, Hale encouraged such activities as calisthenics, archery, and swimming.

One of Hale's most frequent uses of the metaphor of an expanding women's sphere involved community service. From very early in her editorial career, Hale encouraged women to do for their community the kind of work they did within their homes. She often commended women's charitable organizations, such as Boston's Fatherless and Widows' Society, which raised four thousand dollars and helped more than one hundred widows and their children, and a women's organization in North Carolina that raised twelve hundred dollars to build a church (*LM*, Jan. 1828, 48; Feb. 1828, 96). Hale's position on women's expanding sphere therefore bridges what we would now probably characterize as conservative and more radical positions. On the one hand, Hale's vision of women's function in their expanding public roles focused on social service rather than personal fulfillment. Conversely, nineteenth-century women's benevolence groups created what Barbara J. Berg has called a "vibrant feminist ideology" by allowing women to begin to work within the public domain. By showing upper- and middle-class women the conditions among poor women, moreover, these groups fostered a unity based on gender.[10]

For much of her career, Hale generally preferred that women enter the public sphere not as individuals but within groups. According to Hale's theory of sexual difference, such a strategy maximized the strengths of women's essential moral superiority over men. While the achievements of men's groups were inevitably diminished by the selfish competition natural to their members, women within an organization could work cooperatively. Furthermore, a women's group provided protection for its members; an individual woman in the public sphere, in contrast, risked being contaminated by men's greed and corruption.

Indeed, when describing women's sphere, Hale emphasized the sense of community and cooperation among women, in contrast to the competitive world of men. One essay published in 1828, titled "Female Character," for example, suggested that since women had "amiable" rather than competitive dispositions, they were less given to "hatred and suspicion" or "envy and jealousy." Suggesting the association of women with companionship and concern for others, the essay explained that women had "powers and feelings of sympathy" that were "blunted or impaired" in men (*LM*, May 1828, 194–201). Similarly, an 1829 essay, "The Friendship of Woman," associated women's "natural traits" with the "emotions of friendship." Men, in contrast, were identified with selfishness, fame, and competition. Such distinctions made women's groups especially powerful: women were "not drawn aside by the temptations of business, the envy of superiority, and the silly struggle for honors and preferments" (*LM*, Dec. 1829, 560).

Hale's frequent championing of two groups demonstrates her confidence in the power of women's organizations. Consider, first, her involvement with the Bunker Hill Monument Association. Begun in 1825 but halted several times because of insufficient funds, the drive to build a monument was revived in 1840, when a group of women, including Hale, organized a women's fair to raise money. Held in Boston's Quincy Hall for seven days in September 1840, the fair raised more than thirty thousand dollars—enough to complete the monument.[11] Here, as elsewhere in her celebrations of an expanding women's sphere, Hale relied on domestic and separatist rhetoric. Still, although the goods sold at the fair—mostly needlework, clothing, and food—reinforced conservative associations of women's sphere with domesticity, the fair itself clearly challenged this identification by demonstrating women's ability to manage themselves within the public economic world. The public nature of their endeavor was highlighted by the fair's daily paper, the *Monument*, which Hale edited. That the fair's goal was a political act—the construction of a monument commemorating the American Revolution—further emphasizes what Hale would have called women's expanding sphere. While not totally divorced from more traditional definitions of womanhood—these women, after all, earned money to honor men—the fair brought the women into public, political, and economic arenas.

Hale's involvement with the more overtly political Seaman's Aid Society, likewise, was based on the idea that because women were essentially different from men their sphere of influence should be expanded. Organized by Hale in January 1833, this Boston women's group sought to improve the lives of the city's seamen and their families by founding schools, a library, and a boardinghouse. Its boldest act was to fight the exploitation of workers by opening a clothing shop that sold seamen's garments made by the sailors' wives. As a result of the cooperative efforts, the shop was able to pay higher wages to the women and charge lower prices to the sailors—in direct competition with the established stores, known as slop-shops.[12]

As president of the society from 1833 until 1841, when she moved from Boston to Philadelphia, Hale emphasized that women could enter the public sphere and even participate in its competitive production. In her *Sixth Annual Report of the Seaman's Aid Society*, Hale directly confronted those who would restrict women to the domestic sphere, and she extolled the organization as a model of women's public work:

> It has been asserted by a disparager of our sex, that women are unfit for the details of business which requires method and exactness—that they always prefer fancies to facts, and detest all figures save those of poetry and the dance. But I trust we shall show that, in the prosecution of this

benevolent plan, we have not shrunk from the duty of investigating facts, or the labor and care of exact calculation. Our only fear is, that the reader may think we are too minute in details. Yet, without this minuteness, we cannot hope to make our plan of charity rightly understood.[13]

The concentration here on "facts," "figures," and "exact calculation" and the financial charts that follow this passage demonstrate Hale's belief that women could work successfully within the public realm of finances. Furthermore, rather than disguising the public nature of the organization's achievements, Hale insisted on visibility. Defending her emphasis on "particulars," Hale proclaimed her intention of keeping "the whole ground fairly and fully before the public." [14]

In addition to encouraging women to exert their influence through benevolence organizations, Hale also advocated increased opportunities for wage-earning labor. Significantly, her plans for such labor did not require that women work in groups, though she still defended such reforms on the basis of an essential sexual difference. When defending the rights of women to become teachers, for example, Hale emphasized that women already performed instructional duties at home. Women who became teachers, therefore, were not taking away the "work of men"; they were simply regaining the work that already should have been theirs. Hale's identification of teaching as women's work, not men's, is quite clear: in an essay identifying the three vocational categories appropriate for women, Hale stated quite simply that women "should be qualified for [teaching], and employed in it; if not entirely to the exclusion of male teachers, yet certainly in a tenfold proportion" (GLB, March 1852, 228).

Hale's second category of vocations in this same essay—women as "preservers"—employs a similar extension of women's domestic duties beyond the home, and again this extension allows for women to work individually outside the home. Arguing that women had always been responsible for providing health care at home, Hale proposed that women become physicians (GLB, March 1852, 228). As she explained elsewhere, women had already demonstrated their "eminent success in practising the healing-art" (GLB, Feb. 1857, 180). In yet another essay on physicians, Hale established even more clearly the idea that health care was women's responsibility: "The study of medicine belongs to woman's department of knowledge; its practice is in harmony with the duties of mother and nurse, which she must fulfil. It is not going out of her sphere to prescribe for the sick; she must do this by the fireside, the bedside, in the 'inner chamber,' where her true place is. It is man who is there out of his sphere" (*GLB*, March 1852, 187). Hale's direct challenge to the male-dominated medical profession here reveals the extent to which her vision of an expanding women's sphere conflated public and private. On the one hand, she described the idea of women as physicians in very domestic terms. On the other, she suggested that the male medical profession be transformed into part of women's sphere. As Nancy Woloch points out, obtaining a license to practice medicine in most states after the 1820s required a degree from a medical college. Such a policy excluded women from functions they had previously performed.[15] Rather than limiting women's opportunities, then, Hale's ideology of separate spheres attempted to restrict the opportunities of men.

In an essay supporting the Ladies' Medical Missionary Society in Philadelphia, Hale took a similar approach to midwifery. Not only did she argue that women belonged in this occupation, but she also proposed that men be prohibited from it. Hale noted, with approval, the society's decree that the Bible "recognizes and approves *only woman* in the sacred office of *midwife.*" Noting the difference in infant mortality between a Boston hospital run by men and a hospital of maternity in Paris managed by a woman, Hale concluded that "the practice of midwifery by men is not only injurious, but destructive of human life" (*GLB*, March 1852, 185–86). Hale's campaign responded to women's declining right to practice midwifery, which by the 1820s was legally restricted to graduates from medical schools. Such a policy barred women from a profession they had previously dominated.[16] Rather than accepting the intrusion of men into the birthing room, Hale envisioned a return to earlier days when childbirth occurred among women, in a world completely separate from men.

Hale's third general vocation for women in this essay is that of "*helpers.*" Although the term itself, like *preservers*, connotes women's traditional functions within the home and even subservience, Hale's definition encompassed duties within the public realm, specifically

managerial positions. Again, Hale based her argument on separatism and traditional women's functions. She argued, for instance, that
women "should be intrusted with the management of all charities
where their own sex and children are concerned." That Hale defined
these charities in a very broad sense is clear by the examples she
offered. She encouraged women to manage savings banks, explaining
that women would be better able to serve "the poor depositors" than is
"now the fashion" (*GLB*, March 1852, 228). Elsewhere she argued that
women should supervise hospitals, colleges, and post offices. Clearly,
Hale could include within the helper category virtually any vocation in-
volving public service. Again Hale proposed that public positions typically associated with men be redefined as occupations within women's
public sphere.

The terms Hale used to describe these occupations demonstrate the
centrality of an essentialist ideology of gender in her thinking. In the
same way that she used the term *domestic science* to undercut an assumed dichotomy between private domesticity and public professionalism, Hale used domestic imagery when discussing women's professional careers. When describing her own editing and writing duties, for
instance, she frequently employed images of the home and housework.
In a letter to the editor signed "H***" in the first issue of the *Ladies'
Magazine* (and thus presumably written by Hale), editing duties are
compared to making "a feast." The letter provides a "recipe" for effec-
tive editing that "never fails of adding a flavor to the best prepared
meal, and even making the most ordinary one palatable" (*LM*, Jan.
1828, 43).[17] Even more telling are the names she used for professional
women. In the same way that she referred to herself as an "editress,"
Hale used terms like *doctress* and *authoress*, and she wrote editorials
encouraging others to do the same. In part, this crusade, which took
place relatively late in her career, stemmed from her disdain for the
term *female*, which she claimed demeaned women by referring to animals. (Hale campaigned to rename Vassar Female College simply Vassar College.) In addition to disliking the term *female*, Hale denounced
terms like *female doctor* because they failed to suggest the combination
of womanhood and professionalism implied in *doctress*. According to
Hale, *doctress* was "a pleasant, soft word, explaining the rank and the

sex, mingling, in our idea, of the woman and her vocation, tenderness with respect." The title *female doctor*, on the other hand, was "a compound idea" with one word "meaning an animal, the other a man" (*GLB*, Aug. 1857, 177). Unwilling to identify herself by male definitions of occupations, Hale chose titles that emphasized her essential difference from men. Significantly, Hale preferred terms that emphasized what she called tenderness, suggesting her commitment to an ideology of sexual difference based primarily on women's inherent morality rather than strictly biological or "animal" differences.

Hale's categories and examples of women's wage-earning work suggest the degree to which she identified her audience as middle class, desiring professional occupations. Although she certainly recognized the importance of financial rewards for work—especially for widows with children to support—her vision of women's professionalism focused more on what women could do for society than on what jobs paid well. In doing so, Hale ignored the needs of most nineteenth-century American wage-earning women, 70 percent of whom were servants.[18] Hale instead focused on those women who already had some degree of financial security—those who could afford to undergo training—and who already had considerable education.

Hale's interest in professional occupations, specifically managerial roles, however, also suggests her concern that women's culture must be self-determined. When arguing for improved education for girls, which Hale viewed as transmitting women's culture, for instance, she insisted that women supervise the schools. She conceded the possibility that "gentlemen [might] be employed as professors and lecturers occasionally," if "it be found necessary" to do so, but she insisted that "a lady should always preside as directress" (*LM*, March 1829, 133). As she declared in another essay, "Man's fiat cannot fix woman's sphere; she must go to the word of God, to the precepts of the Saviour to learn her moral duties, and she must judge for herself how she can best perform them" (*GLB*, Nov. 1837, 229). While Hale maintained that women must be obedient to God, she gave women—not men—the responsibility for determining God's plan.

While Hale did employ a separatist and essentialist ideology in order to extend women's sphere, there was at least one activity for which she

believed women were not intended: participation in political parties.
An oft-repeated story about the *Lady's Book* asserts that it never mentioned the Civil War. Although recent scholars have proved this tale
erroneous, both the *Ladies' Magazine* and the *Lady's Book* did attack
women for becoming political activists.[19] An essayist writing in the
*Ladies' Magazine* in 1828 disclaimed any "intention of writing *politically*," asking, "What business has a lady's paper with politics?" (*LM*,
Aug. 1828, 338). Similarly, one editorial in the *Lady's Book* in 1852 argued that women should vote only "by influencing rightly the votes of
men" (*GLB*, April 1852, 293).[20] In addition, Louis Godey once notified
his readers that the printing office had orders to inform him of any
political allusions, because, as he explained, "the ladies object" (*GLB*,
March 1856, 273).

Such responses are particularly problematic, since Hale's editorial
columns frequently treated a wide range of political issues, including
married women's property rights and congressional support of women's
higher education. The paradox arises, in part, out of Hale's understanding of politics. While fully endorsing women's involvement in political
issues, Hale did not want women to participate in political parties. As
Paula Baker has explained, political parties in the nineteenth-century
United States were generally defined in masculine terms. With politics
identified with "saloons, barber shops, and other places largely associated with men," the parties themselves served as "fraternal organizations that tied men together with others like themselves." These political parties, moreover, relied heavily on rhetorics of warfare: "Parties
were competing armies, elections were battles, and party workers were
soldiers."[21] A two-part story by T. S. Arthur, titled "Before and After the
Election" and published in the *Lady's Book* in November and December 1849, illustrates a corresponding image of American party politics.
Both accompanying plates depict scenes consisting entirely of men,
and the story itself presents political campaigns as little more than
abuses of power. In the first installment, Patrick Murphy, a recently
naturalized Irish immigrant, is being wooed in a bar by a candidate
for a state legislature. Honored by the candidate's attention and believing his offer of a job, Patrick leaves his own job, only to find his

candidate unsuccessful. When in the second installment Patrick turns to the former candidate in search of a new job, he is rebuffed. Those controlling political campaigns bribe and lie, the story suggests, and they have utter contempt for the electorate (*GLB*, Nov. 1849, 342–45; Dec. 1849, 390–92).[22]

Obviously, women's participation in such male-dominated and crudely competitive activities would have threatened Hale's understanding of separate spheres and essentialism. Becoming involved in such partisanship would inevitably lead women to act like politicians and voters—that is, competitively and ultimately corruptly. Such women would obviously not be acting morally. Since Hale defined women's morality as *the* essential difference between men and women and party politics as essentially immoral and divisive, she found no use for women in politics directly. A woman's only option, Hale insisted, was to influence the vote indirectly, through husbands, brothers, and sons. Only then could women remain essentially different from men.

Hale's understanding of politics and her commitment to an essential difference between the sexes help explain why she reacted so strongly against women fighting for suffrage. By arguing for "equality," these women rejected Hale's notion of sexual difference. Ironically, however, they often used a rhetoric that Hale herself had employed decades earlier—namely the Enlightenment-based philosophy that the mind has "no sex." Most notable here, of course, is the "Declaration of Sentiments" adopted by the 1848 Seneca Falls convention, but many suffrage leaders, including women editors, relied on similar rhetorics. In contrast to Hale's own pleas for difference and morality, Mary A. Livermore's *Agitator* (1869) is filled with Enlightenment-like references to equality and rationality. When another paper objected to women's suffrage, the *Agitator* responded with an essay filled with references to the Enlightenment philosophies of the Declaration of Independence:

> The rights which our fathers called "inalienable," are usually called natural, as distinguished from political rights, and they are not limited by sex. No one will deny that a woman has the same right to "life, liberty, property and the pursuit of happiness," that man has. If so, she has the same right to all that protects her life, liberty and property that a man has. We

think no one will deny that all persons, women as well as men, are born with an equal claim to these natural rights, and an equal claim to every kind of protection of these natural rights. (*Agitator,* 10 April 1869, 4)

Though Hale had at one time shared some of the philosophical under-pinnings of such an argument, by the 1860s and 1870s she was unwill-ing to return to her pre-Victorian rhetoric of equality. Her editorials about the "woman question" repeatedly insisted on essential sexual difference. Thus she once described that "small band of women" who were arguing for suffrage as "persistently ignor[ing] the great and radi-cal differences between the sexes." Reaffirming the "moral and mental differences" between men and women, Hale issued a call to action, urging "every woman who believes the mission of her sex to be in a sphere apart from politics to speak out" (*GLB,* Jan. 1872, 93).

The question to ask here, I think, is why. Why did Hale so ada-mantly reject the idea of women voting, even when she herself was constantly encouraging women to expand their sphere of influence? Why did she not use her essentialism to argue, say, that women should vote precisely because they might vote differently than men? Though many factors undoubtedly contributed to Hale's opposition to suffrage, two seem particularly relevant here. First, Hale's own sense of her-self as an "editress" writing to what she understood to be a univer-sal "woman" was seriously undermined by the rhetoric of suffrage. If women could vote and therefore engage in partisan politics, then the universal "woman" Hale constructed must not exist. If women could argue over politics just as men did, then they must not share an essen-tial moral nature. Significantly, the idea that women might not have an essential moral nature threatened the magazine that dominated Hale's literary career. The *Lady's Book* was always, of course, aimed at a par-ticular group of women—white, middle-class, and mostly Protestant women who either were or aspired to be married. But Hale always assumed that such women represented a universal woman; thus she defined women by what she assumed they shared rather than by their individual differences. That Hale was never able to make the transition to the rhetoric of women's difference and individuality is suggested by the gradual decline of the *Lady's Book* in the years following the Civil

War. Though it survived until 1898, it never regained the popularity it enjoyed in the antebellum period, when Victorian essentialist ideology of gender was at its peak.

Hale's objection to women's involvement in politics was also influenced by her experience and understanding of the Civil War. For Hale, the daughter of a soldier of the Revolution, the threat of the breakup of the Union was nothing short of the catastrophic result of male partisanship. Though Hale did not generally comment on the nation's political tensions or the war itself in the *Lady's Book*, she did occasionally use the magazine to advocate national unity. When arguing for establishing Thanksgiving as a national holiday before the war's outbreak, Hale repeatedly portrayed it as a time for the nation to come together. If the entire nation could share a holiday—literally sit together and share a meal—Hale believed it could avert the impending war. She asked in 1859, "If every State should join in union thanksgiving on the 24th of this month, would it not be a renewed pledge of love and loyalty to the Constitution of the United States, which guarantees peace, prosperity, progress, and perpetuity to our great Republic?" (*GLB*, Nov. 1859, 466).

As idealistic and naive as such a plan seems now, Hale's plea underscores both her belief in women's proper involvement in the political process and her subsequent rejection of women's suffrage. If direct political involvement meant partisanship that could and did lead to war, then she saw no reason why women would even want to become active participants in the political process. That some of her most vocal opposition to suffrage in the *Lady's Book* appeared in the postwar years suggests her own desperate attempts to avoid among women what the nation itself had experienced. Thus, rather than envisioning women as voters, Hale imagined women as easing partisanship through indirect involvement. One of Hale's editorial essays in 1870, "Woman's Mission in War," made such a vision explicit. Arguing basically that men make wars and women end them, Hale declared: "When the time arrives for war to be no more, its cessation will have been brought about by the power of Christian love, acting mainly through the influence of woman, to whom the blessed office of peace-maker seems to be naturally committed." Though Hale did not refer specifically to suffrage here, the implication is clear in the context of questions about women's suffrage in the post–Civil War era. If women were to fulfill their "mission of peace-maker, healer, and consoler," they must remain separate from activities that cause war—namely party politics (*GLB*, Dec. 1870, 555).

But the idea that women must remain separate from politics and war-making posed other problems for Hale, for the Civil War resulted, after all, not only from partisan politics but also from a moral debate about slavery. If Hale's understanding of party politics prohibited her from active participation, her association of women with morality re-quired the exact opposite: if the political debate was about morality, then according to Hale's ideology of gender, women had no choice but to participate. Put simply, the Civil War posed a serious dilemma for Hale and her theory of separate spheres: What should women do when partisan political debates intersected with moral ones?

Hale's own responses to slavery suggest the limits of her essentialist ideology, for she was unable to come to any certain conclusion about the question of women's place in the national debate about slavery. Hale's own position reveals her divisions: although she opposed slavery, she rejected the abolition movement as too partisan. Yet in keeping with her association of women with morality, Hale herself did not remain silent on the subject. Her own *Northwood*, first published in 1827, treated slavery as an important, though not primary, subject. Similarly, early in her editorial career, Hale confirmed her belief that women could write about slavery. In a review of a Mrs. Carey's *Letters on Female Character* in 1829, Hale announced that the book, primarily about women's edu-cation, contained "some remarks respecting the moral effects slavery is producing on the white inhabitants of the South." Clearly hostile to partisanship, Hale mourned the fact that those who opposed slavery could not speak out without "incurring the odium of acting from politi-cal or party motives," but she held to the idea that women might be able to escape such accusations: "But the ladies may surely be permitted to speak or write freely on the subject; nor will their efforts be without effect, if they are as faithful and capable as Mrs. Carey" (*LM*, June 1829, 283–84). Hale's own subsequent editorial columns supporting the American Colonization Society confirm her willingness to express her views publicly. Even during the 1850s, when slavery became an increasingly divisive political issue, Hale continued to write on the subject. In her revision of *Northwood* in 1852, for example, she added two long chapters that provide an extended discussion of slavery, and in 1853 she published *Liberia; or, Mr. Peyton's Experiments*, in which she promoted African American emigration. Still, even in these texts, Hale showed some apprehension about her position as a woman writing on slavery. She ends the 1852 edition of *Northwood*, for example, by insisting that hers is no "partizan book" and claiming a moral rather than a political position:

> "Constitutions" and "compromises" are the appropriate work of men: women are the conservators of moral power, which . . . preserves or destroys the work of the warrior, the statesman, and the patriot.
>
> Let us trust that the pen and not the sword will decide the controversy now going on in our land; and that any part women may take in the former mode will be promotive of peace, and not suggestive of discord.[23]

Similarly, in *Liberia* Hale repeatedly presented colonization as a primarily religious rather than a political plan, describing the early Liberian settlers, for instance, as "pilgrims." [24]

But even such attempts at focusing on peace and morality rather than partisan politics proved insufficient within the *Lady's Book*, where Hale showed even more restraint. In an 1852 review of John Fletcher's *Studies on Slavery, in Easy Lessons*, Hale acknowledged "how carefully we have always avoided all participation in the discussions" on slavery. Though promising her view on Fletcher's work, which evidently used the Bible to defend slavery, Hale avoided expressing any opinion of slavery itself. She insisted that her remarks were only on the "ingenious merits of the defence" and not "the merits of the institution." Hale's equivocations continued: "Without committing ourselves either in favor or against his conclusions in regard to the question under consideration, we have no hesitation in saying that he has produced a learned and able work, and one which, if generally read, would at least throw oil upon the turbulent waves of sectional and sectarian controversy, and induce calm and sober reflection in the minds of all who are heartily interested in the cause of humanity, and in the permanent advancement and security of freedom" (*GLB*, Nov. 1852, 485). As clear as Hale's disdain for "sectional and sectarian controversy" is here, her solution to the moral dilemma of slavery is not.

Hale's ideology of gender was unable to help her resolve the dilemma of whether women should become active in the debate about slavery. Although early in her editorial career she maintained the possibility that women could speak on slavery, she became increasingly uncomfortable with that position as slavery became associated more and more with partisan politics. Within her own books, however, she continued to express her views on slavery into the turbulent 1850s. Although Louis Godey discouraged political statements in the magazine, his self-proclaimed position as censor of the *Lady's Book* does not, to my mind, adequately explain Hale's inconsistent treatment of women's proper involvement in the nation's debate about slavery. Regardless of Godey's own position, Hale faced a serious quandary in discussing slavery in the *Lady's Book*. While Hale was comfortable discussing moral issues, the informal and intimate sisterly relationship Hale envisioned between herself and her readers clashed with her understanding of politics as a male-dominated competitive arena. If she were to engage in political debate with her readers, she would destroy the informal and intimate relation that she enjoyed with them. Though Hale was never able to resolve this dilemma, she did construct a response: in the early 1850s she maintained her right to speak publicly about slavery in books for a general audience; in the gender-specific world of the *Lady's Book*, however, she assumed the position of "editress," avoiding political controversy. After 1853 Hale avoided the subject of slavery altogether—as both editor and author.

Like other constructions of gender, then, Hale's essentialist view of sexual difference and her corresponding commitment to separate spheres proved both limiting and empowering. Though she was never able to craft a comfortable position as a woman speaking on partisan issues, she did use her essentialist and separatist ideology to address other issues related to women. By insisting on the importance and difficulty of women's work within the home, Hale defended significant improvements in women's education. While celebrating domestic work, however, she did not present it as the only opportunity that women had. Rather, she portrayed women's work outside the home as important, and she argued for extending the range of such employment. Thus, although some of her contemporaries believed that the notion of separate spheres explained women's proper confinement within the home, Hale defined that concept in order to imply the differences between men's and women's work. Therefore, she thought, women's public wage-earning labor, including her own editorial work, could—and should—be defined by gendered separatism. And however much Hale's opposition to women's suffrage may appear now to be an internalized acceptance of women's supposed inferiority, in the context of her own rhetoric and the historical conditions in which she worked, such a position was consistent with her belief about the role of women as the nation's moral guardians. Indeed, not unlike radical feminists of the twentieth century who dismiss the political yearnings of their more liberal sisters, Hale rejected politics not because she believed women were unable to manage society's affairs but because she held a cynical attitude toward men's behavior and accomplishments in politics. While her rhetoric proved limited and ultimately unhelpful to the suffrage leaders following her, Hale's separatism and essentialism formed an empowering and flexible ideology that she used to argue for increased opportunities for herself and her readers.

# 4

## The Professionalization of Authorship

Though Hale devoted much attention to women's education and work, many of the editorial columns written during her fifty years as editor focus specifically on literary matters, offering everything from sketches of popular writers to recommendations on the latest books. Just as Hale's theory of sexual difference formed the foundation for her essays on women's education and work opportunities, so it provided the basis for many of her ideas about literature, and if her ideology of sexual difference again sometimes limited her, it also served as a powerful underpinning, as she offered sometimes radical definitions of the author, the reader, and the text. In some of these efforts, Hale foregrounded her essentialism and separatism—as in her construction of the woman reader; in others Hale's ideology of gender is less apparent. Nonetheless, Hale's theory of sexual difference exerted a powerful influence in all of her literary investigations.

Hale's treatment of authorship is one area in which the influence of her gender ideologies is not immediately apparent, and with good reason. However much she defined both the *Ladies' Magazine* and the *Lady's Book* as women's spaces separate from men's, the literary world in which she worked was never exclusively female. Living in two literary centers, Boston and Philadelphia, Hale knew many of the nation's writers, both men and women. Some of these writers, including Oliver Wendell Holmes, Lydia Sigourney, and Edgar Allan Poe, became her friends. Others, such as John Greenleaf Whittier and Henry Wadsworth Longfellow, Hale knew primarily by publishing or reviewing their works. Regardless of the nature of Hale's relationship with writers, she consistently earned their respect. Oliver Wendell Holmes, for instance, admired her "perseverance and spirit in literary labor" and praised how much she had done, "always with a high and pure aim," and Charles Dickens wrote to her, expressing his appreciation for a tribute she had written of him and for those "sympathies" that they "cherish[ed] in common." Even writers who at times disagreed with Hale usually valued her work. Elizabeth Oakes Smith, who suffered Hale's censure for speaking publicly, still described Hale as a "mentor" and praised her patronage of young writers.[1]

Such tributes are hardly surprising, for throughout her career Hale advocated improved conditions for authors. William Charvat has succinctly defined the conditions of professional authorship: "The terms of professional writing are these: that it provides a living for the author, like any other job; that it is a main and prolonged, rather than intermittent or sporadic, resource for the writer; that it is produced with the hope of extended sale in the open market, like any article of commerce; and that it is written with reference to buyers' tastes and reading habits."[2] Though not the only person working toward such conditions, Hale consistently supported professional authorship: she respected authors' financial concerns by treating the literary product as a commodity, yet she refused to portray writing simply as a commercial act. Rather, she repeatedly insisted that authors deserved everyone's praise and support. Moreover, while her theories of gender influenced her notion of authorship, she promoted a vision of professional authorship beneficial to men and women writers.

Recognizing authorship as a profession was a relatively new idea in the United States when Hale began her editorial career in 1828. As many scholars have demonstrated, throughout the 1820s most writers, editors, and publishers accepted the eighteenth-century ideal of the scholarly gentleman, thus equating literary pursuits with leisure activities. This gentleman might write, said Charvat, but he "never wrote for money, never put his name on what he wrote, and rarely even condescended to put what he wrote in print." Although these "gentlemen" authors might have held professional status within their communities, they maintained this social position as doctors or ministers, not as authors. This notion of authorship is antiprofessional in virtually every sense: writing does not demand, or deserve, lifelong commitment, and the literary product lacks economic value.[3]

Although by the time Hale began her editorial career a few writers—most notably James Fenimore Cooper and Washington Irving—had successfully challenged the idea that writing was a leisure activity, all writers seeking professional status, including Cooper and Irving, faced serious obstacles. With publishers not yet able to finance publication, authors of the 1820s either had to pay printing costs themselves and hire a distributor or had to find a patron willing to risk the initial investment. The difficult task of raising the finances to print a work, moreover, was simply an author's first hurdle. With the rail system not yet established, authors and publishers relied on rivers for distribution. Thus service did not reach certain parts of the country, and distribution was interrupted each winter when the rivers froze. As a result, reaching a national audience was extremely difficult, even for the most popular writers. As late as 1845 Lydia Sigourney complained that her books were unavailable even in Hartford, Connecticut, where she herself lived.[4]

Conditions for professional authorship in the magazine industry in the 1820s were not much better than in book publishing. Work was rarely signed, payment remained extremely unusual, and even if one editor acknowledged authorship and offered payment, another was likely to reprint the material without authorial permission or compensation. Writers in the periodical industry also faced difficulties in finding a national audience. The Post Office Act of 1794 allowed magazine publishers to distribute through the mail, but the act did not result in real improvements, in part because postal rates, paid by the subscriber, were high. With most magazines before 1825 depending on local subscribers, periodicals, like the book industry, offered authors little chance of a national audience.[5]

In this antiprofessional climate Hale began editing the *Ladies' Magazine* in 1828. She immediately enacted three specific policies that significantly contributed to the professionalization of literary pursuits. First, while most magazine editors relied on pirated material, Hale accepted only original submissions. Second, she rejected the ideal of the anonymous writer and encouraged attribution, thereby allowing writers to build the reputation necessary for professional status. Finally, Hale supported an author's right to be paid for the written work. These three policies assume the basic premise of professional authorship—that the author deserves compensation for the literary work, which itself is recognized as having an economic value.

As part of her belief that good-quality magazines should not be simply a collection of reprinted material, not only did Hale accept only original material in the *Ladies' Magazine*, but she also used her editorial columns to condemn the practices of the so-called scissors editors, who relied on pirated work. Her critique of such practices is implicit, for example, in this description of the *Ladies' Magazine:* "This periodical is not a compilation, a mere 'omnium gatherum' of the shreds and clippings of all the old newspapers in the nation. The work is to be wholly original articles" (*LM*, Jan. 1829, 5). Like so many of her policies and positions, Hale's condemnation of the "scissors editors," who relied heavily on British material, was motivated in part by her own patriotism. In the introductory issue of the *Ladies' Magazine*, Hale insisted that her magazine must be "national—be American" (*LM*, Jan. 1828, 3), and she repeatedly described support for American authors and American magazines as nothing less than the nation's civic responsibility. Hale insisted that readers should "support generously, with national pride, the efforts of our own talented writers" (*LM*, July 1830, 320).

In return for such support, writers themselves had to aspire to an original American literature. More than a decade before Ralph Waldo Emerson's more famous pleas, in 1830 Hale insisted that the "greatest obstacle to the production of works of originality among us is this—our writers copy European models" (*LM*, June 1830, 286). Rejecting an imitative model for art, Hale used the *Ladies' Magazine* to encourage writers to aim for originality. One essay in 1830, for instance, argued that "original ideas are the greatest productions of an improved intellect. It is an evidence of high and noble feeling that the human mind labours within itself, and does not depend upon others; but soaring above every source of reflection and intellectual aid except those which its own improved powers afford, creates individual and original ideas" (*LM*, Sept. 1830, 407). Significantly, Hale denounced imitating even writers she greatly admired. Although she often praised Felicia Hemans's poetry, she criticized those who copied her style: "We entirely disapprove of imitations; they are the bane of all real excellence" (*LM*, Jan. 1828, 31).

To celebrate authors further, Hale also encouraged editors to identify them. In 1829, when anonymous and pseudonymous submissions remained common, Hale criticized a gift annual for omitting the names of contributors: "Credit ought to have been given to authors *whose* writings are inserted" (*LM*, Jan. 1829, 48). Again, the practice of crediting authorship improved a writer's opportunity to gain professional status; without public recognition, writers had no means of achieving popular acclaim. Despite her proclamations favoring attribution, however, Hale did not always identify her own contributors in the *Ladies' Magazine*. Much of the material, especially in the early years of the magazine, was either unsigned or identified only by initials. Nevertheless, Hale's reliance on unidentified contributions does not necessarily indicate a lack of interest in crediting authorship. She may simply have wanted to hide the fact that she wrote most of the magazine herself. In this way, the lack of identifiable writers may have worked to promote the idea, at least, of professional authorship. If readers accepted the pretense that many different writers contributed to the publication— by no means a certainty—they would have thought the number of published writers was higher than it actually was. Since Hale's readers did sometimes become writers, they may have submitted material based on the assumed success of others. As the number of signed submissions increased, these readers certainly had more reason to be optimistic about publication.

As part of her campaign within the *Ladies' Magazine* to establish authorship as a profession, Hale was one of the first magazine editors to encourage adequate compensation, though she was only partially successful in paying her own writers. Hale probably did pay regular contributors like Lydia Sigourney, who sent her work only where she would receive compensation, but Hale's resources most likely prohibited standard reimbursements.[6] Still, Hale did encourage her readers to consider authors' financial needs. In a review of Hawthorne's *Fan-*

*shawe* in 1828, for example, Hale asked readers not to "depend on obtaining [the book] for perusal from a circulating library, or from a friend," but to "purchase it." Hale argued that the "time has arrived when our American authors should have something besides empty praise from their countrymen" (*LM*, Nov. 1828, 526). Similarly, when reviewing the gift annuals the following year, Hale repeated her plea that "books must be *paid* for as well as *praised*" (*LM*, Nov. 1829, 529).

Hale's understanding of authorship in the 1820s and 1830s fused romantic and commercial considerations into a truly professional model of authorship. Hale understood the author to be a gifted, original individual—a genius—as in romantic definitions of authorship, rather than, as in older models, a transmitter of cultural truths. Hale's vision of the author as a genius differed from that of some of her contemporaries, however, in regard to its relation to the market economy. As R. Jackson Wilson has observed, many nineteenth-century writers viewed the commercial aspects of authorship with considerable disdain, seeing the market as "a foul thing, holding out nothing to the true artist but a temptation to compromise the promptings of genius in order to win the favor of the 'multitudes.'"[7] In contrast to such views, Hale envisioned the author as part of, though not reduced to, market conditions. Her support of adequate compensation for authorship is therefore consistent with the more romantic view of the author as an original individual. Because she believed the author to be a genius, she saw the product of literary labor as property, intellectually valuable and belonging to the author. This definition is, in short, a professional one.

Hale's vision of the professional author helped create a new relationship between reader and writer. While the eighteenth-century writer, subsidized by the patronage of friends and family, generally knew his or her audience intimately, the nineteenth-century professional writer appealed to a much larger and often indeterminate readership. As an editor and author, Hale positioned herself within this larger, less familiar audience by appealing specifically to women—and to a lesser extent to children—with whom she could then establish an intimate relation. Hale's sisterly editorial voice should thus be understood in the context of her concern for professionalizing authorship. In contrast to some of her contemporaries, who viewed the market and the "multitudes" as "foul," Hale crafted a far more agreeable understanding of the mass audience, precisely because she worked within a gender-specific context. By using the sisterly editorial voice and by writing primarily for women, with whom she assumed she shared an essential nature, Hale could deny that her audience was distant and unfamiliar, even while she benefited financially from her ability to appeal to a large national constituency. Hale was thus able to define professional authorship without accepting the idea of a distant and impersonal audience. Ironically, then, while the sisterly editorial voice and the professional model of authorship assume vastly different relationships between reader and writer—one intimate and familial, the other impersonal and economic—Hale's editorial voice and her work for professional authorship were, in fact, mutually dependent strategies.

In this context, Hale's move from the *Ladies' Magazine* to Louis Godey's *Lady's Book* in 1837 marks a pivotal, if often unacknowledged, shift in the history of authorship, for it was with the *Lady's Book* that Hale was best able to combine her sisterly editorial voice with professional standards of authorship. Before Hale's management, the *Lady's Book*, like most periodicals of the 1830s, did nothing to encourage professional authorship. Indeed, during its first seven years it consisted primarily of unacknowledged reprints, unattributed work, and, of course, the famous embellishments. Nowhere in its editorial columns did Louis Godey encourage financial and professional support for authors, as Hale did in her *Ladies' Magazine*. When Hale assumed editorial control of the *Lady's Book*, she brought her editorial policies concerning authorial rights to her new and more popular publication. Thus began one of the longest and most far-reaching campaigns to improve conditions for American writers.

It was a campaign similar to that in the *Ladies' Magazine*. With Hale as editor, writers in the *Lady's Book* were generally identified, and the magazine also shifted to publishing original material.[8] Refusing to publish reprints remained one of the magazine's strongest editorial policies. For decades Hale announced that would-be contributors should not submit material published elsewhere, and the *Lady's Book* repeatedly boasted its policy of "never insert[ing] articles that have appeared in other journals" (*GLB*, March 1857, 277). The policy about reprinted material was so firm, in fact, that the magazine even avoided reprinting its own material. In 1865 Louis Godey announced receiving repeated requests for Eliza Leslie's short story "Mrs. Washington Potts," published in the magazine in 1832, when Godey was editor (*GLB*, July 1865, 88; Aug. 1865, 182). The piece appeared again in 1866, only after Godey asked for and evidently received subscribers' approval.

Besides printing only original material, the *Lady's Book* supported authorial rights to the literary product by copyrighting its contents, beginning in 1845. It was the first American magazine to do so.[9] Writers seeking professional status must have viewed the action favorably. Without copyright protection, authors had little control over their work. The decision to protect the *Lady's Book*, however, was hardly motivated solely by writers' needs; the magazine also suffered when its contents appeared in other periodicals. While the *Lady's Book* paid for the work, competing editors used it for free, thus adding to their own popularity without increasing their costs. Still, the fact that copyright protection was advantageous to both the *Lady's Book* and its writers reveals an important facet of the magazine's support of professional authorship. Unlike the many scissors editors who exploited writers, Hale and Godey proved that fair treatment of writers benefited the magazine. That *Graham's Magazine* immediately followed suit and copyrighted its pages suggests the extent to which the *Lady's Book* influenced national patterns regarding literary authorship.

Although some newspapers strongly objected to the copyrighting of the *Lady's Book*, the move simply extended the growing acceptance of copyrighting within the book industry.[10] Most writers did not take advantage of the Federal Copyright Act when it was passed in 1790, but by the 1840s editors, writers, and publishers generally acknowledged authors' rights to books. In his 1843 book, *Popular Technology; or, Professions and Trades*, for example, Edward Hazen denounced the old idea of treating "literary productions" as "public property," and he described publishing "without making the authors the least remuneration" as "literary piracy." In contrast to such "piracy" in "ancient times," Hazen celebrated the current status of authorship—most notably copyright laws that protected authors' rights to their own productions. Hazen acknowledged that financial rewards remained insuf-

ficient at times, yet he praised the conditions for authors in the United
States, citing the improvements in the previous ten years. What Hale
and Louis Godey did, in effect, was apply this perception of authorship—and ownership of the product—to periodicals.[11]

The writers themselves profited from the policies at the *Lady's Book*,
which, along with *Graham's Magazine*, was widely seen as providing
the most "liberal" rates.[12] Although little is known about the specific
rates paid by the *Lady's Book*, the two magazines probably offered comparable fees. According to Frank Luther Mott, George Graham paid
between four and twelve dollars per page of prose and between ten and
fifty dollars per poem. The *North American Review*, in contrast, offered
a dollar per page during the same period. At both *Graham's* and the
*Lady's Book*, famous writers could bargain for even higher wages. After
declining Hale's offer of twenty-five dollars per poem in 1850, James
Russell Lowell successfully negotiated a thirty-dollar rate.[13]

Some writers, including Edgar Allan Poe, depended heavily on publication in the *Lady's Book*. Hale's relationship with Poe began in 1830,
when she wrote a favorable review of his *Al Aaraaf*, calling Poe "a
fine genius."[14] When Hale's son met Poe at West Point, she began to
follow his career more closely, and she remained one of his most favorable reviewers. Hale helped Poe even more by publishing his work. In
1844 Poe contributed several works to the *Lady's Book*, including "The
Oblong Box," and in 1845 the *Lady's Book* published both his short
stories and a series of essays on literary criticism. Poe's work appeared
in thirteen consecutive issues beginning in November 1845. Among his
more notable contributions to the *Lady's Book* were "The Literati of
New York City" and "The Cask of Amontillado" in 1846. Poe's work
continued to appear in the *Lady's Book*, although at a slower pace,
until after his death; "The Lady Hubbard" appeared posthumously in
December 1849.

According to Poe's biographer Hervey Allen, the *Lady's Book* provided Poe his main source of income in 1845 and 1846, when he was
a constant contributor. Hale's other literary connections helped Poe
as well. When he submitted "The Oblong Box" to Hale's gift annual
*The Opal*, she accepted the short story for the *Lady's Book* and then
asked Poe to submit another piece for the gift book. In a letter thank-

ing Hale for the *Opal* offer in 1844, Poe called her price of fifty cents per page "amply sufficient." He probably received considerably more for the submissions to the *Lady's Book*. According to Isabelle Webb Entrikin, Poe generally earned between four and five dollars per page of prose, and near the end of his career, he received up to fifty dollars per poem.[15]

Poe's dependence on the *Lady's Book* in the mid-1840s was not unique. Harriet Beecher Stowe, Eliza Leslie, Nathaniel P. Willis, Catharine Sedgwick, Henry Theodore Tuckerman, William Gilmore Simms, William Kirkland, and William Cullen Bryant all published in the *Lady's Book* during the 1840s. Many authors worked primarily in periodicals during the decade, in part because of the crisis in the book industry at the time. Although many writers continued to publish books, the depression following the Panic of 1837 caused the collapse of many publishing houses, which could not compete with the cheap British reprints flooding American markets. Only at the end of the 1840s did the American book publishing industry stabilize.[16]

Amid the instability of book publishing in the 1840s, women's magazines, especially the *Lady's Book*, were securely established. The demand for national women's literary magazines was so high, in fact, that it supported the *Lady's Book*'s two most successful competitors, *Graham's Magazine* (1826–58) and *Peterson's Magazine* (1842–98). Whereas the book industry reached a literary peak in what is often described as the American renaissance of the 1850s, the magazine industry's greatest literary achievements occurred in the previous decade, especially in women's magazines like the *Lady's Book*.

To see how authors worked within the women's magazines to establish themselves as professionals, consider the careers of two writers, Lydia Sigourney and Harriet Beecher Stowe, both of whom depended on periodical publication. Sigourney's desire to establish herself as a professional author is particularly important because it preceded similar efforts by other writers in the 1840s. Like many other early nineteenth-century women writers who turned to writing for financial reasons, Sigourney published her first book, *Moral Pieces*, in 1815 with the hope of supporting her parents. Although she apparently suspended her professional hopes in 1819, when she married, because her husband, Charles, wanted writing to be her hobby, financial difficulties soon renewed Sigourney's desire to be a professional author. Turning increasingly to magazines, by 1830 Sigourney contributed regularly to more than twenty periodicals, including Hale's *Ladies' Magazine*.[17]

Almost immediately Hale began celebrating Sigourney's success and her contributions to the magazine. In an essay on the Sigourney home, described as Charles's, Hale called Sigourney a "fine genius," and later she portrayed her as one of the nation's "distinguished literary ladies" (*LM*, Nov. 1832, 482; Jan. 1834, 48). Although the fact that many of Sigourney's contributions were identified solely by initials may suggest some impulse on her part to remain an amateur writer, Hale's own account of Sigourney's career suggests that even then she was building the kind of public recognition necessary for professional status. In an essay honoring Lydia Sigourney written after her death, Hale recalled how Sigourney "became the favorite poetess of our American literature; her name, or her *initials*, gave reputation to newspapers and literary journals, and her books were household treasures" (*GLB*, Oct. 1865, 358).

In many ways, the careers of both Sigourney and Hale depended on Sigourney's becoming a poet recognizable to an audience. In this way their relationship benefited both equally. For Hale, the primary reward, especially during the early years of the *Ladies' Magazine*, was much-needed material. As Sigourney's popularity grew, Hale could publicize her as a means of attracting readers. In return, Sigourney received what was probably a reasonable wage.[18] Much more important, however, she enjoyed an opportunity to establish and strengthen her relationship with her audience. Although Sigourney did not limit her poetry to women's magazines, women were her primary audience, and in the late 1820s and early 1830s Hale controlled the nation's longest-surviving women's magazine. If Hale's own testimony is reliable, her readership actually extended nationally; in 1832 Hale boasted a subscription list that "extended to every part of the union" (*LM*, Aug. 1832, 384). By appearing regularly in a magazine as successful as Hale's *Ladies' Magazine*, Sigourney set in motion a cycle that would maintain her readers' interest. The perpetual national exposure afforded by magazines increased the demand for her books and for her submissions to gift annuals.[19] The success of her books, in turn, strengthened her ability to improve magazine subscription rates. By working in both the book and periodical industries, Sigourney was able to establish herself as a professional poet. Had she worked solely within the book industry, it is unlikely she would have earned enough money or gained the national reputation necessary for professional status.

The almost symbiotic nature of Hale and Sigourney's relationship is evident by the poet's dealings with the *Lady's Book* in the early 1840s. A longtime contributor to the magazine, Sigourney was listed as one of the magazine's editors between 1840 and 1842. Sigourney was quite literally selling her name to the *Lady's Book*. Without any editorial duties, she received five hundred dollars annually—not to mention increased publicity—in exchange for contributing regularly and for having her name appear on the magazine's title page. For its part, the magazine benefited from having such a popular poet on its "staff." Both magazine and poet, then, depended on the success of this professional author.[20]

Although to maintain her professional status Sigourney was forced to sustain a frenetic writing pace, her work within the magazine and book industries did improve conditions for professional authors.[21] As a poet who appealed to a growing readership, Sigourney helped popularize American poetry. Indeed, Sigourney should share the credit now often reserved for Longfellow. Even before his success, Sigourney created markets for future poets and proved to editors and publishers that poetry could be profitable.[22] In addition, Sigourney helped establish professional authorship by inspiring poets themselves to seek such status. Hale herself asserted in an obituary essay written for Sigourney that the writer "left a noble example for the daughters of America who enter on the career of letters" (*GLB*, Oct. 1865, 358). Indeed, Sigourney inspired and served as mentor not only to "daughters" but also to "sons," including James Gates Percival and John Greenleaf Whittier.[23]

Like Sigourney, Harriet Beecher Stowe depended upon periodical publication throughout her career. Much of her early work appeared in magazines, and many of her novels, including, of course, *Uncle Tom's Cabin*, were published serially. Stowe focused so much on periodical writing, in fact, that she was relatively unconcerned by the commercial failure of her first book, *The Mayflower*. Although critics have sometimes dismissed Stowe's early magazine work, her career before *Uncle Tom's Cabin* reveals that she developed her professional status within the periodical industry. Her first magazine piece appeared in Cincinnati's *Western Monthly Magazine* in 1833. In the following year Stowe won that magazine's short story contest for her "New England Sketch" and received a fifty-dollar prize. During that same year the Cincinnati *Chronicle* began reprinting her work.[24] Like many writers, Stowe was working toward professional status that assured financial success. In December 1838 she said of her writing, "I *do* it for *the pay*."[25]

Contrary to some current misconceptions, Stowe did achieve national recognition well before the publication of *Uncle Tom's Cabin* began in 1851. Indeed, during the 1830s and 1840s she contributed regularly to the gift annuals, including the *Christian Keepsake*, the *Christian Souvenir*, Lydia Sigourney's *Religious Souvenir*, and the *Violet*. Stowe's work also appeared in three national magazines. Her first contribution to the *Evangelist*, a Presbyterian magazine based in New York, appeared in 1835, and she continued publishing there, at least occasionally, until 1851. Before its publication of *Uncle Tom's Cabin*, the *National Era* also published four of Stowe's pieces.[26]

Although the *National Era* would soon dominate Stowe's reputation, the *Lady's Book* influenced her career in the late 1830s and the 1840s more than any other magazine. Her first signed piece in the *Lady's Book*, "Trials of a Housekeeper," appeared in January 1839, and three other pieces were published later that year. Stowe continued to write steadily for the *Lady's Book* for the next few years: two works were published in 1840, three more in 1841, and another in 1842.[27] Before *Uncle Tom's Cabin*, Stowe published more in the *Lady's Book* than in any other magazine.

The *Lady's Book* must have been particularly attractive to Stowe, who was seeking professional status. With a circulation much larger than the *Evangelist* or the *National Era*, the *Lady's Book* provided Stowe access to a large audience. That audience, furthermore, was well suited to Stowe, who, like many of the other writers for the *Lady's Book*, wrote fiction that emphasized domesticity and familial relationships. Stowe's dealings with another magazine—the *Boston Miscellany*—demonstrate the importance of the *Lady's Book* in establishing her as a domestic writer nationwide. According to a letter from Stowe to her husband, Calvin, written in 1842, the editor of the *Boston Miscellany* offered her twenty dollars for every three pages of material he published—an offer that Stowe described at the time as "the best" she had received. As Noel Gerson explains, however, Stowe refused the offer because she was disturbed by the magazine's image. Specifically, Stowe objected to the fashion illustrations, especially one depicting a woman wearing a low-cut dress.[28] In addition to offering Stowe a readership, then, the *Lady's Book* provided her with a specific image. By publishing in that magazine, Stowe could identify herself with the other professional women writers who appeared there—writers who, like Lydia Sigourney, maintained a moral and domestic perspective and who were financially successful.

Although Hale did contribute to the successful careers of writers like Poe, Sigourney, and Stowe, she did not encourage all writers. In fact, she often used her editorial pages to discuss the difficulties associated with professional literary careers. While clearly discouraging to some would-be writers, Hale's editorials about authorship may have helped writers like Poe and Stowe even more than her publication of their works, for in these editorials Hale repeatedly rejected the idea that anyone could become an author. Like any other occupation that required training, talent, and hard work, authorship, according to Hale, deserved professional respect.

Hale's editorial support for professional authorship is evident in her many descriptions of a continuum of writers, ranging from the amateur to the professional. She made clear distinctions between "anonymous or voluntary contributors" and "regularly engaged and paid writers" (*GLB*, April 1840, 190), and she accepted the idea that the two groups deserved different treatment. Although she advocated adequate compensation, Hale did not generally pay beginning writers, and she explained that commissioned work would receive her first consideration. Writers who submitted material on a "voluntary" basis should expect longer delays (*GLB*, Dec. 1840, 282). In another editorial, Hale offered three categories of writers whose work she had refused. The first class, identified as "*Promising*," demonstrated "literary talent," and Hale recommended "persevering study." Those in the second category, "the *mediocre,*" exhibited no such promise, though Hale conceded the possibility of eventual success. For the unfortunate writers in the final category, "*Hopeless,*" Hale offered no prospects of public acclaim and urged them to write only for their own benefit (*GLB*, June 1841, 282).

Implicit in these categories is Hale's notion that along the continuum of writers is the authorial apprentice. Clearly, for Hale, neither talent nor ambition alone could guarantee literary success. Even those with "literary talent" had to dedicate themselves to "persevering study," and as Hale explained in another editorial, many "persons mistake a desire, for the ability to perform" (*GLB*, March 1852, 229). Hale's interest in a writer's apprenticeship also emerged in the instructions she repeatedly offered to would-be contributors. In one essay, she admonished correspondents for not writing "as they would speak," and she suggested that they abandon their ideas of needing "a lofty theme, and long words and pompous descriptions" (*LM*, Feb. 1829, 92). Similar notions of an apprenticeship appear in the published announcements Hale made regarding submissions. Although she kindly omitted the authors' names, Hale published titles of rejected manuscripts, along with brief explanations—"dull" or "boring" or "imperfect versification," for example. At times, those rationales were rather severe. She rejected one manuscript titled "My Life" on the grounds that it was "a very useless one, as described" (*GLB*, June 1857, 562). However harsh such a practice may seem today, beginning writers appear to have accepted Hale's practice as part of their training. Frances Hodgson Burnett, whose first published story appeared in the *Lady's Book*, apparently read the announcements of rejected manuscripts in hope of improving her writing.[29]

Throughout her descriptions of the authorial apprentice, Hale presented herself as the master writer responsible for instructing apprentices and maintaining professional standards. As an editor, Hale had the authority to command that arduous preparation. Significantly, when guiding younger writers in the process of becoming professional authors, Hale repeatedly abandoned the sisterly editorial voice she used with readers and invoked the persona of a protecting but strict parent. Like the parent who knows that what a child wants is sometimes not best, Hale once explained that "contributors sometimes offer their first fruit. They should thank us for declining it." Similarly, Hale once rejected a story with the explanation that "the author must not be discouraged. She can write better" (*GLB*, March 1865, 280; Feb. 1841, 96). Hale's persona as the master writer parallels the kind of apprenticeship she envisioned as the basis of mother-daughter relationships. While these mothers trained daughters to become housewives and mothers, Hale taught younger writers to become professional authors.[30]

Even in some of its fiction, the *Lady's Book* presented editors as responsible for maintaining professional standards. One of several humorous depictions of the editorial process, the 1860 story "Scene in 'Our' Sanctum; or, A Peep Behind the Curtain," signed only by "One Who Has 'Been Thar,'" emphasizes the abundance of unpublishable material submitted to magazine editors. Unable to face the submissions alone, two men read aloud to each other in order to divide the work and to allow one the pleasure of smoking. As the editors read, they interject their own aggravations and beg each other to read more rapidly. One poem defines hope as "hopeful, ever hoping," which is later rhymed with "never moping"; two others are titled "What the Trees Said?" and "Written on a Daisy When Confined by Sickness." A similar story, titled "How We Filled the Columns," featured rejected manuscripts such as "Lines on a Drowning Newfoundland Dog" and "The Ensanguined Wedding Ring and Bloody Lock of Hair" (*GLB*, Aug. 1860, 139–44; March 1865, 232–37). Although these two narratives achieve their humor at the expense of inexperienced writers, the effect of the story is similar to the stance taken in Hale's editorial columns. Writing is portrayed as an arduous task, requiring talent and experience, and the editor has the responsibility to maintain professional standards of authorship.

A similar vision of authorship is evident in Hale's use of the term *scribblings*. In contrast to Nathaniel Hawthorne, who used the word to complain about the financially successful writers of the day, Hale used *scribblings* to refer to unpublishable, amateur writings. In one editorial she explained that she would accept only "carefully prepared articles— not 'scribblings'" (*GLB*, April 1865, 373). Although Hawthorne clearly wished to enjoy commercial success himself, his and Hale's uses of the term *scribbling* imply a significantly different understanding of author-

ship, specifically in regard to its economics. Hawthorne's insistence
that he would be "ashamed" of himself if his works proved as popular as the women's "trash" suggests that he believed that writers paid
well for their work were somehow inferior.[31] In contrast to Hawthorne's
financially successful "scribbling" writers, Hale's scribblers were amateurs who worked quickly and easily; professional writers, in contrast,
earned their salaries, not because they pandered to their audiences but
because they had talent *and* worked hard. Thus, however much Hawthorne wished to earn his living by writing, his association of payment
with lack of true artistry is based on an eighteenth-century model of
the leisured gentleman author. Hale, on the other hand, envisioned a
truly professional model of authorship.

Although she was most concerned with distinguishing amateur and
professional writers, even professional writers had to submit to Hale as
the authority responsible for maintaining standards. Hale claimed to
reject a model of reviewing based on finding fault, but she repeatedly
voiced her objections to published writings, though never with the kind
of savage tone she associated with male critics. In virtually every essay
on Cooper, for instance, Hale focused on style, faulting his *Notions of
the Americans*, for example, for its "affectation" and "artificial manner
of detailing unimportant events, and of describing common scenery"
(*LM*, Sept. 1828, 431). In her review of *The Bravo*, Hale summarized
her overall opinion of Cooper's technical abilities: "We do not pretend
greatly to admire the style of Mr. Cooper. His dialogue is frequently
encumbered with unnecessary words, and there seems to be an incon-
gruity in the solemn manner of expression, which he so pertinaciously
puts into the mouths of all his characters, the ignorant as well as the
learned" (*LM*, Jan. 1832, 45). Cooper was by no means the only professional writer who earned Hale's reproofs. Although Hale praised
Herman Melville's *Moby-Dick* as a "perfect literary whale" (*GLB*, Feb.
1852, 166), *Pierre* so frustrated her that she wrote her review in a brutal
parody of Melville's style.[32]

That Hale criticized writers as popular as Cooper and those like Melville, whose talents she praised highly elsewhere, demonstrates once
again her belief in the difficulty of authorship. Even when faulting
writers, Hale strengthened their position as professionals: her criti-

cisms reminded readers that writers who achieved success especially deserved support and respect. Regardless of her treatment of individual writers, Hale urged readers to remember the rarity of literary success and to think of the author as a professional, who, like the physician or minister, had dedicated his or her life to acquiring the necessary skills.

Hale's response to women writers deserves particular attention, because she is sometimes quoted as limiting women's authorial opportunities, and indeed her periodical essays did at times question women's literary ambitions. In an essay in the *Ladies' Magazine* published in 1829, for example, Hale declared that she had "no wish to tinge all her sex *blue* . . . to turn our country into a great literary factory, and set all our young ladies to spinning their brains," and in an 1852 essay about women writers, Hale argued that "a good pair of stockings, or a well-made petticoat, is a much better thing than a feeble attempt at literature" (*LM*, Jan. 1829, 3; *GLB*, March 1852, 229). Similarly, both Hale's editorial columns and the fiction of the *Lady's Book* tended to denounce writers, especially women, who pursued authorship for fame or wealth.

These published concerns notwithstanding, nothing in Hale's own career suggests that she had any misgivings about women pursuing professional authorship. Unlike those women writers Mary Kelley has described as showing ambivalence about publicity, Hale frequently promoted herself before the public as a professional writer and editor. She published many autobiographical sketches and exhibited considerable interest in furthering her reputation. Hale's sense of herself as a professional author is further demonstrated by her response to a personal letter requesting a complete edition of her works in 1855. In her reply Hale explained that no such edition existed "as yet," but she described how her books might be purchased, and she classified her "large number of books" by which were "most important" and "most popular." Hale evidently continued to hope for a collected edition of her works. She collected her manuscripts, letters, and papers throughout her life, and her will appointed her children as literary executors.[33] Similarly, Hale's correspondence with her book publishers reveals that she was comfortable and capable in handling the business aspects of her profession. In her letters to Harper and Brothers regarding the publication of *Woman's Record,* for example, Hale skillfully clarified responsibilities, offered suggestions about the size of the book and its promotion, negotiated her payment, and proposed other projects. She even chastised the publisher for delaying her book: "It will become obsolete. One or two of the ladies, ranked with the *living* when I completed my task, are now *dead.*"[34]

Although Hale did sometimes discourage other women from becoming authors, generally her responses to women writers were consistent with her own professional identity. Indeed, Hale's prudence was based not on any ambivalence about the propriety of literary women but on her recognition of the obstacles facing all professional writers. In warning women about these difficulties, Hale again presented authorship as a profession. Writing, she maintained, was not for the "feeble" but for the talented. A fairly typical essay propounding this view is Alice B. Neal's "American Female Authorship," published in the *Lady's Book* in 1852. Neal, like Hale, unquestionably supported women writers. Asserting that the "time is gone past when literary tastes or pursuits are admitted as a stigma upon the social relation of any woman," Neal declared that "there is nothing inconsistent in a mind that can fashion a dainty lyric and trim a becoming cap." Neal urged readers to let "the needle and the pen lie side by side," for "they will not wrangle" (*GLB*, Feb. 1852, 147).

Despite her enthusiasm, Neal cautioned women dreaming of literary achievement. Responding to what she called women's "mania" for authorship, Neal outlined what new writers could expect, beginning with the lack of adequate financial compensation. She refuted those who considered authorship "a means of subsistence" or a way of "winning fortunes" and urged women "to look soberly at the fact": "There are perhaps ten or twelve ladies in our own country who have adopted literature as a profession. Six of these . . . by giving all their time and energy to their labors, by an industry which few professional men dream of and few ladies can imitate, realize a comfortable, barely comfortable, income, as a reward of years passed in battling with disappointments and patient waiting upon the fancies of a capricious public." As further proof, Neal offered the example of one of the nation's "most finished and elegant writers," who taught many hours a day "to supply deficiency of income." Although Neal acknowledged that such poverty "ought not to exist where so much talent is displayed," she reminded readers that such work was but "meagrely paid for" (*GLB*, Feb. 1852, 145, 148).

In addition to warning readers about the lack of financial rewards, Neal emphasized the difficulty during the apprenticeship period, especially in book production, where the market was "crowded" and "the stamp of magazine approval" had become "almost essential." Writing, she argued, was "an avenue closed to all but those who are content to serve a laborious apprenticeship, or who can afford to print as well as write, asking no remuneration. Of course, there are exceptions to all that we have here stated. . . . But these exceptions only prove the general rule, that authorship, as a profession, is the last to be chosen, if speedy or ample remuneration is expected; for the salary of many a governess equals, if not exceeds, the largest income we have ever known an American authoress to receive" (*GLB*, Feb. 1852, 148). Although Neal focused here on the difficulties of authorship, her warnings, like Hale's, imply considerable praise for the professional author who had endured the "laborious apprenticeship" and conquered the many obstacles.[35]

Hale's support of professional women writers is also evident in her use of the term *genius.* Like most nineteenth-century reviewers, she used *genius* to indicate the highest level of literary achievement, but unlike many of her contemporaries, she was likely to use the term equally for men and women. As Nina Baym has observed in her study of nineteenth-century reviewers of novels, *genius* and *woman* were often perceived as incompatible expressions. While reviewers enthusiastically endorsed signs of genius in men, they often treated similar traits in women uneasily. As Baym explains, women writers were praised for how well they expressed womanhood in general rather than for their individual voices or visions. Whereas individuality was admired among male writers, the primary standard for greatness among women writers was representativeness.[36]

Hale, in contrast, frequently described women writers as geniuses, and she associated female genius with boldness and originality—qualities other reviewers often found problematic in women. In *Woman's Record* Hale characterized Charlotte Brontë as an "original genius" and praised *Shirley* for its "original and striking thought" and its "free, bold spirit, that charms by its spontaneous vigor." Similarly, although Hale objected to Rochester's characterization in *Jane Eyre*, as did many reviewers, she acknowledged the novel's "vigour, animation, originality, an arrest that never flags." Hale also celebrated risk-taking in women writers, another trait generally acclaimed only in men. In a sketch of Sara Jane Lippincott ("Grace Greenwood"), for example, Hale glorified the bold pursuit of literary excellence. An "inferior genius," Hale explained, "would have been satisfied with the honours won," and a "fearful mind would have hesitated to risk, by any effort to widen her sway, a failure."[37]

Essays in the *Ladies' Magazine* and the *Lady's Book* also demonstrate that Hale did not consider genius and women mutually exclusive. One early essay in the *Ladies' Magazine* described "originality of thought" as "the polar star of our female writers" (*LM*, Sept. 1830, 407). Even essays about literary men associated women with genius. An unsigned 1833 essay, titled "True Genius Always at Home" defined the literary "man of genius," using domestic rhetoric associated with women. According to this essay, the man of genius "constructs a domain of his own; and no man is so truly at home as in his own abode. He draws around him a hallowed circle, and in it he moves, and lives, and breathes. The scenes are his own, the atmosphere is his own, every thing within it is his own—immortally his own. Others may wander there, and gaze and admire, but they must still acknowledge that it is his. He only, as its rightful possessor, can stand within it with the proud consciousness that he is *at home*" (*LM*, Feb. 1833, 53–54). Given the association of women with domesticity throughout the *Ladies' Magazine*, the use of the metaphor *at home* here to define the male genius demonstrates that genius is not an exclusively masculine trait. Quite the contrary—this essay implicitly creates a feminine definition of genius.

Although *genius* and *feminine* were compatible terms in Hale's view, she did employ her understanding of an essential sexual difference to differentiate between male and female genius. In one editorial in 1857, Hale specifically refuted the idea that "genius has no sex." According to Hale, men's and women's writings demonstrate distinct differences, with women's writing exhibiting a tenderness and morality impossible in men's. Significantly, Hale documented this female writing even among writers whom she did not associate with a Christian aesthetic. Writing of George Sand, for instance, whom Hale depicted as lacking appropriate Christian influence, she insisted that "the superior moral sense of the woman is clearly discerned." Likewise, Hale explained that the "woman's nature" of Madame de Staël was "as clearly defined in her writings as it could have been in the form of her hand, or in the tone of her voice" (*GLB*, Feb. 1857, 177). Although Hale claimed that both men's and women's writings were "delightful," she did imply a hierarchy, with women's writing achieving the higher status:

> Is not moral power better than mechanical invention? Is not the love, which purifies the heart and makes the sanctity of home, stronger even than the "red right arm of war"?
>
> Why should women wish to be or to do or to write like men? Is not the feminine genius the most angel-like? (*GLB*, Feb. 1857, 178)

The notion of a separate "feminine genius" was, of course, hardly unusual among nineteenth-century critics, but Hale's description of that genius as "stronger" than men's does differ significantly from the assertions of most of her counterparts, who generally regarded women's genius as inferior to men's.

While Hale's celebration of feminine genius challenged contemporary cultural definitions, in other ways her understanding of female authorship corresponded with limited expectations of women's ability. Specifically, Hale expected great women writers to be models not only of authorship but also of domesticity. Like many other nineteenth-century reviewers, Hale exhibited considerable interest in women's— but not men's—private lives, and in her essays on women writers, Hale shifted from biography to literary text with no sense of disjunction. Furthermore, when describing the function of biographies, Hale insisted that personal details should take precedence over women's public accomplishments: "The private histories of eminent persons are always sought after with eagerness; and were this passion for biographical literature, rightly fostered and directed, it would have a most powerful influence in promoting the intellectual and moral improvement of women. But to do this, greatness, in its worldly sense . . . must not be the object of eulogy; or rather, the domestic virtues must possess a prominance [*sic*] in the pictures which are held up for the admiration and consequent imitation of women" (*LM*, Sept. 1829, 393). As Baym explains, such practices were common among nineteenth-century reviewers, and biographical information and essays about women writers' private lives were frequent features in magazines.[38]

Although Hale's biographical essays frequently exhibited admiration of women like Lydia Sigourney, who demonstrated that there was "no incompatibility between literary pursuits and domestic duties" (*GLB*, Oct. 1865, 358), the focus on a woman's private life clearly restricted women writers. Women's literary successes were praiseworthy only when combined with domestic achievements. Male authors, in contrast, had no such requirements and were judged solely on the basis of their writings. Much of the fiction in the *Lady's Book* suggests the difficulty—and even the impossibility—of combining these accomplishments. An unsigned story, for example, titled "Why I Am Not an Authoress," tells of Nellie, a young writer, working on her first novel. At first Nellie abstains from all domestic and social obligations in order to pursue her writing: she refuses party invitations, neglects her clothes and hair, and wears permanent ink stains on her hands, earning her the nickname Miss Fingerblotter. When her family finally convinces her to attend a ball however, Nellie's life is transformed. She falls in love, agrees to marry, and eventually abandons her writing because her husband has advised her to "relinquish public fame" for a "happy domestic life." Neither Nellie nor her husband considers the possibility that she could be both a writer and a wife (*GLB*, April 1857, 314).

As clear as Nellie's choices are, the writer's position about Nellie's choice between marriage and writing is far from certain, since the story itself undercuts the supposed opposition of domestic and literary goals. Although the narrator has supposedly denounced writing, her story—told in the first person—is published in the *Lady's Book*. By mentioning her marriage, the narrator indicates that the writing took place after her wedding and her supposed renunciation of literature. Although the story was probably written by someone other than Hale, in many ways it embodies Hale's ambivalence about women writers and domesticity. On the one hand, Hale generally warned women not to pursue literature single-mindedly, insisting that they always fulfill their domestic duties. On the other hand, she did encourage women to move beyond their domestic spheres. She published the work of women writers, paid them generously, and welcomed them to the commercial world of authorship.

A similar ambivalence emerges within Hale's expectation that women writers should be moral as well as domestic. Although she sometimes praised books by men without considering the books' morality—including Poe's *Tales of the Grotesque and Arabesque,* Melville's *Moby-Dick,* and Thoreau's *Cape Cod*—she rarely gave the same treatment to books by women.[39] Indeed, when defining the goals of female authorship and genius in *Woman's Record,* Hale emphasized what she called "the moral effect of mental power." She explained, "The genius which causes or creates the greatest amount of good to humanity should take the highest rank."[40] Similarly, in an essay memorializing Lydia Sigourney's "poetic genius" in the *Lady's Book,* Hale declared that "piety is essential to the genius of a woman" (*GLB,* Oct. 1865, 358).

Hale's position here on the moral integrity of women writers coincides with her general theory of sexual difference. According to Hale's *Woman's Record,* all women—including those who write—should focus on moral instruction. Hale praised Charlotte Brontë primarily, then, not for her literary technique but for being "an instructress"—"the noblest pursuit of woman"—and Alice Carey, she asserted, was a "guiding angel." Conversely, women writers who neglected their duties as society's moral guardians troubled Hale, regardless of whether or not they were geniuses. When describing George Sand, for instance, Hale acknowledged her "genius of an order capable of soaring to the most exalted heights," yet she regretted that Sand lacked the "saving influences of moral and Christian training." Disapproving of Sand's interest in politics, which Hale viewed as corrupting, she wished that Sand's "genius should teach truth, and inspire hearts to love the good." If Sand applied herself in this way, Hale insisted, she could expect "a mightier effect on her country than any plan of social reform political expediency could devise."[41] Hale's treatment of the woman author, then, matches her portrait of all women: they should provide moral instruction.

Undoubtedly, Hale's association of women writers with morality and domesticity was restrictive. Her belief that some women writers had transgressed the bounds of proper femininity demonstrates her limited notion of female authorship. But scholars have been too quick to dismiss Hale's theory of authorship. Writers and critics have long prescribed limits to literature's aims, and religion and morality have been quite common criteria for determining literary worth. However limited, Hale's association of morality and literature implies a radical rereading of authorship. Although she was particularly concerned with women writers' morality, Hale expected all great writers—regardless of sex—to fulfill her moral standards. When describing William Cullen Bryant as "one of the brightest lights of American genius," Hale focused on the "truth of moral sentiment" in his poetry (*LM*, April 1832, 185). Given Hale's theory of sexual difference, which posited women as society's moral force, her concern for moral truth in literature elevated the status of women writers. According to Hale, the best writers had the greatest positive effect on readers. Since women were society's natural teachers and moral leaders, she concluded, women were more likely to achieve literary greatness than men.

Such a conclusion might explain why Hale continually discussed the gender of writers who were women, but did not do so for men. Whereas many nineteenth-century reviewers belittled the literary accomplishments of women, Hale's position assumed that women's moral superiority gave them—not men—the greatest potential for literary excellence.[42] To be a great writer, a woman must only be true to her natural abilities. A man, on the other hand, must aspire to womanhood. In contrast to earlier ideas of the author as a scholarly gentleman, therefore, Hale advocated a feminized model of authorship.

Hale's ideas of feminized and professional authors were directly related. Unlike writers like Hawthorne, who could secure government appointments when their writing provided insufficient income, women writers had few, if any, options for paid labor. As Hale well knew, if women were to write, they would have to be paid; and if they were paid, they would write. The professionalization and feminization of authorship, in other words, were mutually dependent strategies.

Hale's contributions to the professionalization of authorship challenge some basic assumptions of American literary historians about the role of women's magazines. Hardly on the fringes of the literary world—as is so frequently assumed—the *Ladies' Magazine* and the *Lady's Book* played leading roles in the construction of literary professionalism and helped establish the careers of many of the nation's writers, both men and women. Authorship, considered by some periodicals of the time as little more than a hobby, became in the pages of Hale's magazines a profession, requiring years of study, a difficult apprenticeship, and enormous talent. In addition, Hale redefined authorship as a pursuit appropriate for women, in contradistinction to the male-identified notions of the author, such as the eighteenth-century ideal of the scholarly gentleman. In creating the idea of a professional woman author, Hale changed the way society imagined all writers.

# 5

## Women's Reading

Hale's efforts to depict authorship as a profession, requiring talent and training and deserving of financial rewards, would have been largely unsuccessful without the dramatic changes taking place during the first half of the nineteenth century in the production of print materials. Certainly, without the technological developments that reduced publishing costs, books and periodicals would have remained beyond the means of most U.S. citizens. Even more essential to Hale's redefined author was a readership. Lee Soltow and Edward Stevens have estimated that 25 percent of Americans at the beginning of the nineteenth century could not read or write; by 1840 that rate had dropped to an estimated 9 percent, creating what John Tebbel has described as "the largest reading audience anyone had ever seen." This new readership and the newly professionalized author were, to a great extent, mutually dependent: what one wanted to sell, the other wanted to buy.[1]

The increase in women's literacy during this time helped define the new readership. At the beginning of the nineteenth century less than 50 percent of American women could read and write, and the gap between men's and women's literacy rates remained high. Kenneth A. Lockridge's study of literacy in New England indicates that approximately 90 percent of men but less than 50 percent of women could read and write at the end of the eighteenth century. By 1860, however, that gap had decreased to an estimated 2 percent, and women's literacy rates had reached over 90 percent.[2]

With their new skills, women were frequently identified *as* the new readership. Nathaniel P. Willis, for example, insisted that it "is the women who read."[3] In 1846 the *Lady's Book* declared: "Women are, in our country, the readers" (*GLB*, Jan. 1846, 1). By the end of the century the association between women and reading had become strong enough even to influence architectural design. The family-centered sitting room gradually replaced the once masculine home library, with its heavy furniture and scholarly clerical image, as the primary site for reading.[4]

Hale edited the *Ladies' Magazine* and the *Lady's Book* during the rise of this woman reader, and in this chapter I will examine how she defined women's reading in the two magazines. By revising contemporary views of the woman reader, Hale presented an ideology of women's reading that challenged the subordination of women, while at the same time it assumed and reinforced middle-class values. Separatism provided the basis for this vision of the woman reader, as it did for Hale's theories of women's authorship. Rather than promoting a universal theory of reading, applicable to both men and women, Hale defined reading in the context of her theories of gender and sexual difference.

I would like to begin by describing how my study differs from recent theoretical attempts to define the woman reader. Such projects have grown out of the dialogue between various reading theorists and feminists who, like Annette Kolodny, have argued that "reading is a *learned* activity which . . . is inevitably sex-coded and gender-reflected." Like Kolodny here, most feminist critics agree that reading as a woman is not the inevitable experience of readers who are biologically female. Although I applaud the focus on how gender affects the reading process, I am troubled that most definitions of the woman reader portray her solely as someone who has self-consciously learned to reject the masculine reading process society has imposed upon her. To many critics—from Judith Fetterley to Jonathan Culler—women cannot read "as women" without first unlearning to read "as men." However much these theories of reading attempt to undermine androcentric reading practices, by defining a woman reader only through her difference from and rejection of the male model, they unwittingly reinforce the perception of the male perspective as normative and the female one as deviant. Merely a transformed male reader, this woman reader lacks any independent and positive existence. Significantly, the overwhelming acceptance of this particular model of women's reading reflects the similar reading experiences of these critics. However diverse their areas of expertise, most scholars currently exploring the idea of a "woman reader" have been influenced by the androcentric literary canon. It is hardly surprising, then, that they portray the woman reader as a re-created man. That, in essence, has been the narrative either of their own reading experiences or of the experiences of many of the women readers they know. But while androcentric and misogynistic texts certainly do pose problems for the woman reader, we cannot define the woman reader solely by those conditions.[5]

Indeed, an entirely different construction of the woman reader emerges if we select another group of women readers. Unlike today's feminist literary critics who have read within an androcentric academy and whose very presence in that reading community has been questioned, the subscribers to the *Ladies' Magazine* and the *Lady's Book* lived within a culture that associated women with reading and that encouraged women to read texts written by women. The recent scholarly definitions of the woman reader cannot fully account for the representation of women's reading in these periodicals precisely because they often do not address variances of reading communities. Like other scholars who have questioned the idea of a universal category of "woman reader" by investigating differences of race, class, and sexuality, I will focus on the effect of historical and cultural contexts on definitions of the woman reader. Such an investigation will not, of course, provide much insight into the activities of actual women readers, but public pronouncements of women's reading can reveal cultural expectations of women's behavior and generalized assumptions of gender and its effect on literary culture.[6]

Four of the most dominant representations of women's reading in antebellum America reveal the historical contexts from which these representations emerged. The image of the woman reader as maternal social servant, for instance, combined earlier notions of republican motherhood with a Victorian emphasis on women's role as the nation's moral guardians. These discussions of women's reading generally emphasized devotional material. Whether teaching religious or patriotic virtues, the woman reader here was assumed to be a public servant, who benefited from her reading only indirectly—in the building of a stronger family and a better nation.

Similarly, the popular antebellum image of the woman reader as genteel lady arose from contemporary issues of middle-class economic growth. In this view, the woman reader was not seen as particularly beneficial to society, but she also posed no social threats: she read at home and avoided provocative or controversial material. Her primary motive, moreover, was to fill her time, and she never aspired to learned status. Such a presentation of the woman reader illustrates the relationships between reading, gender, and economic class. The genteel woman was able to project her membership within a privileged class by reading. Unlike her contemporaries who worked outside their own homes—in factories or in other people's homes—or even those who could not afford domestic servants themselves, the genteel lady could mark her class by reading, which itself was defined solely as a leisure activity. This image of women's reading was especially pronounced in women's magazines that emphasized fashion. Like a fashionable dress, a book in a woman's hand marked her—or more precisely her husband or father—as one who had the economic means to consume rather than produce goods. Books could function as similar signs of economic power when displayed in the home. Owning many books, especially those with elegant bindings, indicated financial success, and the public display of these books in cases and in family portraits served as visible signs of high economic standing.[7]

Throughout the antebellum period, these views of the woman reader as public servant and as genteel lady often overlapped, in part because both images portrayed women's reading as desirable. In Susan Warner's popular novel *The Wide, Wide World* (1850), Alice Humphreys—the ideal woman who acts as the young Ellen Montgomery's model—reads as both the leisured lady and the maternal missionary. As a genteel lady, Alice displays her books and remarks on them while giving Ellen a tour of the house. Boasting that "all these are mine," Alice describes her "precious" books as her "greatest treasure." As *precious* and *treasure* both suggest, Alice values her books as a typical genteel lady does: she cherishes them for the personal pleasure they bring her during her leisure time as well as for their economic value. In her roles as Ellen's surrogate mother and a good Christian, however, Alice also adopts the maternal and missionary duties of the woman reader. She acts as Ellen's tutor, and on Sundays she visits two old women, "reading and explaining the Bible" to them. As part of her maturation as a woman, Ellen accepts these roles: following Alice's example, she becomes devoted to books and acquires more of her own, and after Alice's death, she continues the Bible readings for the two old women.[8]

In contrast to these images of a maternal and a genteel reader, two negative representations of the woman reader survived into the nineteenth century. First, the woman reader appeared as a domestic idler. Rather than fulfilling the duties of a wife and mother, this woman reader engaged in frivolous activities at the expense of her family and household; she remained, essentially, an adolescent who had not yet accepted her maternal responsibilities. This image of the domestic idler frequently focused on reading novels. Thus a poem by John Ware, published in the *North American Review* in 1817, satirized women who abandoned their domestic duties for fiction, leaving their brothers or husbands with "elbows ragged, or undarned hose" (*North American Review*, Nov. 1817, 109). Similarly, a mid-nineteenth-century valentine depicts a woman, described as "the lazy novel reader," surrounded by domestic chaos: a kettle boils unwatched, socks need darning, and cobwebs hang in a corner of the kitchen.[9] Like the image of the woman reader as maternal social servant, the image of the domestic idler assumes—by contrast, of course—the importance of women's social responsibility.

The emphasis on women's acceptance of their social and familial duties is also evident in the second negative image of the nineteenth-century woman reader—that of an intellectual "blue." In the second half of the eighteenth century the term *blue stocking ladies* referred to a group of learned women in London—including Elizabeth Vesey, Elizabeth Carter, and Hannah More—who met for intelligent conversation. Originally associated with fashionable parties for women readers and writers, *blue* assumed a pejorative meaning by the nineteenth century.

Although the "blue" derived her pleasure from intellectual rather than entertaining or religious pursuits, she, like the domestic idler, was frequently charged with failing to fulfill her responsibilities as a woman. She had a penchant either for philosophy—a field considered too masculine for a proper lady—or for a professional career in writing, an ambition leading to neglected domestic duties. Unlike the idler, however, the "blue" was seen as unfeminine as well as nondomestic. While the domestic idler's crime was an immature refusal to accept adult responsibilities, the "blue" suffered accusations of manliness. Fanny Fern's 1852 sketch "A Practical Blue Stocking" illustrates, and ultimately refutes, the popular perception of the "blue." Visiting a friend who had "the misfortune to have a blue stocking for a wife," Harry has a vision of "inky fingers, frowzled hair, rumpled dress, and slipshod heels . . . not to mention thoughts of a disorderly house, smoky puddings, and dirty-faced children." Harry's impression of the "blue" is quite typical: he assumes that she lacks all social and domestic skills, being unable to care for her family or even entertain a guest. Harry's fears, however, are unfounded. The house and family are well cared for, and he leaves wishing that the "blue" were his own wife.[10]

To some extent, Hale accepted the values implicit in these images of the woman reader as maternal social servant, as leisured lady, as domestic idler, and as intellectual "blue." Sharing the class assumptions embedded in these four images, Hale did not envision the woman reader as working-class laborer or even political activist. Rather, she expected the woman reader to abide by middle-class values, specifically notions of gentility. Similarly, Hale also celebrated, as do most of these images, women's responsibilities to serve their families and the nation. But the images of women's reading included in the *Ladies' Magazine* and the *Lady's Book* do more than simply affirm already popular definitions. To a considerable degree, Hale manipulated and revised these images to promote her own understanding of essentialism and women's expanding sphere. These revisions of the woman reader thus secured a place for the *Lady's Book* at the center of this sphere.

Hale's indebtedness to and manipulations of popular constructions of the woman reader are evident throughout her magazines. One engraving in particular—the 1861 frontispiece of the *Lady's Book*—warrants close analysis (figure 3). Depicting women in six different settings, this engraving demonstrates that, like many of her contemporaries, Hale enthusiastically endorsed notions of women's responsibility to serve others. In five of the scenes, the women engage in activities clearly defined as social service—offering water to a wounded soldier on a battlefield, visiting a prisoner, rowing toward a sinking ship, nursing the ill, and helping a poor family. Amid these scenes appears a sketch of a woman reading. She is seated, reading a book with two children by her side. A younger child plays with a toy nearby—reinforcing the association of the reader with motherhood. As in the other five scenes, here the woman performs a socially responsible activity. She reads not for her own pleasure or benefit but as a mother, teaching her children.

Though this engraving does emphasize women's role in serving families and society, its definition of such roles conforms to Hale's notion of women's expanding sphere. Rather than confine women's social function to the domestic world, the engraving claims the public spaces of hospitals, battlefields, prisons, and even the open sea as appropriate places for women, and the enclosure of these scenes in circles reinforces the association with women's expanding sphere. Serving a similar function are the five female figures that frame the engraving. Depicted as ideals on pedestals, the five women are identified in the accompanying essay as actual women, including Dorothea Dix, who fought to improve conditions among patients in mental hospitals, and Florence Nightingale, who aided soldiers of the Crimean War. Thus the engraving presents the expanding women's sphere as both an ideal and an already realized actuality.

Though the woman reader shown here with her family does not leave her private domestic space, that scene too suggests women's expanding sphere, and it specifically implies the importance of reading in that expansion. Certainly, by reading to her children and educating them, the woman is presented as one able to influence the world around her. Moreover, by bringing materials from outside the domestic space into the private familial world, the woman is assumed to have knowledge of things beyond the home. Thus, just as Hale's notion of women's expanding sphere claims public spaces for women, so reading itself undermines any certain boundary between public

Figure 3. Frontispiece of the *Lady's Book*.
From *Godey's Lady's Book*, Jan. 1861. Courtesy of the
University of Illinois at Urbana-Champaign.

and private: though experienced primarily in a private space, reading inevitably takes people, at least imaginatively, beyond their private,
familial world.

But the role of reading implied by this engraving does not simply
concern the one scene depicting a woman reading. On the contrary—
the entire engraving is presented as something to be read. Each of the
six scenes, after all, narrates a story, the overlapping spheres encourage the reader to make connections among the individual scenes, and
the title of the accompanying editorial, "Our Plates and Their Lessons," practically orders people to make meanings of these visual texts.
In both the engraving, in this sense as a text itself, and the accompanying essay, Hale identified the role of the *Lady's Book* within this
expanding women's sphere. Twice in the editorial Hale suggested the
importance for women of remembering other women's heroic deeds.
Calling the frontispiece a "MEMORIAL of benevolence and worth, of
fame justly won by women," Hale insisted that their "names and deeds
are worthy to be kept in perpetual remembrance" (*GLB*, Jan. 1861, 77).
Only inspired by the memory of these women could other women be
encouraged to act in similar ways. Here Hale's *Lady's Book* emerged
as an instrument playing a key role in the expanding women's sphere,
for the *Lady's Book* ensured the remembrance of heroic women like
Dix and Nightingale. Women's reading, then, is not defined here solely
by a woman's familial responsibilities. Indeed, women read in part to
learn about women's culture, with readers of the *Lady's Book* focusing
specifically on the idea of an expanding women's sphere.

Significantly, this break from a purely maternal image of reading is
suggested in the engraving itself. In the background of the family scene
another woman is reading. As if to indicate her existence independent
of her social relations, this woman stands alone, presumably reading
for her own pleasure and benefit. Though she is an independent reader,
this woman's individual pursuits do not disrupt the domestic world.
Rather, the mother and children read alongside her. Though it is not
certain that she is reading about other women, her reading, like the
reading of the *Lady's Book* itself, extends beyond any strict definition
of social service.

This one engraving, then, presents multiple definitions of women's reading. In its depiction of a woman, presumably a mother, reading to children, the engraving conforms to the popular image of women's reading to serve their families. In its association of reading with women entering public space, however, the engraving defines social service in the context of a much expanded women's sphere. As a text itself that celebrates heroic women, this engraving also defines reading as one of the central and binding activities of women's culture. And finally, in its portrayal of a woman reading alone, the engraving validates reading as an activity that gives pleasure to individual women.

Though these are the primary ways Hale envisioned women's reading within her magazines, this engraving alone does not suggest the implications of these various definitions nor the complexity with which Hale responded to other popular images of women's reading. For example, Hale's portrait of women's familial reading reveals her objections to the popular image of the woman reader as domestic idler. While images of the idler assumed that reading threatened domestic stability, Hale argued repeatedly that reading was an inherent part of domestic and family life. In 1865, for example, the *Lady's Book* declared: "We must have books. They are necessary as bread to the full life of the home circle" (*GLB*, April 1865, 372).[11] Visually, the magazine's association of domestic life with reading was reinforced by the many plates featuring mothers, children, and books. One fairly typical plate, titled "Maternal Instruction" and published in 1845, portrays a woman, presumably a mother, surrounded by books (figure 4). She holds one book and points to another, held by the young child she is instructing; a third book rests on the floor. The older daughter in the background reinforces the association of women's reading with domestic life, specifically maternal instruction. Standing both physically and symbolically between the mother and the younger child, this daughter serves a dual role: as a daughter she reviews some basic lessons; as a potential mother herself, she is also learning how to become a teacher.

The short essay accompanying this plate defines more clearly Hale's challenge to the idea that reading threatened the domestic world. While the domestic idler read fiction to the neglect of her housework, this essay emphasized women's intellectual reading. Not surprisingly given Hale's background in republican ideology and her commitment to

Figure 4. "Maternal Instruction."
From *Godey's Lady's Book*, March 1845. Courtesy of the
University of Illinois at Urbana-Champaign.

educational reform, the essay framed women's familial responsibilities and intellectual reading in the context of improved education for women. Thus, only with efforts "to enlighten and improve the minds of females" would women achieve their true potential in teaching their children and thus create "a very different state of society" (*GLB*, March 1845, 108).

In addition to challenging the image of women readers as domestic idlers, this association of women's reading with intellectual development and social influence undercut many of the assumptions of the genteel lady and the intellectual "blue." While the leisured lady consumed reading material primarily to entertain herself, the woman reader in the *Ladies' Magazine* and the *Lady's Book* was expected to enrich her mind. Conversely, while the intellectual pursuits of the "blue" threatened her femininity, this woman's intellectual reading extended her feminine influence in good Victorian fashion. Thus, a column published in 1837, "The Ladies Mentor," celebrated women's intellectual reading as benefiting society in a specifically feminine manner: "Instead, therefore, of there being any danger that the intellectual and moral progres [*sic*] of woman will make her, what is termed, masculine, we hold that her enlightened influence . . . will, by making men better Christians, make them more like women" (*GLB*, Nov. 1837, 230). This image of the woman reader again implies an expanding women's sphere. By making men more like women, the woman reader here extends her influence beyond the domestic space.

The idea that women's reading could help to transform the world was popular in Hale's magazines. Though at times the magazines defined that transformative function by focusing on women's influence on their children, other essays suggested a broader view. For example, an essay titled "Good Reading" by a Professor Hart, which was included in Hale's editorial column in February 1867, urged women to "cultivate assiduously the ability to read well." Focusing specifically on skills of reading aloud, Hart asked: "Did you ever notice what life and power the Holy Scriptures have, when well read? Have you ever heard of the wonderful effects produced by Elizabeth Fry among the hardened criminals of Newgate, by simply reading to them the parable of the Prodigal Son?" Continuing his appeal, Hart celebrated the

"power" of good readers, mentioning specifically the ability "to minister to the amusement, the comfort, the pleasure of dear ones" (*GLB*,
Feb. 1867, 191–92).

Hart's celebration of oral reading fits well with the image of reading
throughout Hale's magazines. On the one hand, the emphasis on social
service conformed to traditional notions of the woman reader as one
who fulfilled her civic, religious, and familial responsibilities. On the
other hand, Hart's construction of the woman reader challenged, as did
so much in Hale's magazines, any definition of women's sphere that
confined them to the private domestic world. Hart's address here to
the graduates of a Philadelphia girls' school assumed that women have
the "power," even the responsibility, to leave their domestic space and
enter public, often male-dominated domains. Thus, while the image of
the woman reader as social servant generally assumed that a woman's
audience would be her children, Hart portrayed women who read publicly to adult men and had the power to transform them.

Although the *Ladies' Magazine* and the *Lady's Book* celebrated the
benefits to society and family of women's reading, both magazines also
repeatedly recognized reading as an appropriate leisure activity. The
author of an 1831 essay titled "My Books" asserted that books could
relieve the boredom and loneliness that some women experienced in
the home: "While men can seek relief from care or sorrow in active
duties or public amusements, women are confined by the decorums of
society to the seclusion of home—often a cheerless and solitary seclusion. What resource remains for them? There is none to be compared
with that which books afford." In addition to easing the solitude of
domestic life, books provided women some relief from the "wearisome
monotony of in-door life—where like the mill-horse she must daily
tread the same round of duty." The writer, identified only as "S****,"
argued that books also provided this necessary pleasure even in the
best circumstances, when a woman was "surrounded by friends and
the advantages of rank and fortune." Even in such situations, "woman
has many hours, which the gayest life cannot supply with amusement."
Those activities traditionally relegated to women—such as going to the
theater and dances—could not fully satisfy them. Reading, in other
words, made *all* domestic life tolerable. In contrast to the image of

the domestic idler who was accused of squandering her time, here women's reading offered an alternative to "frivolous amusements" and an antidote to idleness itself (*LM*, Sept. 1831, 407–8).

Still, although recognizing women's individual motives for reading, both the *Ladies' Magazine* and the *Lady's Book* suggested that such reading should be regulated by genteel expectations. An 1831 essay, "Reading," urged women to select their materials with "judgment and good taste and discretion." Only those works that performed the task of "ennobling and purifying the human soul" were recommended, and the reader was warned to banish anything "unworthy [of] a mind of delicacy, good taste, and moral sentiment" (*LM*, March 1831, 135). In urging her readers to be careful in their selections, however, Hale did not suggest that women alone had such a responsibility. On the contrary, the reviews frequently instructed men to follow similar genteel standards. A review of *Memoirs of Vicocq, the Secret Agent of the French Police* in 1859, for example, warned readers that it "is certainly not a book for gentlewomen to read. Such being our opinion, we cannot conscientiously recommend it to gentlemen. Perhaps we are prudish" (*GLB*, Oct. 1859, 373).

The *Ladies' Magazine* and the *Lady's Book* never abandoned genteel values, but they did not limit genteel reading to polite entertainment. Indeed, to have the social influence Hale desired, women had to read widely. Thus in 1837 Hale described the "invention of printing" as a "blessed era for woman" precisely because of the range of knowledge it afforded women: "The multiplication of books has, in some degree, destroyed that monopoly of knowledge which men would engross, while learning was confined to manuscripts and the schools. As soon as books were accessible, the female mind received a new impulse" (*GLB*, Nov. 1837, 230). Similarly, *Mrs. Hale's Receipts for the Million* advised women to vary their reading to include "poetry, story, biography, history, essays, and religious works." [12] A fairly typical "Editors' Book Table" in the *Lady's Book* recommended an equally broad spectrum of fiction, poetry, and nonfiction prose, the latter of which included such works as Alexis de Tocqueville's *Democracy in America* and volumes on U.S. history, mental disorders, and practical mechanics (*GLB*, July 1840, 47–48). Other nondomestic subjects suggested elsewhere in the

*Ladies' Magazine* and the *Lady's Book* included surgery, anatomy, the rules of chess, botany, and government organization. Thus, in contrast to earlier American women's magazines that limited women's reading to domestic subjects and entertainment, the *Ladies' Magazine* and the *Lady's Book* provided their women readers with a precise formula for reading that combined domesticity with intellectual development and emphasized the variety—rather than the limits—of women's reading.

Not coincidentally, Hale's vision that women's reading should be intellectually rigorous and diverse corresponded precisely to her understanding of magazines, and she frequently recommended other periodicals to her readers. As early as 1829 Hale endorsed five other periodicals: the *North American Review*, the *Journal of Education*, the *Western Monthly Review*, the *Edinburgh Review*, and the *Quarterly Review* (*LM*, May 1829, 246–48). Not one of these was the light miscellany traditionally sanctioned for women's reading, and all sought an intellectual audience. Two of them, in fact—the *Edinburgh Review* and the *North American Review*—were considered the most seriously intellectual periodicals of the time. Explaining even more clearly the importance of periodicals in making women's reading diverse and intellectually demanding, Hale argued in 1857: "The advantages of this *flying literature* are great to the people of America. It gives them an extent and variety of general information never met with among the *peoples* of other countries. It is the chief source of woman's intellectual culture" (*GLB*, Dec. 1857, 557). Using patriotic rhetoric reminiscent of the eighteenth-century celebrations of the maternal woman reader as national hero, Hale offered an expanded definition of women's reading. No longer limited to light entertainment and material intended for children or identified solely by her social relations, this woman read as an individual and for intellectual development. As "flying literature," periodicals performed a specifically patriotic function: they gave American women the freedom to explore a "variety of general information." In some ways, Hale's emphasis on the diversity of magazines may have been a response to the attacks against the domestic idler, who was accused of single-minded, obsessive reading. Unlike a novel, a magazine, Hale suggested, would enrich a woman's mind without making reading an obsession.

In addition to encouraging women to read intellectual magazines, Hale urged them to read newspapers—material traditionally considered as appropriate for men, not women.[13] In *Mrs. Hale's Receipts for the Million*, for example, Hale advised the "lady of the house" to "insist" on a subscription to a newspaper.[14] Similarly, the November 1858 "Godey's Arm-Chair" urged women to read newspapers because they provided an "education with the actual world and its transpiring events." Godey insisted: "Let her have an intelligent opinion, and be able to sustain an intelligent conversation regarding the mental, moral, political, and religious improvement of our times. . . . Let the whole family—men, women, and children—read the newspapers" (*GLB*, Nov. 1858, 474). Such recommendations illustrate how Hale's theory of reading coincided with her concern for women to expand their sphere beyond the domestic world. Neither devotional nor purely entertaining, the newspaper generally reported on the world of politics and business—two spheres outside the realm of traditional domesticity.

Hale defended such diverse and intellectual reading partly by insisting that it be balanced with domestic responsibilities. T. S. Arthur's "Managing a Blue," published in the *Lady's Book* in 1846, illustrates how the woman reader was expected to combine the intellect of the "blue"—but not her lack of femininity—with the domesticity of the republican mother and genteel lady. The protagonist, a "decided *blue*" named Miss Phoebe Gray, had "spent nearly all of her time for years in reading," especially in philosophy. Kant, Carlyle, Goethe, and Schiller were among her "favorite authors, and she read them until she had quotations enough on her tongue's end to frighten away half the men who approached her." Run they do, for Miss Gray's habit of humiliating others in conversation makes more than one man of the town "feel as small as a seed potatoe" (*GLB*, Dec. 1846, 261).

This beginning seems to promise the typical condemnation of the "blue," for the woman reader is incapable of maintaining any social relations. Indeed, the plot initially suggests such a punishment of the woman. Miss Gray experiences humiliation herself when a young physician, whom she had embarrassed for not knowing Macaulay, seeks revenge by interrogating her on medical subjects. Once aware of the error of her ways, Miss Gray becomes the model of feminine sociability, introducing in conversation only those subjects of "common interest." As a reward for her transformation, Miss Gray befriends and eventually marries the same doctor who had humbled her. At the end of the story, Miss Gray, now "Mrs. Doctor Philips" is "as little like the blue, Phoebe Gray, as can well be imagined" (*GLB*, Dec. 1846, 264).

As much as this story condemns the antisocial "blue" and rewards the domestic, socially conscious woman, it does not denounce women's intellectual reading. Quite the contrary—Miss Gray and Dr. Philips cultivate their friendship by reading in each other's area of expertise. Dr. Philips reads "general literature," and Miss Gray studies "scientific subjects, and those relating specially to animal and vegetable physiology." Miss Gray's "error," then, is not her reading; more diverse materials, after all, are part of the solution. Rather, her mistake is that she neglected her duties as a woman, to be sociable and kind (*GLB*, Dec. 1846, 264). In this story and elsewhere in Hale's magazines, then, the ideal woman reader is assumed to combine her rigorous studies with her domestic and feminine responsibilities.

T. S. Arthur's suggestion that Miss Gray should read with Dr. Philips reveals a fairly common nineteenth-century strategy concerning women's reading. In part because reading was recognized as a means of inspiring passionate and even erotic responses, nineteenth-century women readers were often portrayed within a social setting. A family sitting room was expected to domesticate women's pleasure in reading. Any erotic possibilities were thus tamed as the women were either under the watchful eye of husbands, fathers, and brothers or themselves responsible for watching young children.[15] Though, as I have shown, Hale certainly celebrated women's reading in such familial contexts, her magazines did not preclude the possibility of a pleasurable component of women's reading, and women's leisured reading was occasionally described with sexual imagery. One essay published in 1854, titled "The Benefit of Reading," portrayed a woman named Aunt Sallie who lives happily amid her garden and her books, and her life is associated with fertility. Her rooms are "perfect greenhouses," filled with plants that "bear fruit." Like her flowers, Aunt Sallie's books provide her with great pleasure. "The charm of the house," they "replenish the fountain of youthful and affectionate sympathy with all

that has beauty and life," and "they have well repaid her in the cheer-
ful energy which they have kept green through the winter of her life"
(*GLB*, July 1854, 79).

On the one hand, this image of a woman reading for pleasure challenged cultural expectations about women's sexuality. Aunt Sallie, after
all, has found a source of pleasure independent of the permission, assistance, or even knowledge of any man. On the other hand, Aunt Sallie's
circumstances minimize the threat of private pleasure. As an older
woman who never married and lives alone, Aunt Sallie has no familial
duties and thus can pursue her personal wishes more freely than the
woman who has responsibilities as wife and mother. Aunt Sallie's pleasure, then, threatens no one, for she remains, as the essayist reminds
us, an "old maid" (*GLB*, July 1854, 79).

Visually, the idea of women reading privately for pleasure was reinforced by fashion plates that depicted individual women with books,
such as "Visiting Dress," published in the *Lady's Book* in 1865 (figure 5).
The elaborate designs of the dress and the hat suggest a pleasurable
rather than a utilitarian activity. Similarly, although the dress is supposedly designed for socializing, the woman's attention to her book,
its small size, and its placement on her lap all contribute to the sense
of privacy. The size of her skirt, moreover, creates a barrier of sorts,
protecting her from intruders. Ironically, the large skirt hiding much
of the woman's body seems both to deny and to make possible a physical, erotic element in her reading. With a more revealing dress, the
presence of a book might have been too suggestive.

Though it sometimes portrayed women reading by themselves, the
*Lady's Book* more frequently depicted reading for pleasure occurring
among groups of women. Though obviously in a social setting, the
woman reader here was not denied personal pleasure. An engraving
published in 1846, for instance, shows three women readers (figure 6).
One woman holds a large book on her lap, while the other two women
look on. Like the typical genteel lady, these women have surrounded
themselves with luxuries: they wear fine clothing and jewelry, and an
urn sits on a table behind them. The book, moreover, has an expensive
binding, complete with clasps.

These luxurious details do more than indicate the social standing

Figure 5. "Visiting Dress."
From *Godey's Lady's Book*, Oct. 1865. Courtesy of the
University of Illinois at Urbana-Champaign.

Figure 6. "A Reading Party."
From *Godey's Lady's Book*, Oct. 1846. Courtesy of the
University of Illinois at Urbana-Champaign.

of the women; they also suggest the pleasure of reading together in a group. The expensive binding and clasps, for example, imply that the book is especially treasured. The intimacy of the setting and the title of the engraving—"A Reading Party"—also suggest a certain sensuous, even sensual, pleasure. Although these women are not permitted purely individualistic pleasures, they do experience a degree of freedom not imagined in other portraits of the woman reader in social settings. Neither governed by husbands or fathers nor limited by the needs of children, they read in a community of equals.

Other engravings in the *Lady's Book* also emphasize the enjoyment associated with reading groups of genteel women. Indeed, the *Lady's Book* itself was presented as a publication that had a primary place within women's reading groups. An engraving published in 1854 features a group of three women and one girl waiting for the arrival of the *Lady's Book* (figure 7). As in other engravings, reading here appears as a communal and pleasurable activity, and the women's informal dress—their hats are off—suggests a high level of intimacy.

In virtually all of these reading groups, the women's pleasure is inherently tied to the separatist nature of the groups themselves. Many plates, including "A Reading Party," signal this separatism not only in the enclosed domestic space in which the women appear but also by the material objects of women's culture—art objects such as urns, fancy clothing, and needlework. Even "The Arrival of the *Lady's Book*," which places its reading group outdoors, expresses a separatist ideology. Seated by what appears to be the porch of a house, the women are separated physically from the town featured in the background, and two fences emphasize their isolation. Even the man who is bringing the magazine to them remains distant. Presumably, this separatism allows for the group's intimacy and the pleasure associated with reading together as a group.

Because the *Lady's Book* was a woman-identified magazine—with editor and reader bonded in an equal, same-sex relationship—the description of women coming together to read it suggests the close emotional bonds noted by Carroll Smith-Rosenberg in her study of nineteenth-century American women. Specifically, the intense inti-

Figure 7. "The Arrival of the *Lady's Book*."
From *Godey's Lady's Book*, April 1854. Courtesy of the
University of Illinois at Urbana-Champaign.

macy of these women's reading groups parallels the way that nineteenth-century women described their own friendships. In their letters and diaries, women described their intense love for their female friends, often in romantic language. Such relationships, Smith-Rosenberg argues, encouraged personal development not likely to occur through women's interaction with men: "Women, who had little status or power in the larger world of male concerns, possessed status and power in the lives and worlds of other women." [16] While ignored or belittled in the public sphere, a woman could develop a sense of self-worth through her intimate relations with other women.

Although Smith-Rosenberg does not discuss women's reading groups specifically, a similar sense of self-worth was suggested in the *Lady's Book*. Certainly the editorial *we*, which was repeatedly identified as female, invited women readers to share the authority of its woman editor. In the editorial pages of the *North American Review*, in contrast, the *we* assumed that both the writer-editor and reader were educated, literary men; the writer hoped to persuade the reader that *his* position on a particular issue was the rational one for all members of that *we*. Although conventional in magazines edited by men—for the *we* was defined as male—the identification of reader with editor challenged patriarchal assumptions of power when the normative, intelligent voice was female. The *we* of the *Ladies' Magazine* and the *Lady's Book* referred to Hale and other women. By accepting Hale's authority as editor, the readers assumed some of that power for themselves, for they shared her perspective as a white, middle-class, literate woman.

The association of woman reader and woman editor suggests that, unlike many other women's magazines, which followed the father-daughter model, the *Ladies' Magazine* and the *Lady's Book* were based on the same-sex bonds described by Smith-Rosenberg. The structure of both magazines matches their representation of women's reading groups. Like the three women in the engraving reading a volume together, the readers of the *Lady's Book* engaged in an activity in which they were among other women as equals. Even the woman reading the *Lady's Book* alone in her own home joined this group in her identification with Hale. Like the actual women friends whom Smith-Rosenberg has described, the women readers of the *Lady's Book* were assumed to speak and to listen to one another, valuing their own lives and experiences.

This relationship assumed between editor and reader and among readers influenced Hale's understanding of the reading process. Early in her editorial career, as she was developing the idea of an expanding women's sphere, Hale sometimes presented reading in ways similar to Judith Fetterley's idea of the resisting reader. The 1832 essay "Reading," for example, criticized readers who relied on "the opinions of great and wise men" rather than thinking for themselves. As the author, "S.J.," explained: "The indolent reader prefers the easiest way of reading, which is to let his thoughts run on in the same stream with the author's, or rather, not think at all; not troubling himself to inquire whether in this assertion or that remark the author is right or wrong" (*LM*, Jan. 1832, 32). Similarly, an 1833 essay titled "Musings of an Invalid" urged women readers not to accept passively the material they read. The danger of passive reading, as the author, "J.," explained, was the risk of overidentifying with the author. Passive readers who did not take time to "reflect" could be "take[n] up" by a "fascinating writer, who utters his sentiments in spirit-stirring phrases." If this were to happen, readers might "hurry on, with heedless impetuosity over lines, paragraphs and whole pages and volumes." Without reflection, the reader could "swallow down error, as a blind man drinks a bowl of poison" (*LM*, June 1833, 243).

Although not explicitly named, gender is an implied factor, especially in the second example. The impression of recklessness certainly conjures up images of the domestic idler, who voraciously feeds her appetite for fiction. The identification of the reader as female but the author as male, moreover, reinforces the idea that, especially for women, good reading is an active process, even one that requires resistance. Indeed, in contrast to these images of blindness and recklessness, good reading was associated with self-consciousness, sight, and depth: "When we read, we should do it with care and deep thought. We should go to the bottom of the thing. We should analyze and compare. We should place the opinions broached, side by side, with the result of our own experiences, and from them draw the inference. We should not pass by a single sentiment without a full understanding of it, and a full investigation of its truth" (*LM*, June 1833, 244–45). Thus, like Fetterley's resisting reader, this "good" reader maintains control, never granting authority to the writer, who is an outsider.

As the positive images of women's reading groups suggest, however, Hale did not maintain this emphasis on resistant reading. Quite the contrary—as she became increasingly committed to the idea of a separate women's culture, in which women read the work of women writers in the company of other women, the idea of resistance grew far less appealing and far less necessary. One letter written to Louis Godey in 1852, for example, described the "pleasure with which the 'Lady's Book' is received by a circle of our ladies," who take turns reading the magazine aloud to the entire group. According to the writer, the women meet for "the express purpose of listening to its contents," which they "devour" with "gusto" (*GLB*, April 1852, 297). While the idea of such ravenous reading was unthinkable to Hale in a nonseparatist community of readers, women who met together to read women's texts could be afforded such pleasures. No doubt such a shift was at least partially related to the fact that Hale's editorial career depended on women choosing to read women-identified texts. Hale could advertise her own magazine, then, by emphasizing the pleasure of this kind of reading.

The relation between Hale's own position as an editor of a women's magazine and the image she presented of women's reading is evident as well in the 1857 title plate of the *Lady's Book* (figure 8). With its claim that "mothers take the *Lady's Book* for their daughters whose mothers took it for them," this engraving establishes the magazine at the center of women's culture. By reinforcing the intergenerational element of women's culture both in its written text and in the multigenerational family scene, this engraving also serves as an advertisement for the magazine, attesting to and requesting its continuance through several generations. In addition to supporting the continued existence of the *Lady's Book*, this engraving also stands as a paradigm of the magazine's representation of women's reading. Certainly the intergenerational scene here defines women's reading in the context of familial responsibilities and establishes reading as a necessary component of domestic life rather than a threat to its stability. The description of the magazine as "a library in itself" as well as the globe, the inkstand, the

Figure 8. Title plate of the *Lady's Book*.
From *Godey's Lady's Book*, Jan. 1857. Courtesy of the
University of Illinois at Urbana-Champaign.

heavy books, and what appears to be a telescope in the lower right-hand corner of the plate suggest Hale's interest in the intellectual rigor of women's reading. The pairing of art and musical objects at the bottom left of the plate likewise reveals Hale's interest in diverse reading and the idea that women's culture, like women's reading, must maintain a balance between the intellectual and the so-called ornamental arts. That the young boy in the plate ignores the women reading, moreover, implies the separatist nature of women's culture. But as in so many of the images of women's reading in the *Lady's Book*, that separatist women's culture here is based on the idea of an expanding women's sphere. Though the domestic scene is itself bounded by an oval, the open window suggests the expansive nature of women's reading. By bringing in ideas and information from the public sphere and, even more important, by the influence of women readers on family and society, reading breaks down any certain division between public and private spheres. The spires of a public building—a church or an ornate library, perhaps—that top the domestic scene also suggest this fluidity between public and private spheres. While associating women's culture with the domestic space, this engraving refuses to confine that culture. On the contrary, it portrays women's culture as diverse and expansive, and the existence of the *Lady's Book* in the public realm reinforces the idea of a public women's culture.

Certainly this image of women's reading reveals its significant cultural differences from late twentieth-century theories of women's reading. While such theories have generally assumed that the woman reader has rejected the ideological position of reading as a man, in Hale's depiction no such transformation is necessary. Reading was defined as part of women's culture, and from a very early age girls were assumed to be reading women's texts in the company of others of their sex. These images were, of course, bound by Hale's own cultural contexts. Assuming that women accepted both middle-class notions of gentility and the primary responsibility of raising children, Hale could not imagine the woman reader to be, say, a politician, a factory worker, or even a devotee of French novels. Still, Hale did not simply reaffirm popular definitions of the woman reader. She recognized women's existence apart from domestic and social relations, challenged the presumed intellectual inferiority of women, and encouraged women to explore nondomestic worlds. No longer denied access to varied materials, the nineteenth-century woman reading the *Ladies' Magazine* and the *Lady's Book* assumed control of her own reading material, experienced personal pleasure, furthered her intellectual development, and, in the process, extended herself beyond the domestic sphere. That such transformations of the woman reader proved viable to others is evident by the popularity of the *Lady's Book*. Still, Hale's manipulations of other popular images were hardly disinterested. Without reimagining women's reading as familial and intellectual, as varied and pleasurable, Hale's magazines would never have thrived.

# 6

## Hale's Aesthetics of Poetry and Fiction

Though Hale envisioned women's reading as intellectual and diverse, her magazines, especially the *Lady's Book*, are often remembered as publications that served their readers an utterly monotonous fare that pandered to the worst literary tastes. Almost without exception, scholars have described the contents of Hale's magazines as little more than sentimental trash, as "mawkish, moralistic fiction" and "doubly mawkish, moralistic poetry."[1] Contrary to such descriptions, however, neither of Hale's magazines favored the stereotypical features of sentimental literature. Rather than finding overtly moralistic narrators or simplistic situations and melancholy characters, subscribers to the *Ladies' Magazine* and the *Lady's Book* were likely to read direct complaints about and even parodies of these very features. In a manner anticipating Mark Twain's parody of sentimental conventions in "Ode to Stephen Dowling Botts, Dec'd," one sketch in the *Lady's Book* featured a poem titled "Lines on a Retiring Crab." Describing the crab's death as a "cruel fate" caused by the "fierce and hunger driven hate / Of an epicure's pate," the poem ridicules the emotional and melancholy reaction of the speaker, who wonders whether the crab had been her "mother's favorite daughter," "dragged" from her "native water" (*GLB*, Aug. 1860, 140–41).[2]

The *Ladies' Magazine* and the *Lady's Book* did not assert their literary aesthetic simply by attacks of this kind. Rather, the editorials and essays articulated a fully conceived aesthetic of poetry and fiction.

Hale's theories of each genre differed, of course, but they shared an understanding of literature based, in large part, on her view of women as essentially moral, and both aesthetics complemented her treatment of the author and the reader. Because she wanted authors to be financially supported by their readers and because she defined women's reading as rightfully balancing domestic responsibilities and personal pleasure, Hale's aesthetics of poetry and fiction highlighted moral and pleasurable effects on the reader. Thus, although denouncing virtually all of the stereotypical conventions of sentimental literature, Hale emphasized the importance of sentiments. Indeed, the intersection of morality, sentiment, and gender was the foundation of Hale's aesthetic.

Hale's reputation for publishing "mawkish" verse is based, at least in part, on the general standards of nineteenth-century editors. As many scholars, most notably Emily Stipes Watts, Alicia Suskin Ostriker, and Cheryl Walker, have noted, nineteenth-century editors generally praised women for their modest poetic attempts and their emotional rather than intellectual abilities, while honoring male poets when they ambitiously pursued intellectual truths. In anthologies of American women's poetry—including Caroline May's *The American Female Poets* (1848), Rufus Griswold's *The Female Poets of America* (1849), and Thomas Buchanan Read's *The Female Poets of America* (1849)—editors generally defined feminine poetry as substandard, lacking power and vigor. Such a definition placed strict limits on the woman poet or, as she was frequently called, the poetess. Bound by expectations of modesty, unassertiveness, and melancholy emotionalism and denied ambition and rational thought, she was expected to produce poetry spontaneously and to strive for "light" verse. Never granted the status of a great poet, the poetess was not far removed from Mark Twain's Emmeline Grangerford, who produced endless elegies without even having to think and who, in the process, embodied and produced images of women's weakness and passivity.[3]

Hale is generally assumed to have promoted this restricted image of women's poetry, and not without reason. Numerous scholars have cited Hale's comment from an 1829 review that "the path of poetry, like every other path in life, is to the tread of woman, exceedingly circumscribed." In this review of *Guido, a Tale: Sketches from History*

*and Other Poems*, written by Emma Embury, though signed simply
"Ianthe," Hale contended that the woman poet "may not revel in the
luxuriance of fancies, images and thoughts, or indulge in the license
of choosing themes at will, like the lords of creation. She must never,
for the sake of a subject, forget or forfeit the delicacy of her sex." In
assessing the appropriate themes of women's poetry, Hale proclaimed
satire unsuitable and urged any woman poet to be "very circumspect
if she attempt to strike the soft lyre of love," and she expressed her
preference for poems that paint "domestic scenes and deep emotions."
Hale's warning to all women wishing to compose verse itself assumed
a restricted notion of women's poetry: "Neither anger, ambition, or the
love of *fun* must ever inspire a woman." The only appropriate motive,
Hale insisted, was "some deep, affectionate impulse" (*LM*, March 1829,
142–43).

However much Hale's caution about the themes and motives of the
woman poet recalls the restrictions on the poetess, her understanding
of women's poetry in this review and elsewhere challenged the basic
premise of that tradition—namely that women poets should aim at
writing light verse. Hale's primary criticism of Embury's volume was
that it trivialized women's emotional lives by emphasizing the romances
of young women. "Love," Hale insisted, "should not have been thus
exclusively the burden of her song; it is not the sole business of life,
nor is a disappointment of the heart the most terrible affliction that can
befal [*sic*] the children of men." Critical of the focus on the "discarded
lover" and the "disappointed damsel," Hale urged Embury to portray
a much greater range of emotional experiences, such as "the kind husband who has an ill-tempered wife" or "the agony of feeling which
the fond, faithful wife must endure who has a drunken husband" (*LM*,
March 1829, 143).

Hale's suggestions for new themes were clearly limited to domestic, specifically marital, relations, but these suggestions also urged
women poets to abandon a romantic, and largely sentimental, tradition of defining women only by their ability to acquire a husband.
While traditional love poetry, Hale implied, generally ended with the
heroine's wedding, she encouraged women poets to investigate marital
life itself. No longer a light topic that ended predictably and bliss-

fully, marriage in Hale's view was a complex subject more worthy of the woman poet's attention than the simple concerns of the forlorn lover. Hale's discussion of Embury's "The Mother's Farewell to Her Wedded Daughter," a poem Hale praised, demonstrates that she expected emotional richness from women poets. Rather than portraying a wedding as an inherently idyllic occasion—as one might expect from the stereotypical sentimental poet—Embury presents the wedding as a time of considerable tension: the mother in the poem "fears" for her daughter's happiness and mourns her leaving, yet chooses not to "pale" her daughter's "cheek" with her concerns. The poet's decision to focus on the mother's point of view, rather than the daughter's, further intensifies the challenge to the convention that the woman poet should avoid emotional complexity. As Joanne Dobson has observed, few nineteenth-century texts by women focused on the experiences of married women, yet here Embury wrote a poem that rejects the conventional perspective of the blissful bride, and Hale praised her efforts.[4] While the poem implies that marriage is a woman's destiny, it does challenge the then-popular restrictions on women's poetry. In addition to questioning the happiness assumed in traditional love stories that end in marriage, the poem insists that readers consider the experiences of an older woman in a moment of considerable anxiety and ambivalence. While many nineteenth-century editors expected the woman poet to offer little more than idealized, simplistic visions of life, Hale applauded Embury's poem, which emphasizes and never resolves this moment of considerable conflict (*LM*, March 1829, 143).

The difference between Hale's understanding of women's poetry and that of many of her contemporaries can be seen by comparing her review of Embury's *Guido* with a review of the same volume published just a few months after Hale's essay in the *North American Review*. While this reviewer was much more laudatory than Hale was, the *North American* praised the volume because—not despite—it was "light literature." As the reviewer explained, Embury's poetry neither illuminated "the deep places of human nature" nor offered a "high and far philosophy," but functioned "simply and solely to please." Though earlier in the essay the reviewer had explained that the great poet should "stamp upon the heart, the sublimest truths of moral and intellectual being," the lack of such truths in *Guido* evidently caused this reviewer no concern. The reviewer expressed "pleasure" and "pride" in the "productions of our fair country-women," who had taken "possession of the whole domain of light literature, as if it were theirs by a peculiar and exclusive right." In contrast to Hale's review, then, which insisted that women's poetry be more than beautiful, light verse, this review clearly assumed a poetic hierarchy based on gender: men's poetry must express "the sublimest truths," but women's poetry could be praised simply for being "beautiful" and "light" (*North American Review*, July 1829, 232–41).

Hale's later essays challenged even more directly the idea of women's poetry adopted by many of her contemporaries. In her essay "Woman the Poet of Nature," published in the *Lady's Book* in 1837, Hale directly refuted the idea that women's poetic achievements were naturally inferior to men's.[5] Rather than describing the highest poetic achievement in masculine terms, Hale created a feminized critical discourse for poetry. She defined the duties of all poets, in fact, just as she described ideal womanhood. Poetry, like women generally, promoted patriotism, religion, and social responsibility: the "office of true poetry is to elevate, purify, and soften the human character, and thus promote civil, moral and religious advancement." Indeed, like women, poetry improved society "by inculcating reverence and love towards God, . . . awakening the spirit of national aggrandizement, . . . [and] teaching the true relations of men to each other." While she acknowledged that some poets rejected such aims, Hale insisted that, however popular they might be, they would "die and be forgotten" (*GLB*, May 1837, 193). In contrast to the reviewer of the *North American Review*, then, Hale did not equate feminine poetry with limited achievement. On the contrary, she asserted that all poets, especially the great ones, should strive for feminine goals.

Believing that women had an innate advantage in this regard, Hale inverted the hierarchy used by many of her contemporaries, who assumed men's poetry to be innately superior to women's. Indeed, Hale argued that women, not men, were "morally gifted to excel" in poetry. Although she recognized exceptions, she believed that generally "the poetry of man" focused on the individual "intellect," "passions," and "pride," but the "poetry of woman" expressed the greatest human truths, including "impressions of the Beautiful and the Good," "the love of truth and nature," and "faith in God" (*GLB*, May 1837, 194–95).[6] Such a distinction between men's and women's poetry reinforced the genteel association of women with emotions and men with intellect, but Hale believed that men's poetry was capable of greater human truths only when it accepted a feminine perspective. Like a mother or wife who exerted a positive moral influence on her family through love, poets, according to Hale, achieved their highest calling when they appealed not to readers' rational faculties but to what might be called their sentiments—their "impressions," "faith," and "love." Significantly, this understanding of poetry's aims did not imply that it had a didactic purpose. Indeed, elsewhere Hale distinguished between "didactic" poetry and that which achieved its moral purpose through "indirect influence" (*LM*, Feb. 1829, 73).

Within her gendered vision of poetry's aims, Hale offered her own narrative of its history. According to Hale, poetry began as a male-dominated form and then blossomed under the influence of women. In the "heathen world," she argued, the woman poet had "no place": "Her harp cannot move stones, or tame beasts. She must wait till the flowers bloom and the birds appear." Thus, the greatest poets of this time were men, namely Homer and Virgil, who presented "the lofty and complete picture of national aggrandizement." In the Judeo-Christian world the woman poet emerged. Celebrating the Bible as the first pious poetry, Hale noted the achievements not of David or Solomon but of Deborah: "The song of Deborah is one of the most beautiful and sublime poems to be found in holy writ" (*GLB*, May 1837, 193).

According to Hale's literary history, women's voices transformed and ultimately improved poetry, especially in its subject matter: "War, the chace, the wine-cup and physical love are the themes of song in which men first delight and excel; nor is it till feminine genius exerts its power to judge and condemn these, always earthly, and often coarse and licentious, strains that the tone of the lyre becomes softer, chaster, more pure and polished and finally, as her influence increases, and she joins the choir, the song assumes that divine character which angels might regard with complacency." Although she associated men here with a greater topical range, Hale directly refuted the charge that she restricted women poets. She objected to those "critics who always speak of the 'true feminine style'—as though there was only one manner in which ladies could properly write poetry," and she noted the variety of such poets as Felicia Hemans, Mary Howitt, Jane Taylor, Letitia Elizabeth Landon, Lydia Sigourney, and Hannah Gould. Furthermore, Hale explained that although women poets have a more limited "range of subjects" than men, "in the manner of treating those within her province, she has a freedom as perfect as his." Relying heavily on an essential sexual difference that refuted notions of women's inferiority, Hale insisted that "the delicate shades of genius are as varied and as distinctly marked in one sex as its bold outlines are in the other. There are more varieties of the rose than of the oak" (*GLB*, May 1837, 194).

Demonstrating how Hale's critical discourse about poetry contradicted the association of her magazines with stereotypical sentimental literature is not the same, of course, as evaluating the poetry within the magazines themselves. To test the consistency between Hale's selection of poetry and her editorial rhetoric, I have analyzed the poems by Lydia Sigourney published in the *Lady's Book* between 1840 and 1842, during the time that she was listed as one of the magazine's editors. I take Sigourney as my focus here because, although scholars have recently corrected the image of Sigourney as an embarrassingly elegiac versifier, much of her magazine work is generally thought to have conceded to the expectations of light poetry.[7] Indeed, Sigourney herself declared that she gave magazine editors those "slight themes that were desired."[8]

The thirty-nine poems Sigourney published in the *Lady's Book* during these three years, however, fulfill not an aesthetic of "light" poetry but rather the powerful feminine poetics promoted in Hale's editorial columns. While Sigourney's most frequent topics—death, religion, and nature—correspond to stereotypical sentimental literature, her treatment of those subjects does not. Consider first her poems about death. The sentimental tradition often associated with the *Lady's Book* featured poems about the idealized deaths of mothers and children. The prevalence of dying children accounts for the excessive grief often noted in sentimental literature. The pairing of women and children in this tradition, moreover, suggests the degree to which women, like children, were portrayed as passive, emotional figures and, especially, as victims, either unable to withstand the emotional trauma of their lives—thus they often die from heartache—or incapable of protecting themselves from the brutal world around them. In this sample of Sigourney's poems, however, more poems focus on the deaths of adults than of children, and women are less often memorialized than men. While Sigourney's exploration of death and its influences on others corresponds with the conventions of the sentimental poet, then, her poetry does not assume women's victimization and passivity, nor does it equate women with children.

Rather than focusing on women's passivity, as does stereotypical sentimental literature, Sigourney's poetry repeatedly insists on women's strength. The widows who appear in Sigourney's death poetry are portrayed as strong, surviving women. In "On the Death of Lieutenant David E. Hale"—a poem honoring Sarah J. Hale's son—the mother grieves the loss of her adult son but in doing so assumes the role of strong survivor, who has outlived him and her husband (*GLB*, Jan. 1840, 32). Similarly, in "The Widow's Charge, at Her Daughter's Bridal," Sigourney transforms a normally patriarchal ritual—the father's giving the bride away—into a matriarchal one, with the mother instructing the husband to be (*GLB*, May 1840, 224). In contrast to the excessive emotionalism noted within the sentimental tradition, Sigourney's poems also suggest women's strength by portraying widows and other grieving women who control their emotions. In "The Kind Neighbor" the speaker refuses to indulge in "bitter grief" because it would displease her dead neighbor (*GLB*, Feb. 1840, 94). Even "The Owlbar Cottage"—a poem depicting a young woman's death after the drowning of her lover—ends with an image of the woman's parents coping with their grief. Although they "steep their bread in tears," they continue to work in the fields: "Habit-led, / They sow and reap, and spread the rustic board" (*GLB*, Sept. 1841, 120). Controlling one's emotions is, of course, neither a better response than an expression of grief nor a sign of strength. Still, Sigourney's move away from excessive grief does seem to be a rejection of the stereotypes of sentimental literature, perhaps as a way to insist on women's strength.[9]

Sigourney's poetry in the *Lady's Book* also challenged the association of women with passivity in its portrayal of women's public authority. Consider "Jotham's Parable," a poem based on Judges 9, which tells the story of Abimelech, who becomes king of Shechem by killing all but one of his brothers. Hardly the pious verse of the sentimental tradition, this poem tells the story of Jotham, the only surviving brother, who responds to Abimelech's disloyalty to God by cursing Shechem with fire and destruction. Within three years Jotham's curse is fulfilled: Abimelech is killed, and the town is demolished. Although the poem does imply the disastrous effects of disloyalty to God, as does Judges 9, it hardly conforms to the image of nineteenth-century women's religious verse. Rather than presenting a simplistic moral—or any moral, for that matter—the poem narrates political and historical struggles for power. Moreover, these are struggles in which women are intimately involved. As Abimelech invades the town of Tabez, a woman throws a large stone on his head, breaking his skull. Although his wound is fatal, Abimelech asks a servant to stab him with a sword so that no one will know he was killed by a woman. The servant obliges, and Abimelech dies (*GLB*, July 1840, 44).

Despite Abimelech's attempts to erase this woman's actions, she—not a man—fulfills God's wishes, and she does so with an act requiring great strength. By literally carrying and throwing the stone, the woman figuratively bears the weight of justice, and the biblical story suggests that women hold great political and religious power, even if men might try to deny them public recognition. The poem does not emphasize the woman's role; the speaker refers to the woman's deed rather cursorily when describing how the stone, "by a woman thrown," and a "servant's deadly thrust, / Avenged the usurper's ruthless deed." Still, Sigourney's decision to repeat this particular biblical story implicitly challenges the perception that women's poetry should champion only the dying, passive, female victim. After all, Sigourney's "Jotham's Parable" portrays a woman who murders with God's blessing (*GLB*, July 1840, 44). Sigourney's choice to title her poem using the word *parable* enhances that challenge to stereotypical images of women's inherent weakness. The biblical story, appearing as it does in the Old Testament, is not a parable in the sense of being either a fictitious story or one of the teachings of Jesus. Sigourney's intention in using *parable* is not clear, and she never identifies what the parable teaches. Certainly from the perspective of twentieth-century feminism, however, the poem reads as a parable of Sigourney's own patriarchal culture that ignores and erases women's engagement with history and politics.[10]

Sigourney published a number of poems in the *Lady's Book* that portray women's power within public realms, often while insisting on the connection between women's private and public lives. In "Queen Maria Christine's Farewell" Sigourney presents from both a public and private perspective the queen's departure from Spain in 1840. Appearing as both a mother and a queen, Maria Christine describes her pain as she "resign[s]" her "sceptre" and the "sterner sacrifice" of leaving her children. The connection between private and public realms is heightened by the image of Maria Christine's daughter, Isabella, who remains in power. Maria Christine leaves Isabella, asking all Spaniards to be "tender, and be true" to this "sacred trust" that she as "mother, and the queen" offers. Although the poem shows Maria Christine heading to exile in France, it does not imply a loss of women's power. The power structure is, in fact, matriarchal. By presenting Maria Christine as both monarch and mother, Sigourney offers her readers a means of claiming the queen's power. Her royal and maternal roles are intertwined, and readers who identify with her maternal feelings are also imagining themselves as queens (*GLB*, May 1841, 206).

Similarly, in "On Seeing, at Holyrood Palace, the Candelabra Which Mary, Queen of Scots, Brought from France," Sigourney encourages readers to identify with the subject's political power by describing the speaker's search for a personal connection with Mary. The speaker stands within the castle and then literally follows Mary's path, hoping to hear her "echoed footsteps." The relics of Mary's political life— the castle, the prison cell, the moat—do not succeed in bringing the speaker close to Mary. Only the "household vestige slight" can do so— Mary's chair, her couch, her sewing box, the basket of children's clothing, her closet. Once the speaker finds Mary's personal life amid these relics, she achieves the union she had been seeking, realizing that Mary shared the "joys that none but mothers taste." In connecting with Mary's personal life, the speaker is also able to envision the queen's political role. With the image of Mary as mother in her mind, the speaker finds that Mary's "pangs," "faults," and "fearful doom" come "thronging back, with magic power." The final image of Mary in the poem, as "Old Scotia's bright and smitten flower," reflects the integration of Mary's public and private roles. Her place within "Old Scotia's" history established, Mary also appears as a flower, a traditional image of women's personal femininity (*GLB*, Feb. 1841, 68).

Sigourney's own image as a poet during this three-year period parallels the public personae of her poem's speakers. During her editorial tenure she traveled to England and Scotland, and she publicized her travels in the *Lady's Book* by identifying the location of her poetry's composition and by writing poems about foreign subjects (e.g., "Excursion to Chester," "On Seeing Mrs. Fry at Newgate Prison," and "Sheep on the Cheviot Hills"). Hardly the unambitious poetess confined to her home and scribbling verses, Sigourney appears as a world traveler, sending verses from London and Edinburgh. That image as a world traveler, moreover, establishes Sigourney's place within the literary community. Several of these poems connect her to literary history—"To Wordsworth. Written at Rydal Mount," "Hawthornden. Recollections of the Poet Drummond, Who Formerly Resided There," and "On Visiting the Grave of Sir Walter Scott." In each of these poems, the speaker describes herself as searching for and being enriched by the contact with the literary present and past. In "To Wordsworth" Sigourney expresses her gratitude that she "found" Wordsworth in his "lake-girt bower," and she describes how his "music thrill'd [her] heart" (*GLB*, Jan. 1841, 34). Refusing the marginal position of the sentimental poet, Sigourney confirms her membership in a large literary community.

The fact that the public voice arises in these poems from a woman's personal and emotional experiences suggests much about the aesthetics of poetry within the *Lady's Book*. The speakers are not the stereotypical sentimental heroines, on the margins of society, forever destined to be invisible and self-effacing. On the contrary, they use their private experiences to claim the authority of public discourse. As they do so, however, they do not abandon what Hale viewed as their "natural" sensibility. Rather, their "natural" responses to issues of sentiments provide the impetus for the poet's public voice. Thus, the speaker in the poem about Mary, Queen of Scots, identifies with Mary because she understands the emotions of motherhood, and Sigourney becomes a member of the large literary community because Wordsworth's music "thrill'd her heart." While the stereotypical sentimental literature associates this emotional identification with a private, domestic space, here these sentiments are assumed to have power in the public realm.[11]

However much the *Lady's Book* has been invoked as the promoter of a "mawkish, moralistic" tradition, both the editorials and the poetry suggest that Hale's editorial stance recognized and refuted the conventions of sentimental literature. While periodicals like the *North American Review* defined poetry in masculine terms and relegated women poets to light literature, Hale used the pages of the *Ladies' Magazine* and the *Lady's Book* to insist upon quite different standards for poetry, including that by women. Indeed, virtually none of the stereotypical conventions of sentimental literature dominate these magazines. Like many critics, Hale insisted on the place of sentiment, but she favored neither the excessive emotionalism nor the moralistic intrusions so often associated with sentimental poetry. Moreover, the image of women's role differed sharply from that of the sentimental heroine. Here the woman poet as well as the poems' female speakers are portrayed as strong, moral people with considerable public authority. Like the editor herself, the woman poet in the *Lady's Book* emerged as a voice of literary authority, who recognized her place in literature and history and who moved freely between private and public experience.

As disparate as the perception and the reality of poetry are in the *Lady's Book*, so too are those of fiction. Though scholars have not always agreed about the terms of the fiction's failings—having called it overly didactic, emotional, melancholy, and sensational, for example— the *Lady's Book* has been repeatedly portrayed as promoting a simplistic and debased form of fiction.[12] Such assessments mask the complexity and power of Hale's understanding of fiction, which, again, was intimately connected with her theories of gender.

Though Hale's aesthetic of fiction did seek to empower women readers, writers, and editors, it did not challenge popular views to the same degree that her feminized aesthetic of poetry did. Indeed, in many ways Hale differed little from most periodical editors of her time in her treatment of fiction. Like many of her peers, she focused on what she and many other editors called moral tendency. Believing that human beings have innate moral sentiments that are rewarded in life, and should be rewarded in literature, Hale favored narratives that encouraged readers to sympathize with moral characters and that depicted these characters as triumphant. Thus, although the fiction of the *Lady's Book* has been criticized for its heavy-handed narrators, Hale defined moral tendency, as did most midcentury editors, primarily by reference to plot, characterization, and the effect on the reader.[15]

L. A. Wilmer's 1840 essay "Some Thoughts on Works of Fiction" is a virtual paradigm of the *Lady's Book*'s aesthetic of fiction. Certainly Wilmer defined moral tendency, as did most of the magazine's essayists, as a feature of plot, primarily. Wilmer faulted one book because its "only *innocent* character" met "with unmitigated misfortune and die[d] in the most unhappy circumstances." Similarly, he emphasized plot in his assessment of Samuel Richardson's *Pamela*, which he said proved that some novels "which are ostensibly moral, are often the reverse." Despite Richardson's attempt to enforce "the maxim that servant girls, by strict adherence to virtuous principles, may . . . marry their masters," the novel ultimately taught "that an honest and worthy female is *rewarded* by marrying with a wealthy and unprincipled booby, and that the most scandalous outrages are mere trifles in the conduct of a man of fortune and family." According to Wilmer, *Pamela* failed as a moral novel not because of narrative voice or authorial intentions, but because the plot failed to punish Mr. B and to reward Pamela. As Wilmer explained, the heroine deserves far more than to become "the wife of a professed libertine, a desperately wicked fellow, . . . who, even after marriage, gives good reason to suspect that Pamela does not possess his undivided affections." To improve "the morality of the tale," Wilmer recommended a different ending: Mr. B should go to Newgate, and Pamela should marry Mr. Williams (*GLB*, July 1840, 13–14). Such an ending would fulfill Wilmer's understanding of moral fiction.

A review of *Belial* published in 1865 demonstrates how Hale employed this aesthetic when assessing contemporary fiction. Denouncing the novel as "nothing more than an illy-flavored rehash" of "second-rate romances," Hale focused on its plot about a middle-aged married man who falls in love with his fifteen-year-old ward. After waiting "impatiently" for his wife's death, the man marries the young woman. Although Hale generally favored marriage plots in which moral characters triumphed, here she disapproved precisely because the novel rewarded a man who did not honor his first wife: "If the author had made the parties elope before the fortunate event of the wife's demise, and then given approval and blessing to the iniquitous union, the moral of the story could scarcely have been worse" (*GLB*, Sept. 1865, 267). In its happy ending, *Belial* suggests that both the husband and the heroine deserve the reader's sympathy. Because Hale considered such sympathy unearned, she declared the happy ending immoral. Only if the novelist had inspired criticism of the characters could the novel achieve a positive moral tendency.

Although Wilmer's assessment of Richardson's *Pamela* and Hale's review of *Belial* accurately represent the aesthetic of fiction in the *Lady's Book* throughout the antebellum period, neither Hale nor Louis Godey had initially embraced this aesthetic, and the principle of moral tendency was both a compromise of their earlier positions and an indication of their ambivalence about fiction's role in their magazine. Initially Hale and Godey expressed very different attitudes toward fiction. When Hale began editing the *Ladies' Magazine* in 1828, she did not highlight fiction. Though she praised some novels in her reviews, her opening editorial made only a passing reference to "tales," and the magazine tended to feature more essays than fiction. Moreover, the magazine favored sketches, which combined elements of fiction and nonfiction prose. In contrast, when Godey began the *Lady's Book* in 1830, fiction emerged as the magazine's primary genre. In the early years of the magazine, he included as many as seven or eight fictional selections in individual issues, and the magazine itself sponsored a fiction contest. Godey's attitude toward fiction is also suggested by the type of story he published. While Hale favored the semifictional sketch, Godey published many sensational stories, with titles like "The Tiger's Cave" and "The Traitor's Doom."

Several factors account for these differences. First, Hale's early neglect of the short story form may have resulted from her insistence on publishing original works by American authors. Though Americans were certainly writing short stories in the late 1820s, the form was still underdeveloped, and Hale may have been unable to obtain much original American short fiction. Godey, on the other hand, who published—or pirated—British writers as well, may have simply had more material from which to choose. But their differing treatment of fiction also resulted from their own philosophies about their magazines. Hale's early emphasis on women's intellectual abilities and education complemented her preference for the essay. Suggesting why fiction was not highlighted in the *Ladies' Magazine*, Hale explained in one review in 1829 that works of fiction could be "advantageous" but that "they should be considered and treated only as light and amusing productions; they should not be represented as the sources, from which we may or can draw our knowledge, principles, faith" (*LM*, Sept. 1829, 436–37). Godey, in contrast, interested primarily in entertaining rather than influencing his readers, preferred fiction over the more overtly educational essay, and his addresses to readers focused on pleasing the reader with engravings and fashion plates rather than improving her through essays.

In joining their editorial efforts in 1837, Hale and Godey fused their aesthetics of fiction as well. Unlike Hale's opening editorial for the *Ladies' Magazine,* her inaugural essay in the *Lady's Book* identified fiction as a mainstay of the magazine: "We shall talk of novels, and communicate all the interesting tales and stories which our department of fiction will allow" (*GLB*, Jan. 1837, 3). While earlier favoring the essay over fiction, which she associated with "amusement," Hale soon depicted fiction in relation to truth and knowledge. As she explained in 1841, "It is not always wise to lecture, even though we are discussing grave subjects. Truth may, to many minds, be more easily conveyed by exhibitions of character in a story, than in the deductions of a logical essay on morals; and hearts, that would be callous to the reproofs of a sermon, may be melted to penitence by the appeal of a song" (*GLB*, June 1841, 281). Hale's vision of "hearts" being "melted" by "song" rather than a "sermon" demonstrates how her acceptance of moral tendency depended upon her increased emphasis on sentiments rather than rationality. For his part, Godey also changed in his treatment of fiction. In the essay announcing Hale's editorship, he made a strong, and hitherto atypical, appeal to social service. Insisting that the magazine "will do good," Godey explained: "Its influence is directed to promote social refinement, domestic virtues, and humble piety" (*GLB*, Dec. 1836, 283). Soon he applied this new principle of improvement directly to fiction. Implicitly denouncing his earlier association of fiction as amusement, Godey came to reject the idea that the *Lady's Book* should be a "mere story-book": "Those articles of fiction that we do publish, have all a moral tendency" (*GLB*, Feb. 1860, 186).

This idea of a moral tendency provided Hale and Godey the compromise they needed. Though late twentieth-century readers are likely to associate moral fiction with didactic instruction, nineteenth-century readers were likely to see it as pleasing. As Fred Kaplan has suggested, the happy ending in sentimental literature arose from the idea that moral readers experienced pleasure when good characters were rewarded and morally corrupt characters punished.[14] In promoting fiction that had a moral tendency, then, Louis Godey did not have to abandon the idea of achieving a mass readership. Though redefining the nature of such pleasure, Godey maintained his emphasis on pleasing his readers. But if moral tendency provided a way of recognizing and celebrating the pleasure of reading fiction, the principle also did not position the magazine as one that simply amused its readers—an image Hale would have found unacceptable. Rather, moral tendency implied that fiction affected its readers and that, like Hale's editorials, it was capable of inspiring personal, familial, and national improvement. By defining fiction as moral, Hale also ensured a positive association of women with fiction. Indeed, her definition of good fiction is almost identical to her understanding of woman's innate nature: both are essentially moral. This aesthetic of fiction's moral tendency, which assumed that fiction was properly designed to please *and* to influence readers, then, served as the foundation of the *Lady's Book*.

Still, it was an aesthetic built on considerable ambivalence. While capitalizing on the enormous popularity of fiction, this aesthetic implied a distrust of people's abilities to choose the fiction they read. Though readers might be able to decide what pleased them, editors and publishers assumed the authority to determine what constituted moral tendency. As Hale herself declared in 1850, "Novels are now the great vehicle of public sentiment, where politics, religion, or political economy are discussed, and all new ideas, or at least the extravagant opinions of each would-be reformer, are promulgated. In this way the masses are reached, for everybody reads novels; but it is reserved for the magazines and reviews to sift these crude works, [and] select the appropriate for their own readers" (*GLB*, April 1850, 290). Such a position suggests Hale's conflicted response to fiction. On the one hand, the magazine seemed to embrace a democratic impulse in featuring such a popular form. On the other hand, both Hale and Godey were unwilling to resign their authority as arbiters of taste.

The tensions between the goals of pleasing and influencing the reader erupted within the magazine in other ways as well. While some essays and editorials praised fiction's ability to convey truth, others openly denounced any such message. Edgar Allan Poe was just one of the essayists in the *Lady's Book* to reject a didactic aim for fiction. In his 1847 review of Nathaniel Hawthorne's *Twice-Told Tales*, he insisted that readers "are positively offended by instruction" and argued that "the end of all fictitious compositions" is "pleasure" (*GLB*, Nov. 1847, 253). Or as he declared in yet another essay published in the *Lady's Book*, "It is not in the power of any fiction to inculcate any truth" (*GLB*, March 1846, 136).

The magazine's essayists repeatedly tried to navigate between the two ideas that fiction should have a moral tendency and that it should reject any didactic aim by portraying the author's influence as properly indirect. Thus, in one review Hale praised a writer who "infuses into all his writings a spirit of instruction," but she defined the nature of that instruction as "quiet and unobtrusive" (*GLB*, June 1841, 282). Similarly, while L. A. Wilmer's "Some Thoughts on Works of Fiction" described a "positive moral tendency" as "a most excellent circumstance," Wilmer opposed the idea that the "*sole* object of the novelist should be to inculcate lessons of morality." The only way to achieve the difficult task of pleasing the reader while investing the text with moral import was, Wilmer insisted, for the author to adopt a duplicitous role. Indeed, Wilmer's essay is full of rhetoric associated with deceit: "If people are to be cheated into instruction, it must be done cautiously. The medicine must be well disguised; for if once detected, it becomes more distasteful than if offered in its original purity" (*GLB*, July 1840, 13). Though Wilmer attempted to combine instruction with pleasure, ultimately his essay undercut one of the central premises of the aesthetic of moral tendency—namely that moral readers experience pleasure when reading moral texts. By portraying amusement and authorial intervention as conflicting goals, Wilmer implicitly rejected the notion of a moral audience, unsatisfied by mere amusement.

The metaphor of authorial deceit also clashed with the frequent use of a rhetoric later associated with literary realism. Like many other editors of her time, Hale believed that the fiction writer should accurately represent "real" life, and the *Lady's Book* generally faulted writers for characters that were too perfect or for improbable plots.[15] Thus, Wilmer criticized Richardson's characters as "unnatural" and "intolerable" because they were "intrinsically correct" and "perfect" (*GLB*, July 1840, 13). Similarly, Hale denounced what she called "silly novels" for "their apparent renunciation of all reality": she wrote that they "avoid depicting human nature; their heroes and heroines are careful never to speak and act as real people would do; nor do we find in these novels any trains of circumstances leading to such conclusions as occur in the real world. . . . impossible events, situations, and results make up the staple of these books" (*GLB*, April 1857, 370). Though not exactly contradicting the moral aesthetic, this appeal to accurate representation implicitly undercut the idea of fiction as indirectly influencing the reader. While one highlighted the fiction writer's abilities of imitation, the other celebrated powers of deception.

Further suggesting the tension between the ideas of fiction as pleasurable and as morally beneficial, these two models of fiction—as a moral influence and as accurate representation—sometimes appeared simultaneously within individual essays. Wilmer, for instance, basically argued that while fictional works should not be condemned for being a "mere literary toy" with "no moral import," great works exerted a positive moral influence on their readers. Here, of course, Wilmer relied on the notion that writers had to deceive their readers in order to please and influence them. In the same essay, however, Wilmer posited a very different notion of influence, based on the idea of fiction as an imitative art. When explaining why writers should "adher[e] to *nature*" and thus avoid "perfect" characters, Wilmer suggested that fiction influenced its readers far too easily. Readers—specifically "young people" and implicitly young women—who based their "exalted notions of the human character" on fiction were likely to face "ruin." Wilmer then narrated the fairly conventional anecdote of a young woman who expected her suitors to match her idea of "imaginary perfection" and thus refused "several advantageous offers of marriage," only to "repent of her folly" later. Contradicting his claims elsewhere in the essay, Wilmer suggested that a novel should not simply please—should not be a mere "literary toy"—precisely because that toy was likely to affect the reader adversely. Significantly, this threat existed regardless of the author's intentions; even those writers who showed "evident intention" of doing good sometimes produced "pernicious" works (*GLB*, July 1840, 13–15). The only way to avoid this risk, according to Wilmer, was for the writer to adopt a purely mimetic mode. Such confidence in realistic representation challenged his insistence elsewhere in the essay that writers should try to deceive their readers.

The fear that fiction might prove too pleasurable and thereby too influential was clearly related to generalized concerns about women's reading. Although providing a forum for such fears, Hale's aesthetic tempered them as well. Ironically, by promoting a fairly contradictory aesthetic that depicted fiction as deceptive and mimetic, pleasurable and morally beneficial, Hale ultimately minimized those very features thought to be most dangerous to women—namely fiction's imaginative qualities. Such was certainly the strategy of "D.M.," who published an essay titled "Romances" in the *Ladies' Magazine* in 1830. Responding to the idea that novels, especially romances, served as dangerous narcotics, the essayist explained that such objections were "very reasonable" in "the olden time" when "startling tales of giants and enchanters were so much admired, and half believed." The reviewer concluded that these perils no longer existed: "There is now little danger to any who have access to the publications of the present day. The contrast between the two kinds is readily perceived, and the extravagancies of the romance excite, at present, as much ridicule as they formerly excited admiration." The reviewer defined these preferred fictions in realistic terms, distinguishing between works that "raise curiosity by the very strangeness of the circumstances" and "sweet tales, which portray nature and mankind correctly" (*LM*, March 1830, 130–31). The appeal of this aesthetic is clear: if works were defined in supposedly real rather than imaginary terms, then they could pose no danger to women readers.

The high praise and frequent discussion of historical fiction in the *Ladies' Magazine* and the *Lady's Book* further suggest that the realistic rhetoric functioned as a way of defusing fears about women's fiction reading.[16] Indeed, Hale praised historical fiction only when it provided what she believed to be an accurate picture of life. Historical "romances," in contrast, which "misrepresent characters and facts," received her continued disapproval (*GLB*, Sept. 1854, 276). Similarly, in his essay Wilmer focused on the merits of historical accuracy as a way of easing fears about fiction. His account of history writing depended heavily on both a realistic rhetoric and the idea that fiction might exert a positive moral influence:

> If a novel present *just* views of life, it will be most likely to be beneficial in the perusal, for virtue cannot be represented more amiable than it is, nor can vice be exhibited in colours more disgusting than the reality. History itself, in its veritable details, strongly enforces the precept, that good actions usually meet with a reward, even in this life, and that crimes seldom fail to incur their appropriate penalties. If this be the truth, then it is no disparagement to the moral rectitude of a novel, if it approximate to historical accuracy. There is no necessity for presenting unnatural characters and improbable circumstances to make a work of fiction strictly moral. It is, moreover, no dispraise to an author, if his chief design be to exhibit a faithful picture of the manners of some particular age or people. . . . Books of this kind are positively beneficial; and these are almost the only kind of novels that are worthy of preservation. . . . A book of this sort may scarcely be called *fiction*—for though the story itself may be wholly imaginary, all that is important as a matter of record, the peculiarities of the people, &c., are *facts*. (*GLB*, July 1840, 14)

The connections between representational rhetoric and fiction's moral tendency can hardly be more explicit. According to Wilmer, history proved the moral plot—in which the good are rewarded—as essentially realistic. That we now see the sentimental plot's happy ending as "unrealistic" should not cause us to dismiss such a statement as illogical. After all, "realistic" endings are culturally determined, and our insistence that "happy" endings are improbable tells us as much about naturalist, modernist, and postmodern aesthetics as Hale's and Dickens's preferences for happy endings. To "prove" that good things happen to moral people, writers like Hale and Wilmer relied on their perception of history, itself a constructed narrative.

To test these aesthetics of fiction with the fiction actually published by Hale and to allow comparison with the aesthetic of poetry outlined above, I studied the *Lady's Book*'s fiction of 1840–42, focusing my analysis on three months—January 1840, May 1841, and September 1842. In contrast to earlier pictures of the fiction of the *Lady's Book*, which claim that it features intrusive narrators and purely good or evil characters and favors catastrophic conclusions, the fiction in this sample strongly parallels the aesthetic outlined in the magazine's editorials and essays. That is, almost without exception, the stories end happily, by rewarding morally good though not perfect characters, and the fiction itself repeatedly asserts its veracity.

The plot that rewarded the good was consistently crafted within the *Lady's Book* as a love story. These love stories were overwhelmingly presented as what Nina Baym has described as the plot of woman's fiction, in which a heroine, often an orphan, makes her way in the world, depending primarily upon her own efforts and virtues.[17] This pattern is basically a plot of moral tendency. Readers are assumed to be pleased and improved by reading stories in which good characters are rewarded.

If the plots of love and marriage are the primary manifestations of the moral aesthetic, the frequent declarations of veracity attest to the writers' concern about overly imaginative works. The story "Marion," for instance, is subtitled "A Tale of Everyday Life." Similarly, "Kate Percival" is described as "A Tale of Real Life," and the story ends with the narrator's testament: "It was from one who had personally shared in these innocent expressions of joy that the writer learned the main incidents described in the foregoing pages" (*GLB*, Sept. 1842, 131). Thus, like the essays, the fiction of the *Lady's Book* tempers some of its imaginative elements by employing a rhetoric of realism.

Catharine Sedgwick's "A Huguenot Family" demonstrates how the magazine presented historical fiction as both realistic and essentially moral—and thus both pleasing and beneficial. Though the narrative's form, especially the dialogue, suggests fiction, Sedgwick introduces her story as "a true record of some of the harassing persecutions which the Protestants endured," and several times within the narrative she reminds the reader of its realistic basis by referring to specific laws regarding Louis XIV's persecution of Protestants and her unnamed sources, a "log-book" and "the records" (*GLB*, Sept. 1842, 144–45). Though the narration addresses the issue of accurate representation, the plot itself relies heavily on the principle of moral tendency. Not all of the moral characters are rewarded—the heroine, for example, dies—but the heroine's son, Eugene, carries out her wishes and escapes to America.[18] After living in America several years, Eugene marries the daughter of his mother's servant, thus implicitly rewarding her for her virtue. His wife, Marie, thus assumes the role of the woman's fiction heroine. She has endured hardships—poverty, imprisonment— and through her suffering and maturity finds a happiness that includes marriage. Though assumed to be "real" and therefore less dangerous, the story is also pleasurable, for the "natural" sympathies of the moral reader are themselves rewarded.

But it was not solely in historical fiction that writers or readers were content to combine reality with pleasure. Indeed, in many of the declarations of veracity—which tend to define fiction's aim as primarily imitative—the writers, like the magazine's essayists, employed a rhetoric that was at least as romantic as it was realistic. Meeta M. Duncan's "Mildred," for example, argues that seemingly romantic and improbable events can occur in "real" life. When one character accuses another of thinking wild imaginative thoughts, "as if you were reciting a page from that novel you hold in your hand," the other character defends himself by saying, "Novels sometimes tell truths." This story ends by reiterating the realities of romance. The narrator addresses the "dear reader": "Should you doubt or question the probability of our tale, cast your eyes around on the world's bubbling cauldron, and ask yourself if there is aught of romance in it, like the romance of real life?" (*GLB*, May 1841, 230–32). In insisting on the "romance of real

life," this story, like many of the essays in the *Lady's Book*, refuses to
surrender the pleasure of romance. Thus, like the essays and reviews,
the stories themselves imply an aesthetic of fiction based on the ability
to represent reality and to please.

Though the stories tend to support the aesthetic of fiction described
in the magazine's nonfiction prose, the essayists' repeated denounce-
ments of improbable plots are not reinforced in the fiction itself. Three
of the stories in my sample present a significant twist on the woman's
fiction plot by beginning with the heroine's reluctant marriage to a
man she does not love and then by improbably concluding with their
declarations of mutual love. Even more dependent on coincidences
is J. H. Ingraham's "The Milliner's Apprentice; or, The False Teeth,"
significantly subtitled "A Story That Hath More Truth Than Fiction
in It." The story opens as the heroine, Caroline, and her family face
poverty, resulting from the death of her father, Mr. Archer, and the
family's insolvency. Misfortunes continue: the bank fails on the day
Mrs. Archer had planned to withdraw the family's four hundred dollars, and Mrs. Archer becomes ill, leaving Caroline to support the
family. A "cruel landlady" suggests that she turn to prostitution to earn
the twenty-five-dollar rent. Though she finds a purse containing nearly
four hundred dollars, Caroline returns the money and instead sells her
four front teeth to a dentist. The story ends as Caroline accidentally
meets the woman who bought her teeth, the sister of the wealthy man
who owned the lost purse. As it turns out, the man, Francis Astley,
had fallen in love with Caroline when they had previously met in the
milliner's shop where she works, in part because Caroline was the perfect resemblance of a miniature he had purchased in France. Issuing a
final seal bonding these two families, Ingraham reveals another coinci-
dence: Years earlier, Caroline Archer's father had done some "great
and important service" for Francis Astley's father, leaving the Astley
family indebted to the Archers (*GLB*, May 1841, 205).

Clearly this story fulfills its moral tendency by rewarding the noble
Caroline, and like much of the fiction in the *Lady's Book*, it acknowledges the sometimes brutal circumstances of the social world. (The
story suggests that, given the lack of economic opportunity, women
have only their bodies to sell.) Still, the story's plot—like that of many

others in the *Lady's Book*—stretches the realistic rhetoric featured within the magazine's essays on fiction. Both Hale and Godey, after all, repeatedly criticized improbable plots. Certainly this inconsistency between the essays and the fiction itself demonstrates that, as I have already suggested, Hale endorsed a realistic rhetoric not so much because she, like realistic writers later in the century, believed in the absolute principle of accurate representation, but because she wanted to minimize the dangers of highly imaginative fiction. The rhetoric of realism, in other words, was at least in part just rhetoric, masking the deeply imaginative nature of the texts published in the *Lady's Book*.

In other ways, however, these improbable plots demonstrate Hale's deep commitment to moral tendency. No matter how unlikely it may seem for a poor milliner's apprentice to fall in love with the wealthy man whose sister bought her teeth, this plot—like much of the fiction in the *Lady's Book*—suggests that fortunate things can happen when people deserve them. Merit, in other words, not chance, determines one's fate. Obviously, the magazine's fiction does not always reward characters so extravagantly, nor does it necessarily dole out rewards in any just way. Indeed, within the *Lady's Book* the rewards of the moral universe are generally limited to white and properly genteel characters.

For Hale's white, middle-class women readers, however, the aesthetic of fiction described in the magazine's essays would have likely matched their reading experiences of the fiction itself. Assumed to be pleasing and capable of influencing the reader, the fiction in the *Lady's Book* confirmed the Victorian vision of the world as moral. Although in their efforts to please readers without eliciting fears about such pleasures the magazine's essayists and writers relied on sometimes contradictory assumptions, the magazine's central tenet was that writers of fiction could manage to please and influence readers by crafting plots that relied on a system of just rewards and punishments. Because many of the writers and readers understood that system to be realistic, even the most improbable events could be presented as accurate representations of reality.

However untenable such an aesthetic may seem to some readers today, the likelihood that Hale's own readers experienced it as coherent and appropriate is further strengthened by the extent to which it was consistent with Hale's theories of gender. In the same way that her understanding of poetry's aims was based on her vision of women's essential nature, so too did Hale's aesthetic of fiction depend upon her sense of women's moral superiority over men. Like women themselves, fiction and poetry were presented as having an enormous, though often indirect, influence on others and the world around them. Although the alternative aesthetic, promoted by some of Hale's contemporaries, who associated women's literature with mere light amusement, has enjoyed a more lasting reputation, that aesthetic did not go unchallenged. Indeed, in associating the aims of literature with women's expanding mission in the world, Hale helped popularize an aesthetic that empowered women as readers and writers.

# EPILOGUE

## Beyond the *Lady's Book:* Hale's Legacy in the Twentieth Century

In the years I have spent reading the *Lady's Book,* I have occasionally found evidence from the readers themselves that the magazine was, as it often claimed, a treasured part of nineteenth-century women's culture. Flowers pressed within its pages, volumes bound with the owner's name engraved on the cover, and, of course, the extraordinary circulation of the magazine itself all indicate that Sarah J. Hale's Victorian readers shared and valued much of her vision. Throughout this book I have explored the world that Hale created in her magazines—how it worked, whom it empowered, why it proved successful. More than anything else, it was a world defined by Hale's commitment to an essential difference between men and women. Indeed, Hale's editorial authority depended on her perception of herself as an "editress" working among and for other women. By working in a primarily separatist environment, Hale exerted a powerful influence throughout her contemporary literary culture, as she popularized a vision of the writer, the reader, and the text that empowered herself and her readers. Having examined these formulations in nineteenth-century literary culture, I turn now to consider the impact of Hale's work on the twentieth century. It is worth asking, though the answers must remain speculative: What is the legacy Hale left us, and how can we assess its value?

Certainly Hale's legacy has been a lasting one. Though she died in

1879 and the *Lady's Book* folded in 1898, the ideology of sexual difference that she helped popularize has lasted long into the twentieth
century. The idea that, as Hale and many others argued, women are
essentially different from men—specifically more moral and less competitive—still pervades American culture. Even within feminist circles
the influence of Victorian ideologies like Hale's continues. Though
feminists have rightly complicated the arguments, Hale's own shift
from Enlightenment ideologies of women's intellectual equality with
men to a Victorian emphasis on women's essential moral difference
has in many ways been replicated in current feminist debates about
equality and difference.

Still, such a legacy is not necessarily enviable. An essentialism like
Hale's has been used, after all, to limit women's opportunities and
to silence and exclude women. Most frequently excluded, of course,
have been women whose race, class, or sexuality differs from the white,
middle-class, heterosexual woman who has too often served as the basis
for notions of essential womanhood. Ideologies of essential sexual difference have also been used against women writers, when their works
have been seen as offending women's so-called natural moral ten-
dencies. Even those writers embracing an aesthetic like Hale's have
sometimes suffered from it. Writers grounded in a Victorian moral aesthetic, such as Lydia Sigourney, have historically been denied canoni-
cal status. But as Hale's work makes clear, ideologies of essential sexual
difference based on women's supposedly innate moralities have not
been the sole property of antifeminists. However much the Victorian
notion of separate spheres was sometimes employed to restrict women
within the private sphere, that same ideology also helped create a public female space that empowered women rather than limiting them.

It is within the separatist world of women's periodicals that Hale's
legacy seems most enduring. Certainly contemporary radical feminist
periodicals, like *off our backs*, insist, as did Hale, on the power of a
public forum by and for women. Even popular women's magazines,
available at local supermarkets, have managed to continue some of the
traditions Hale helped popularize. Though these periodicals are generally politically conservative and are often designed primarily to sell
products, they can function as an intimate place for women to come

together, listening to and speaking to one another and valuing each other's experiences. Popular women's magazines frequently include information on women's health, for instance, and American women today are far more likely to learn of new developments in contraceptives and in the treatment of breast cancer there than anywhere else in the media. Similarly, modern popular women's magazines, like Hale's more than a century before, also celebrate women artists. *Essence* has included features on En Vogue, Sister Souljah, and Queen Latifah, and the *Ladies' Home Journal* has recently published articles on Reba McEntire and Bette Midler. Likewise, many women's periodicals—both radical ones and newsstand varieties—often support women writers by either publishing or reviewing their work. Thus Judith Ortiz Cofer has appeared in *Glamour;* Gail Godwin in *Redbook;* and Joyce Carol Oates in *McCall's.*

The coverage of women's art in the newly revised, advertisement-free *Ms.* warrants special consideration here. Although the magazine shares neither Hale's ideology of gender nor her politics, its editors, like Hale before them, have insisted on the importance of women's art, including literature, within women's periodicals, and they have challenged any presumed distinction between what is popular and what is art. More than any other women's magazine currently available at most newsstands and grocery stores, *Ms.* has celebrated the work of such women as Pat Mora, Alice Walker, Rita Dove, Barbara Lewis-Marco, Louise Erdrich, June Jordan, Grace Paley, Maxine Kumin, Alison Bechdel, Ama Ata Aidoo, May Sarton, Maya Angelou, Lori Grinker, Toni Morrison, and Adrienne Rich—to name just some of the artists recently featured.

Significantly, this insistence on bringing women's art to a popular audience is not the only similarity between the new *Ms.* and Hale's *Ladies' Magazine* and *Lady's Book.* The editorial column that opens *Ms.* and the voluminous and often intimate letters from subscribers recall Hale's sisterly editorial voice. Similarly, like Hale, the editors of *Ms.* assume that the magazine and its readers have the potential of changing the world, and women are presented as powerful participants in the public and private realms. The world of women's periodicals, then, continues today in many ways as it did during its creation and rise in the nineteenth century. While some continue to define women primarily within the domestic space, other periodicals claim their separatist vision as an empowering one.

The power of a public female space is, then, the greatest legacy of Hale's career, and it is a power that she must have experienced personally. At a time when many middle-class women struggled to find adequate employment and few people of either sex found financial success through literary pursuits, Hale worked successfully as an editor and writer for over fifty years. But Hale's work within a public female space was not simply self-serving. On the contrary, her editorial columns consistently reveal both the power of the sisterly editorial voice and the flexibility of Victorian ideologies of separate spheres. With this editorial voice and Victorian ideologies of gender, Hale used her magazine to create and to comment on literary and women's cultures. That Hale envisioned these cultures as including the professionalization of authorship and improved wage-earning opportunities for women suggests the extent to which she rejected conservative interpretations of separate spheres. Thus, in the same way that this sister editor found her own voice of authority within the public and separatist world of women's periodicals, she also constructed her own magazines in order to extend that power to her readers.

# APPENDIX

# Nineteenth-Century American Women Periodical Editors

This is the only comprehensive list of nineteenth-century women magazine editors ever compiled, yet it should not be seen as exhaustive. The sheer number of nineteenth-century periodicals prohibits a complete survey, and for many nineteenth-century magazines, no issues or even records survive. Moreover, many of the editors who worked anonymously remain unidentified, and biographical information on many of the women editors of the 1800s is scant. For some, I have been unable to determine even their full names. Because some women who edited under their initials alone or under masculine names have probably been overlooked here, only the use of a social title, a Miss or a Mrs., has saved some of these women from continued oblivion.

Although necessarily incomplete, this list does demonstrate the number and the range of nineteenth-century American women editors. The tradition of these editors is marked by its diversity. The women listed here edited periodicals ranging from small manuscript papers to national magazines like the *Lady's Book*, and they worked in virtually every part of the nation. The contents of their periodicals, moreover, range from fashion to phrenology. In order to explore as fully as possible the diversity of women's editorships, I have included both newspapers and magazines, and I have made no distinction between "minor" and "important" periodicals. To do so seems at best premature and at worst another means of erasing the tradition of women editors.

My aim to be as comprehensive as possible is also suggested by my decision to include women who, though not officially recognized as editors, seem to have worked closely with relatives (usually husbands or fathers) who did edit periodicals. Thus I have included, for example, both Jane Johnston Schoolcraft and her Ojibwa mother, Ozha-guscoday-way-quay (given the English name Susan Johnston). Although neither woman was listed as the editor of the *Muzzinye-*

*gun; or, Literary Voyager,* evidence suggests that both had at least some editorial control of this manuscript paper, which focused on Ojibwa culture and was produced by Jane Johnston Schoolcraft's husband, Henry Rowe Schoolcraft, an Indian agent at Sault Ste. Marie, Michigan. As Philip P. Mason has explained in the introduction to *The Literary Voyager; or, Muzzenyegun,* Jane Johnston Schoolcraft not only wrote many of the pieces in the magazine but also served as interpreter for her husband. Her mother arranged for Henry Rowe School-craft to attend tribal ceremonies, and using interpreters to communicate with her son-in-law, who spoke only English, she provided the "editor" with the Ojibwa legends, biographies, customs, and folklore that made up the maga-zine. While Henry Rowe Schoolcraft certainly considered himself the editor, the content of the magazine was in large part determined by Jane Johnston Schoolcraft and Ozha-guscoday-way-quay.

While I have intended to be as inclusive as possible, any list of this type must be based on exclusions as well. For this list, I have defined a publica-tion as a periodical if it was intended to appear on a regular and somewhat frequent basis. Publications appearing annually, like gift annuals, have been excluded, though I have included publications like Elizabeth Palmer Peabody's *Aesthetic Papers* that were intended to be periodicals but appeared only once. I have defined editors as those who managed departments or entire periodi-cals, not those who were primarily columnists, though the difference between editing and writing a column has at times been difficult to determine. Geo-graphically, I have confined myself to periodicals published in what is now the United States, and I have included U.S. periodicals edited by women of other nationalities (like Emma Hardinge Britten's *Western Star*). Periodicals edited by American women published outside the United States, such as Victo-ria Woodhull's London paper, are not included here. I have, however, allowed myself one exception by including Mary Ann Shadd Cary, who edited the *Pro-vincial Freeman,* a Canadian newspaper for African Americans fleeing U.S. slavery. To exclude her newspaper is to ignore an important part of the history of American periodicals. Finally, attempting to include all the assistant and associate editors, and even all the editors themselves, of, say, the many state Woman's Christian Temperance Union papers or local club papers would have made this list impossible to complete. For similar reasons I have not included all the newspaper editors after the Civil War.

To be listed here, a woman must have begun editing a periodical between 1800 and 1899. An editor like Emma Goldman, who began her editorial career in 1906, for example, has been omitted, even though she was born years before some of the women included here. Like any dates of beginning and ending, mine are arbitrary and emphasize certain historical developments at the expense of others. While the wide span of this study does tend to overlook dramatic changes in women's editorships throughout the century, the dates of inclusion also have certain advantages. First, by beginning in the nineteenth century rather than earlier, I have avoided duplicating Marion Marzolf's *Up from the Footnote*, which begins with a study of seventeenth- and eighteenth-century women printers. Second, by identifying women editors throughout the century rather than, say, just the antebellum period, I am able to suggest the rich context in which one should read the *Lady's Book*, which was published until 1898. By including editors of the late nineteenth century, moreover, I have demonstrated that this period was not simply the time of the great male editors, such as Edward William Bok, Samuel Sidney McClure, Frank Andrew Munsey, Walter Hines Page, and Benjamin Orange Flower. Indeed, the number of women editing periodicals during the last part of the nineteenth century suggests the extent to which men's so-called dominance of the periodical industry is a construct of an incomplete literary history.

Each entry consists of the name of the editor and of the publications that she edited. To help identify these periodicals, I have supplied, if possible, a brief description of the magazine or newspaper when the title does not suggest its focus. Because the great number of periodicals has prohibited me from seeing many of them and because some no longer exist, I have relied on secondary sources for these descriptions. I have also provided, whenever possible, the place and dates of publication. As in most bibliographies concerning periodicals, dates of publication, especially ending dates, should be taken as estimates; it is often impossible to judge whether a periodical ended at a particular time or whether we simply have not yet found later issues. Moreover, secondary sources often give conflicting dates. In supplying dates and places of publication, I have relied primarily on Frank Luther Mott's *A History of American Magazines*, Mott's *American Journalism, A History, 1690–1960*, *The Union List of Serials*, Winifred Gregory's *American Newspapers, 1821–1936*, and the On-line Computer Library Center (OCLC). To determine whether a publication is still current, I have consulted *The Standard Periodical Directory* (16th ed., 1993), *The Serials Directory* (7th ed., 1993), and *Ulrich's International Periodicals Directory, 1993–1994* (32d ed.). I have differed from these sources, however, when more detailed studies of individual periodicals were available. In order to suggest the ways in which nineteenth-century women editors often worked together, I have provided cross-references in capital and small-capital letters. I have not attempted to identify every source consulted, but I have ended each entry with a reference to the most helpful sources with which a reader can begin further study of an individual editor. Other sources can often be found by checking the *Biography and Genealogy Master Index*, published by Gale Research, or the *Index to Women of the World from Ancient to Modern Times*. When investigating biographical information about individual editors, however, readers are warned to expect inaccurate and conflicting material. When deciding how to present uncertain material here, I have tried to give the information I believe is most likely to be accurate. I leave it to future studies to determine the wisdom of these decisions.

## Abbreviations

The following abbreviations are used to indicate the sources where readers might begin research on individual editors. Full citations are included in the Works Cited section.

| | |
|---|---|
| *AAPP* | Bullock, *Afro-American Periodical Press* |
| *ACAB* | *Appleton's Cyclopaedia of American Biography* |
| *AI* | Littlefield and Parins, *American Indian and Alaska Native Newspapers and Periodicals* |
| *ALM* | Chielens, *American Literary Magazines* |
| *AMP* | Weichlein, *Checklist of American Music Periodicals* |
| *AP* | *American Periodicals* |
| *AW* | Willard and Livermore, *American Women* |
| *AWP* | Walker, *American Women Poets* |
| *AWW* | *American Women Writers* |
| *BDAE* | *Biographical Dictionary of American Educators* |
| *BDSA* | *Biographical Dictionary of Southern Authors* |
| "BG" | Stearns, "Before *Godey's*" |
| *BLC* | Venable, *Beginnings of Literary Culture in the Ohio Valley* |
| "BWJ" | Snorgrass, "Black Women and Journalism" |
| *CP* | Kelly, *Children's Periodicals of the United States* |
| *DA* | Hanaford, *Daughters of America* |
| *DAB* | *Dictionary of American Biography* |
| *DATB* | *Dictionary of American Temperance Biography* |
| *DLP* | Marzolf, *Danish-Language Press in America* |
| *EFE* | Butcher, *Education for Equality* |
| "EFM" | Stearns, "Early Factory Magazines in New England" |
| *EGM* | Flanders, *Early Georgia Magazines* |

"EPM"      Stearns, "Early Philadelphia Magazines for Ladies"
"EWM"      Stearns, "Early Western Magazines for Ladies"
*HAM* 1–4   Mott, *History of American Magazines*, vols. 1–4
*HBA*       Johannsen, *House of Beadle and Adams*
*J*         *Journalist*, special issue, 26 Jan. 1889
*MAS*       Riley, *Magazines of the American South*
*MBE-YA*    Peel, *Mary Baker Eddy: The Years of Authority*
*MBE-YT*    Peel, *Mary Baker Eddy: The Years of Trial*
*NAW*       *Notable American Women*
*NCAB*      *National Cyclopaedia of American Biography*
"NSW"      Braude, "News from the Spirit World"
"PML"      Stearns, "Philadelphia Magazines for Ladies"
*PPW*       Coggeshall, *Poets and Poetry of the West*
"PWMP"     Vaughan, "Pioneer Women of the Missouri Press"
"RP"       Stearns, "Reform Periodicals and Female Reformers"
*SEAP*      *Standard Encyclopedia of the Alcohol Problem*
"SML"      Stearns, "Southern Magazines for Ladies"
*SS*        Burgess-Olson, *Sister Saints*
*TWW*       Whitton, *These Were the Women*
*UFF*       Marzolf, *Up from the Footnote*
*VTO*       Solomon, *A Voice of Their Own*
*WNAA*      *Who Was Who Among North American Authors*
*WPN*       *Women's Periodicals and Newspapers*
*WT*        Willard, *Woman and Temperance*
*WWA* 1–5   *Who Was Who in America*, vols. 1–5
*WWWA*      *Woman's Who's Who of America*

**Abbot, Anne Wales** Editor of the *Child's Friend* (Boston; 1843–58). (*CP*)

**Abbott, Osee** Editor of the *Pipe of Peace* (Indian school paper; Genoa, Nebr.; 1887–91). (*AI*)

**Adams, Lois Bryan** Co-editor and part owner of the *Michigan Farmer* (Lansing and Detroit; 1843–current). (*PPW*)

**Adams, Lucinda Bragg** Associate editor to Amelia L. Tilghman of the *Musical Messenger* (African American magazine of music; Montgomery, Ala., and Washington, D.C.; 1886–89). (*AAPP;* "BWJ")

**Ahern, Mary Eileen** Editor of *Public Libraries* (Chicago; 1896–1931). (*NAW*)

**Aikens, Amanda L.** Editor of the women's department of the *Evening Wisconsin* (Milwaukee). (*AW*)

**Alcott, Louisa May** Editor of *Merry's Museum* (children's magazine; New York and Boston; 1841–72). (*AW; AWW; CP; NAW*)

**Alden, Isabella Macdonald** Editor of *Pansy* (Sunday school paper; Boston; 1874–96). Editor of the *Primary Quarterly* (Presbyterian paper). (*AW; AWW; CP; NAW*)

**Aldrich, Elizabeth** Publisher and editor of the *Genius of Liberty* (women's reform paper; Cincinnati; 1851–53). Editor of the department "Genius of Liberty" in *Moore's Western Lady's Book* (Cincinnati; 1849–56). See also Mrs. H. G. Moore. ("EWM"; *HAM 2*; "RP")

**Aldrich, Josephine Cables** Founder and editor of the *Occult World* (reform paper; Rochester, N.Y.; 1882–?). (*AW*)

**Aldrich, Mildred** Editor of the *Mahogany Tree* (literary journal; Boston; 1892). (*AWW*)

**Allen, Eliza C.** Editor of the *Mother's Journal and Family Visitant* (New York and Philadelphia; 1836–72). (*HAM 2*)

**Allen, Elizabeth Ann Chase Akers** Assistant editor of the *Transcript* (weekly newspaper; Portland, Maine; 1837–1910). Associate editor of the *Portland Daily Advertiser* (newspaper; Portland, Maine; 1831–1909). (*AW; AWW; DAB; NAW*)

**Ames, Eleanor Kirk** Editor of *Eleanor Kirk's Idea* (women's club periodical; New York; 1892–1905). (*AW; HAM 4*)

**Ames, Julia A.** Editor of the *Union Signal* (temperance journal; Chicago and Evanston, Ill.; 1874–current). (*AW; J*)

**Amies, Olive Pond** Department editor of the *Sunday School Helper* (Universalist paper; Boston). (*AW*)

**Anderson, Annie T.** Publisher of *Western Light* (spiritualist weekly; St. Louis; 1881). ("NSW")

**Anderson, Sada J.** Department editor of Josephine St. Pierre Ruffin's *Woman's Era* (African American women's club journal; Boston; 1894–1903). (*AAPP*)

**Andrew, Elizabeth W.** Assistant editor to Mary Allen West of the *Union Signal* (temperance journal; Chicago and Evanston, Ill.; 1874–current). (*AW*, under Mary Allen West)

**Andrews, Marilla** Editor and publisher of local weekly paper (Gransville, Wis.). Editor of the *Wisconsin Citizen* (suffrage paper; Racine, Brodhead, and Evansville, Wis.; 1887–1919). (*WPN; WWWA*)

**Anneke, Mathilde Franziska Giesler** Founder, publisher, and editor of *Deutsche Frauenzeitung* (German Women's Newspaper) (feminist paper; Milwaukee, Wis., and Newark, N.J.; 1852–54). (*AWW; NAW*)

**Anthony, Susan Brownell** Publisher, with ELIZABETH CADY STANTON as editor, of the *Revolution* (suffrage journal; New York; 1868–72). Associate editor of the *Ballot Box*, later titled *National Citizen and Ballot Box* (suffrage paper; Toledo, Ohio, and Syracuse, N.Y.; 1876–81). (*AW; AWW; DAB; EFE; HAM* 3; *NAW; VTO*)

**Arey, Harriet Ellen Grannis** Editor, with assistance from MRS. C. H. GILDERSLEEVE, of both the *Youth's Casket* (Buffalo; 1852–57) and the *Home* (Buffalo and New York; 1856–60). (*AW; HAM* 2; *CP*)

**Austin, Harriet N.** Editor of the *Laws of Life and Woman's Health Journal* (Dansville, N.Y.; 1858–93). ("RP")

**Ayars, Mary Warren** Editor of the *Woman's Missionary Friend* (Boston; 1869–1940). (*WPN*)

**Bagley, Sarah G.** Editor of the *Voice of Industry* (factory periodical; Boston and Lowell, Mass.; 1845–48). (*AWW;* "EFM"; *NAW*)

**Bailey, Margaret L. Shands** Editor of the *Youth's Monthly Visitor* (Cincinnati and Washington, D.C.; 1844–52). Co-founder and later publisher of the *National Era* (abolition paper; Washington, D.C.; 1847–60). (*HAM* 1; *PPW*)

**Baker, Lucile B.** Editor of *Chat* (St. Joseph, Mo.; 1894–?). ("PWMP")

**Baker, Lydia H.** Medium and possible co-editor of the *Impending Epoch* (spiritualist periodical; Augusta, Ga.; 1866–67). ("NSW")

**Ball, Helen W.** Editor of the *Indian Leader* (school paper; Lawrence, Kans.; 1897–current). (*AI*)

**Ball, Isabel Worrell** Editor of *Chronoscope* (newspaper; Larned, Kans.; 1878–1930). Editorial member of the *Commonwealth* (newspaper; Topeka; 1869–88). Editor of the *Weekly Times* (Kansas City, Mo.; 1869–1901). (*AW; J*)

**Ball, Martha Violet** Assistant editor and then editor of the *Home Guardian* (reform journal; Boston; 1838–92). (*AW*)

**Ball, Mrs. P. W.** Editor of the *Evening Visiter* (weekly focusing on science and literature; Zanesville, Ohio; 1837–?). ("EWM")

**Banks, Mrs. E. K.** Co-editor with ELLA WENTWORTH of the *Literary Journal* (Cincinnati; 1854). (*BLC;* "EWM")

**Bannister, Carrie A.** Co-editor of the *Future State: A Monthly Journal of Negro Progress* (Kansas City, Mo.; 1891–98). (*AAPP*)

**Barber, Catherine Webb** Editor of the *Madison Family Visitor* (newspaper; Madison, Ga.; 1847–64). Editor of the women's department of the *Southern Literary Companion* (Newnan, Ga.; 1859–65). Editor of *Miss Barber's Weekly* (Newnan, Ga.; 1866–?). (*BDSA; EGM;* "SML")

**Barnard, Helen** Publisher and editor of the *Woman's Campaign* (women's rights journal; New York; 1872). (*HAM* 3)

**Barnes, Annie Maria** Editor of the *Acanthus* (juvenile periodical; Atlanta; 1877–84). Editor of *Young Christian Worker* (Methodist Episcopal church periodical). Editor of *Little Worker* (Methodist Episcopal church periodical). (*AW; BDSA; CP; WWA* 4)

**Barnes, Catharine Weed** Editor of the women's department and then associate editor of the *American Amateur Photographer* (Brunswick, Maine, and New York; 1889–1907). Editor of the women's photographic department of *Outing* (recreational magazine; Albany, N.Y., and New York; 1882–1923). (*AW*)

**Barnett, Ida B. Wells** Part owner and then editor of *Memphis Free Speech* (African American newspaper). Editor of the home department of *Our Women and Children* (African American magazine; Louisville; 1888–90). (*AAPP; AWW; NAW*)

**Barney, Mary Chase** Editor and publisher of the *National Magazine; or, Lady's Emporium* (Baltimore; 1830–31). (*HAM* 1; *MAS*; "SML")

**Barrows, Anna** Co-founder and co-editor with ESTELLE M. H. MERRILL of the *New England Kitchen Magazine*, later titled *Everyday Housekeeping* (Boston; 1894–1908). (*BDAE; HAM* 4)

**Barrows, Isabel Chapin** Assistant editor of the *Christian Register* (Boston; 1821–1961), continued as the *Unitarian Register and the Universalist Leader*. Department editor of *Survey* (social service journal; New York; 1897–1952). (*J; WWWA*)

**Barry, Cordelia** Co-editor of the *Age of Freedom* (spiritualist weekly; Berlin Heights, Ohio; 1857). ("NSW")

**Bascom, Emma Curtiss** Co-editor with MARY EATON and HELEN REMINGTON OLIN of the *Motor* (temperance paper; various locations in Wisconsin; 1886–1990). (*AW; WPN*)

**Bateham, Josephine Abiah Penfield Cushman** Editor of the women's section of the *Ohio Cultivator* (farming and family magazine; Columbus; 1845–66). (*AW; DATB; NAW*)

**Bates, Rebecca** Editor of the *Social Circle* (monthly miscellany; Mount Pleasant, Ohio; 1827–?). ("EWM")

**Baumuller, Mrs. O. L.** Editor of the *China Decorator* (fine arts magazine; New York; 1887–1901). (*HAM* 4)

**Beecher, Eunice White Bullard** Editor of the *Mother at Home and Household Magazine* (New York; 1869). (*NCAB; WPN*)

**Bemis, Elizabeth P.** Editor of several educational periodicals, including *Teachers' World* (New York; 1887–1903); *Normal Instructor*, later titled *In-*

*structor* (Dansville, N.Y., and New York; 1891–current); and *Primary Plans* (Dansville, N.Y.; 1903–14). (*HAM* 4)

**Bennett, Mrs. S. R. I.** Editor of the *Advocate of Moral Reform* (New York; 1835–1941). (*HAM* 2; "RP")

**Benson, Frances M.** Editor of *McCall's Magazine* (women's magazine; New York; 1873–current). (*HAM* 4)

**Berry, Caroline Sanderson** Co-editor with LOUISE CUNNINGHAM BOWLES, IDA MAY JACKSON, and MARY ANTISDEL MARNER of the *Milwaukee Journal (Charity Edition)* (1895). (*WPN*)

**Betts, Lillian W.** Editor of the home department of *Outlook* (religious and family magazine; New York; 1870–1935). (*HAM* 3)

**Bingham, Henrietta A.** Editor of the *Ladies' Repository* (Universalist monthly; Boston; 1832–74). Editor of the *Myrtle* (Sunday school paper; Boston; 1851–1900s). (*DA*)

**Birdsall, Mary B.** Editor of the women's department of an *Indiana Farmer* (perhaps the *Indiana Farmer* published from Richmond, Ind., and Indianapolis; 1851–61). Owner of the *Lily* (women's rights journal; Seneca Falls, N.Y., Mount Vernon, Ohio, and Richmond, Ind.; 1849–56). (*HAM* 2; "RP"; *UFF*)

**Bishop, Annette** Co-editor with FRANCES HARRIET WHIPPLE GREEN and others of the *Journal of Progress* (spiritualist weekly; New York; 1853–?). ("NSW")

**Bittenbender, Ada Matilda Cole** Editor of the *Osceola Record* (newspaper; Osceola, Nebr.). Editor of a Farmers' Alliance journal (Osceola, Nebr.). (*AW*; *DATB*; *NAW*)

**Blackwell, Alice Stone** Co-editor with her parents, LUCY STONE and Henry B. Blackwell, and later sole editor of the *Woman's Journal* (suffrage paper; Boston; 1870–1932). Editor of the *Woman's Column* (suffrage paper; Boston; 1888–1904). (*AWW*; *DAB*; *HAM* 3–4; *NAW*; *VTO*)

**Bland, M. Cora** Editor and publisher of the *Ladies' Own Magazine* (Indianapolis; 1869–74). Co-editor of the *Council Fire* (Indian reform journal; Philadelphia and Washington, D.C.; 1878–89). (*AI*; *DA*; *HAM* 3)

**Blinn, Odelia** Co-editor with MARIA HAWLEY, MARY TOMLIN, and MRS. E. MACKWAY of the *Balance* (women's paper; Chicago; 1871–75). (*DA*)

**Bliss, Mrs. James A.** Co-editor of the *Sower* (spiritualist journal; Elmwood Place, Ohio, Detroit, Mich., and Chicago, Ill.; 1889–95). ("NSW")

**Bloomer, Amelia Jenks** Founder and editor, briefly with ANNA C. MATTISON, of the *Lily* (women's rights journal; Seneca Falls, N.Y., Mount Vernon,

Ohio, and Richmond, Ind.; 1849–56). Assistant editor of the *Western Home Visitor* (literary weekly; Mount Vernon, Ohio; 1853–55). (*AW; AWW; DAB; DATB; HAM* 2; *VTO*)

**Blount, Alice S.** Editor of the *American Club Woman* (Milton, Wis.; 1898–99). (*WPN*)

**Bolton, Sarah Knowles** Editor of the *Congregationalist*, eventually known as the *Congregationalist and Herald of Gospel Liberty* (Boston; 1816–1934). (*AW; AWW; DAB; WWWA*)

**Booth, Mary Louise** Editor of *Harper's Bazar* (women's magazine; New York; 1867–current). (*AW; AWW; DAB; HAM* 3; *NAW*)

**Bowen, Mary** Briefly, co-editor with MARY NOLAN of the *Central Magazine* (women's magazine; St. Louis; 1872–75). Co-editor and co-publisher with LAURA WEBB of *South St. Louis* (weekly). ("PWMP")

**Bowles, Louise Cunningham** Co-editor with CAROLINE SANDERSON BERRY, IDA MAY JACKSON, and MARY ANTISDEL MARNER of the *Milwaukee Journal (Charity Edition)* (1895). (*WPN*)

**Bowman, Maggie A.** Editor of the *King City Democrat* (newspaper; King City, Mo.; 1892–1918). Editor of the *Counsellor* (Missouri temperance paper). ("PWMP")

**Bowser, Rosa Dixon** Department editor of JOSEPHINE ST. PIERRE RUFFIN's *Woman's Era* (African American women's club journal; Boston; 1894–1903). (*AAPP*)

**Bradwell, Myra Colby** Founder and editor of the *Chicago Legal News* (1868–1925). (*AW; DAB; NAW*)

**Bragg, Carrie** Editor of the *Lancet* (Petersburg, Va.). (*J*)

**Bres, Rose Falls** Associate editor of *ERA* (women's publication). Editor of the *Women Lawyers' Journal* (New York, Richmond Hill, N.Y., and Chicago; 1911–current). Editor of *Oyez!* (legal and literary magazine; New York; 1916). (*AWW*)

**Briggs, Mary Balch** Editor of *Work at Home* (missionary journal; Albany, N.Y.; 1875–1900). (*J*)

**Britten, Emma Hardinge** Editor of the *Western Star* (spiritualist paper; Boston; 1872). (*HAM* 3; "NSW")

**Britton, Mary E.** Editor of women's column of the *Lexington Herald* (Lexington, Ky.; 1870–current). (*J*)

**Brooks, Mary Burt** Associate editor with MRS. WILLIAM CAHOON JR. and CATHERINE CAMPBELL CUNNINGHAM of the *Woman's Chronicle* (women's rights periodical; Little Rock, Ark.; 1888–93). (*EFE*)

**Brown, Hannah F. M.** Editor of the *Agitator* (spiritualist reform journal;

Cleveland; 1858–60). Editor of the *Little Bouquet* (children's spiritualist paper; Chicago; 1865–67). Editor, with Mrs. Lou H. Kimball as publisher, of the *Lyceum Banner* (children's spiritualist paper; Chicago; 1867–72). ("NSW")

**Brown, Harriet L.** Editor of the *Child's Friend* (Boston; 1843–58). (*CP*)

**Brown, Helen E.** Editor of the *Advocate of Moral Reform* (New York; 1835–1941). (*HAM* 2; "RP")

**Brown, Martha McClellan** Editor of the *Temperance Visitor* (Good Templar magazine; Alliance, Ohio). Editor of the *Alliance Monitor* (weekly newspaper; Alliance, Ohio; 1866–77). (*AW; DATB; NAW*)

**Bruce, Elizabeth M.** Editor of the *Myrtle* (Sunday school paper; Boston; 1851–1900s). (*DA*)

**Bryan, Mary Edwards** Literary editor of the *Georgia Literary and Temperance Crusader* (Washington, Penfield, and Atlanta, Ga.; 1834–61). Editor of the *Semi-Weekly Times*, later titled *Natchitoches Times* (newspaper; Natchitoches, La.; 1859–73). Associate editor and then editor of *Sunny South* (family weekly; Atlanta; 1875–1907). Assistant editor of *Fireside Companion* (story paper; New York; 1866–1907). Assistant editor of *Fashion Bazaar* (New York). Editor of the *Half Hour* (literary monthly; New York; 1897–1900). Editor of the *Old Homestead* (monthly magazine; Atlanta; 1889–94). (*AW; AWW; DAB; HAM* 4; *NAW*)

**Buck, Mrs. A. Truehart** Editor of *Southern Literary Messenger* (Washington, D.C.; 1895). (*HAM* 4)

**Buell, Caroline Brown** Co-editor of *Our Union*, later titled *Union Signal* (temperance journal; Chicago and Evanston, Ill.; 1874–current). (*AW; DATB*)

**Buffum, Adeline** Editor of *News from the Spirit World* (spiritualist paper; Chicago; 1868–70). Editor of the *Religio-Politico Party* (spiritualist paper; Chicago; 1872–73). ("NSW")

**Bullard, Laura Curtis** Editor, with assistance from Augusta Larned and Phoebe Cary, of the *Revolution* (suffrage journal; New York; 1868–72). (*HAM* 3)

**Bumpass, Mrs.** Editor of the *Message* (women's magazine; Greensboro, N.C.; 1855). ("SML")

**Burbank, Katharine** Editor, with assistance from Mrs. Frederick C. Jones and Marie E. Ives Humphrey, of the *Indian Bulletin* (Connecticut Indian Association journal; Hartford, Conn.; 1888–1901). (*AI*)

**Burgess, Marianna** Business manager and then co-editor, at times with Kate Irvine and later Frances Campbell Sparhawk, of the *Morning*

*Star*, later titled *Red Man* (U.S. Indian Industrial School paper; Carlisle, Pa.; 1880–1904). (*AI*)

**Burlingame, Emeline Stanley** Editor of *Myrtle* (children's magazine; Dover, N.H.; 1845–1904). Assistant editor of *Town and Country* (temperance paper; Providence). Editor of the *Missionary Helper* (Boston, Mass., and Saco, Maine; 1878–1919). (*AW*)

**Burns, Mrs. E. V.** Co-editor of the *Woman's Advocate* (Dayton, Ohio; 1869–70) (*Agitator*, Chicago, 10 April 1869)

**Burr, Celia M. Kellum** Literary editor of the *Great West* (weekly literary journal; Cincinnati; 1848–53). (*PPW*)

**Burr, Frances Ellen** Possibly assistant editor of the *Hartford Times* (newspaper; Hartford, Conn.; 1817–1920). (*DA*)

**Burt, Mary Towne** Managing editor and publisher of *Our Union*, later titled *Union Signal* (temperance journal; Chicago and Evanston, Ill.; 1874–current). (*AW*)

**Bushnell, Madeline Vaughan Abbott** Associate editor of *Literary World* (review magazine; Boston; 1870–1904). (*WWA* 5)

**Bushnell, Rose L.** Publisher with MATTIE P. OWEN of the *Golden Way* (spiritualist paper; San Francisco; 1891). ("NSW")

**Butler, Mrs. Frank N.** Editor of the *Woman's Missionary Advocate* (Nashville; 1880–1910). (*WPN*)

**Cadwaller, Mrs. M. E.** Editor of the *Progressive Thinker* (spiritualist weekly; Chicago; 1889–1912). ("NSW")

**Cahoon, Mrs. William, Jr.** Associate editor with MARY BURT BROOKS and CATHERINE CAMPBELL CUNNINGHAM of the *Woman's Chronicle* (women's rights periodical; Little Rock, Ark.; 1888–93). (*EFE*)

**Calhoun, C. C.** Editor of the *Pioneer* (women's rights paper; San Francisco; 1869–73). (*EFE*)

**Calhoun, Cora C.** Editor of the women's department of the *Justice* (African American newspaper; Chattanooga; 1887–88). (*J*)

**Callahan, Martha J.** Editor of the *Woman's Standard* (suffrage journal; Des Moines and Waterloo, Iowa; 1886–1911). (*WPN*)

**Callahan, Sophia Alice** Editor of the temperance column in *Our Brother in Red* (mission paper; Muskogee, Creek Nation, McAlester, Choctaw Nation, Ardmore, Chickasaw Nation, and Oklahoma City; 1882–99). Editor of *Wealaka Wit and Wisdom* (Wealaka Mission School student newspaper; Creek Nation; 1893). (*AI*)

**Campbell, Helen Stuart** Literary and household editor of the *Continent* (general weekly; Philadelphia and New York; 1882–84). Department editor of *Good Housekeeping* (Holyoke and Springfield, Mass., and New York; 1885–current). Co-editor with CHARLOTTE PERKINS GILMAN of the *Impress* (women's reform paper; San Francisco; 1894–95). (*AW; AWW; HAM* 3–4; *NAW*)

**Carr, Mary Clarke** Editor of the *Intellectual Regale; or, Ladies' Tea-Tray* (Philadelphia; 1814–15). ("BG"; "EPM")

**Carse, Matilda Bradley** Founder and president of the Woman's Temperance Publishing Association in Chicago, which published the *Signal* (1880–82), the *Union Signal* (1874–current), the *Young Crusader* (1887–current), and the *Oak and Ivy Leaf* (1887–94). (*AW; DATB; NAW*)

**Carter, Matilda P.** Editor of the *Eastern Magazine* (Bangor, Maine; 1835–36). (*HAM* 1)

**Cary, Alice** Assistant editor and then editor of the *Parlor Magazine* (miscellany; Cincinnati; 1853–54). (*AW; AWW; BLC; DAB; HAM* 2; *NAW*)

**Cary, Mary Ann Shadd** Editor of the *Provincial Freeman* (newspaper for African American refugees; Toronto and Chatham, Ont.; 1853–58). ("BWJ"; *NAW*)

**Cary, Phoebe** Assistant editor to LAURA CURTIS BULLARD of the *Revolution* (suffrage journal; New York; 1868–72). (*AW; AWW; DAB; HAM* 3; *NAW*)

**Cate, Hattie A.** Amanuensis/editor of the *Watchman* (spiritualist paper; Chicago; 1880–91). ("NSW")

**Cather, Willa** Editor of the *Home Monthly* (Pittsburgh; 1894–1900). Copy editor of the *Pittsburgh Daily Leader* (newspaper; 1870–1923). Managing editor of *McClure's Magazine* (general magazine; New York; 1893–1929). (*AWW; HAM* 4; *NAW*)

**Catt, Carrie Lane Chapman** Co-owner and co-editor of the *Republican* (newspaper; Mason City, Iowa; 1861–1910). Co-editor with EVELYN M. RUSSELL and ELIZABETH C. BUNNELL READ of the *Woman's Standard* (suffrage journal; Des Moines and Waterloo, Iowa; 1886–1911). (*AW; WPN*)

**Chamberlain, Laura A.** Editor of *Fashion or Shopping by Mail* (Chicago). (*J*)

**Chandler, Elizabeth Margaret** Editor of the women's department of the *Genius of Universal Emancipation* (antislavery periodical; various cities in Ohio, Tennessee, Maryland, and Illinois; 1821–39). (*AWW; DAB; HAM* 1; *NAW*)

**Chapin, Clara Christiana** Editor of the *Union Signal* (temperance journal; Chicago and Evanston, Ill.; 1874–current). (*AW; SEAP*, under Woman's Christian Temperance Union)

**Chapin, Maria Bowen** Editor, with assistance from EMILY MALBONE MORGAN, of *Far and Near* (journal focusing on women working outside the home; New York; 1890–94). (*HAM* 4; *WPN*)

**Chapman, Maria Weston** Occasional editor of the *Liberator* (antislavery journal; Boston; 1831–65). Editor of the *Non-Resistant* (Garrison's New England Non-Resistance Society periodical; Boston and Milford, Mass.; 1839–45). Co-editor of the *National Anti-Slavery Standard* (New York; 1840–72). (*AWW*; *DAB*; *NAW*)

**Chapman, Minerva J.** Editor of *Youth's Instructor* (religious children's magazine; Rochester, N.Y., Battle Creek, Mich., and Washington, D.C.; 1852–1970). (*CP*)

**Charleton, Helen H.** Editor of the *Wisconsin Citizen* (suffrage paper; Racine, Brodhead, and Evansville, Wis.; 1887–1919). (*WPN*)

**Chase, Mary Maria** Editor of the *Monthly Rose* (Albany Seminary journal; Albany, N.Y.). (*DA*)

**Chenoweth, Mary Hayes** Editor of *True Life* (spiritualist monthly; Edenvale, Calif.; 1894–1903). ("NSW")

**Chevailler, Alzire** Editor briefly of the *International Magazine of Christian Science* (New York and Chicago; 1888–89). (*MBE-YT*)

**Child, Abbie B.** Editor of *Life and Light for Woman* (Christian missionary magazine; Boston; 1869–1922). (*WPN*)

**Child, Lydia Maria** Founder and editor of the *Juvenile Miscellany* (Boston; 1826–36). Editor of the *National Anti-Slavery Standard* (New York; 1840–72). (*AWW*; *CP*; *DAB*; *NAW*)

**Churchill, Caroline Nichols** Editor and business manager of the *Pioneer* (women's rights paper; San Francisco; 1869–73). Publisher and editor of the *Colorado Antelope* (monthly magazine; Denver; 1870s). Founder and editor of the *Queen Bee* (suffrage magazine; Denver; 1879–96). (*AW*; *EFE*; *HAM* 3)

**Claflin, Tennessee Celeste** Co-editor and co-publisher with her sister, VICTORIA CLAFLIN WOODHULL, of *Woodhull & Claflin's Weekly* (magazine advocating women's suffrage, free love, and workers' rights; New York; 1870–76). (*HAM* 3; *NAW*, under Woodhull)

**Clair, Mrs. F. M. W.** Associate editor of the *Banner* (religious paper; Washington, D.C.; 1890s). ("BWJ")

**Clapp, Eleanor Bassett** Editor of *McCall's Magazine* (women's magazine; New York; 1873–current). (*HAM* 4; *WWWA*)

**Clark, Mrs. H. H.** Publisher of the *Winning Way* (spiritualist weekly; Sacramento, Calif.; 1872). ("NSW")

**Clark, Kate Upson** Editor of the *Housewife* (Greenfield, Mass., and New York; 1882–1917). (*HAM* 4; *WWWA*)

**Clark, Mrs. Uriah** Co-editor of the *Spiritual Clarion* (spiritualist monthly; Auburn, N.Y.; 1857–60). ("NSW")

**Clarke, Helen Archibald** Co-founder and co-editor with CHARLOTTE ENDYMION PORTER of *Poet Lore* (literary magazine; Philadelphia and Boston; 1889–1953). (*DAB; NAW*, under Charlotte Endymion Porter)

**Clarke, Mary Bayard Devereux** Assistant editor of *Southern Field and Fireside* (agricultural and literary paper; Augusta, Ga.; 1859–64). Editor of *Literary Pastime* (Richmond, Va.; 1868–?). (*DAB; HAM* 2; *NAW*)

**Clarke, Mary G.** Editor of the *Mother's Journal and Family Visitant* (New York and Philadelphia; 1836–72). (*HAM* 2)

**Clarke, Sarah J.** Editor of MARY BAKER EDDY's *Christian Science Journal* (Boston; 1883–current). (*MBE-YT*)

**Cleveland, Rose Elizabeth** Editor briefly of *Literary Life* (Cleveland, Chicago, and New York; 1884–1903). (*AW; HAM* 3)

**Coffin, Mary Augusta** Editor of the *Olive Plant and Ladies' Temperance Advocate* (New York; 1841–42). ("RP")

**Coggeshall, Mary J.** Editor of the *Woman's Standard* (suffrage journal; Des Moines and Waterloo, Iowa; 1886–1911). (*WPN*)

**Colby, Clara Dorothy Bewick** Editor of a women's column in the *Beatrice Weekly Express* (newspaper; Beatrice, Nebr.; 1870–1912). Founder and editor of the *Woman's Tribune* (suffrage paper; Beatrice, Nebr., Washington, D.C., and Portland, Oreg.; 1883–1909). (*EFE; HAM* 3; *NAW; VTO*)

**Cole, Dora J.** Department editor of JOSEPHINE ST. PIERRE RUFFIN's *Woman's Era* (African American women's club journal; Boston; 1894–1903). (*AAPP*)

**Cole, Miriam M.** Editor with MARGARET V. LONGLEY of the *Woman's Advocate* (Dayton, Ohio; 1869–70). (*DA*)

**Colvin, Mrs. A. S.** Editor of *Mrs. A. S. Colvin's Weekly Messenger* (women's magazine; Washington, D.C.; 1822–23 and 1826–28). ("SML")

**Conant, Hannah O'Brien Chaplin** Editor of the *Mother's Monthly Journal* (Utica, N.Y.; 1836–42). (*AWW; DAB; NAW*)

**Conway, Katherine Eleanor** Editor of the *West End Journal* (religious monthly). Various editorial positions on Catholic newspapers, including the *Catholic Union and Times* (Buffalo; 1872–1939), the *Pilot* (Boston; 1835–?), and the *Republic*. (*AW; AWW*)

**Cook, Irene** Editor of the *Telegram* (city weekly; Baltimore; 1862–1915). (*HAM* 4)

**Cook, Martha Elizabeth Duncan Walker** Editor of the *Continental Monthly* (literary and political magazine; Boston; 1862–64). (*DAB; HAM* 2)

**Cook, Mary Virginia** Editor of the women's department for a South Carolina *Tribune* and for the *American Baptist* (Louisville; 1879–?). Education editor of *Our Women and Children* (African American magazine; Louisville; 1888–90). (*AAPP*; "BWJ"; *J*)

**Cook, Sarah** Co-editor of *Kingdom of Heaven* (spiritualist monthly; Boston; 1874). ("NSW")

**Coolbrith, Ina Donna** Associate editor of the *Overland Monthly* (literary magazine; San Francisco; 1868–1935). (*AW; AWW; DAB; HAM* 3; *NAW*)

**Cooper, Adelaide B.** Editor of *Youth's Instructor* (religious children's magazine; Rochester, N.Y., Battle Creek, Mich., and Washington, D.C.; 1852–1970). (*CP*)

**Cooper, Anna Julia** Editor of the women's section of *Southland* (African American periodical; Salisbury and Winston, N.C.; 1890–91). (*AAPP*)

**Coston, Julia Ringwood** Editor, with assistance from MOLLY E. LAMBERT, SARAH MITCHELL, EARNESTINE CLARK NESBITT, SUSIE I. SHORTER, MARY CHURCH TERRELL, and ADINA E. WHITE, of *Ringwood's Afro-American Journal of Fashion* (Cleveland; 1891–95). (*AAPP*; "BWJ")

**Cowell, Mrs. A. B.** Editor, with assistance from her mother, HITTIE POND, of the *Winthrop Visitor* (newspaper; Winthrop, Mass.; 1880–1905). (*J*)

**Crabtree, Sudie** Co-editor of column with RACHEL SIXKILLER for *Our Brother in Red* (mission paper; Muskogee, Creek Nation, McAlester, Choctaw Nation, Ardmore, Chickasaw Nation, and Oklahoma City; 1882–99). (*AI*)

**Crannell, Elizabeth Keller Shaule** Founder and editor of the *Indian Advocate* (Albany, N.Y.; 1891–96). Founder and editor of the *Anti-Suffragist* (Albany, N.Y.; 1908–12). Founder and editor of the *Church Record* (probably Albany, N.Y.). (*AI; WWA* 5)

**Cridge, Anne Denton** Editor of *Home Gem* (spiritualist monthly for children; Cleveland; 1858). Editor with ELIZABETH M. FOOTE DENTON and others of *Vanguard* (spiritualist weekly; Dayton, Ohio, Richmond, Ind., and Cleveland; 1857–59). ("NSW")

**Croly, Jane Cunningham ("Jennie June")** Numerous newspaper editorial positions with the *New York World* (1860–1931), the *New York Times* (1851–current), the New York *Weekly Times* (1851–95), the New York *Daily Graphic* (1873–89), and the New York *Sunday Times and Messenger* (1843–92). Assistant editor with ELLEN LOUISE CURTIS DEMOREST of *Mirror of Fashions* (New York; 1860–64). Co-editor with ELLEN LOUISE CURTIS

DEMOREST of *Demorest's Monthly Magazine* (fashion magazine; New York; 1865–99). Editor and part owner of *Godey's Lady's Book* (Philadelphia and New York; 1830–98). Founder and editor of the *Woman's Cycle* (club journal; New York; 1889–96). Editor of the *Home-Maker* (New York; 1888–93). (*AW; AWW; DAB; HAM* 3–4; *NAW*)

**Crosse, Sarah** Briefly acting editor and later business manager and publisher of MARY BAKER EDDY's *Christian Science Journal* (Boston; 1883–current). Editor of the *Boston Christian Scientist* (1889–90). (*MBE-YT*)

**Cumings, Calista** Editor of the *Akron Offering* (women's magazine; Akron, Ohio; 1849–50). (Only known source is the magazine itself.)

**Cunningham, Ann Pamela** Founder and editor of the *Illustrated Mount Vernon Record* (monthly devoted to the preservation of Mount Vernon; Philadelphia; 1858–60). (*DAB; NAW*)

**Cunningham, Catherine Campbell** Founder and editor, with assistance from MRS. WILLIAM CAHOON JR. and MARY BURT BROOKS, of the *Woman's Chronicle* (women's rights periodical; Little Rock, Ark.; 1888–93). (*EFE*)

**Curtis, Emma J.** Co-editor with ELLEN W. LAMB, HELEN REMINGTON OLIN, and AMY KELLOGG MORSE of the *Motor* (temperance paper; various locations in Wisconsin; 1886–1990). (*WPN*)

**Curtis, Harriot F.** Co-editor with HARRIET FARLEY (with the assistance of HARRIET LEES) of the *Lowell Offering* (factory magazine; Lowell, Mass.; 1840–45). (*ALM;* "EFM")

**Daggett, Nella I.** Editor of *Home* (Boston; 1877–1908). (*HAM* 4)

**Dall, Caroline Wells Healey** Assistant editor of PAULINA WRIGHT DAVIS's *Una* (women's rights monthly; Providence and Boston; 1853–55). (*AW; AWW; DAB; NAW*)

**Dalrymple, Mary Agnes** Editor of a *Grafton Journal*. Editor of the *Massachusetts Ploughman* (Boston; 1840–1906). (*J*)

**Daniel, Mrs. M. M.** Publisher and editor of *Rising Tide* (spiritualist paper; Independence, Iowa; 1860–65). ("NSW")

**Davidson, Grace L.** Owner of *St. Louis Life*, which she renamed the *Criterion* (literary magazine; St. Louis and New York; 1889–1905). (*HAM* 4)

**Davis, Mary Fenn** Co-editor of the *Herald of Progress* (spiritualist paper; New York; 1860–64). Editor of the *Lyceum Herald* (spiritualist paper; New York; 1865). (*NAW;* "NSW")

**Davis, Paulina Wright** Publisher and editor of the *Una* (women's rights monthly; Providence and Boston; 1853–55). Corresponding editor of the

*Revolution* (suffrage journal; New York; 1868–72). See also SUSAN BROW-
NELL ANTHONY, CAROLINE WELLS HEALEY DALL, and ELIZABETH
CADY STANTON. (*AWW; DAB; HAM* 3; *NAW; VTO*)

**Day, Mrs. F. H.** Editor of the *Hesperian* (women's magazine; San Francisco;
1858–62). (*HAM* 2)

**Demorest, Ellen Louise Curtis** Editor, with assistance from JANE CUN-
NINGHAM CROLY, of *Mirror of Fashions* (New York; 1860–64). Co-editor
with JANE CUNNINGHAM CROLY of *Demorest's Monthly Magazine* (fashion
magazine; New York; 1865–99). (*HAM* 3; *NAW*)

**Denison, Mary Ann Andrews** Co-editor of the *Olive Branch* (Boston; 1836–
60). Possibly editor of a *Lady's Enterprise*, perhaps the *Ladies' Enterprise*
(literary magazine; Boston and Worcester, Mass.; 1853–56). (*AWW; NAW;
NCAB*)

**Denton, Elizabeth M. Foote** Editor with ANNE DENTON CRIDGE and
others of *Vanguard* (spiritualist weekly; Dayton, Ohio, Richmond, Ind., and
Cleveland; 1857–59). ("NSW")

**Devereux, Mrs. C. A. R.** Editor of *Mrs. Devereux's Tips* (society and humor
magazine; Cincinnati; 1893–1909). (*HAM* 4)

**Dick, Sallie E. Jones** Editor of the *Weekly Capital* (Cherokee newspaper;
Tahlequah, Cherokee Nation; 1887–96). (*AI*)

**Dingee, Mrs. M. P.** Editor of the *Wisconsin Citizen* (suffrage paper; Racine,
Brodhead, and Evansville, Wis.; 1887–1919). (*WPN*)

**Dodge, Mary Abigail ("Gail Hamilton")** Co-editor with LUCY LARCOM of
*Our Young Folks* (children's magazine; Boston; 1865–73). Editor of *Wood's
Household Magazine* (Newburgh, N.Y., and New York; 1867–81). (*AW; AWW;
CP; DAB; HAM* 3; *NAW*)

**Dodge, Mary Elizabeth Mapes** Assistant editor of the *Working Farmer* (New
York; 1849–75). Associate editor, with HARRIET BEECHER STOWE as editor,
of *Hearth and Home* (New York; 1868–75). Editor of *St. Nicholas* (children's
magazine; New York, Columbus, Ohio, and Darien, Conn.; 1873–1943). (*AW;
AWW; CP; DAB; HAM* 3; *NAW*)

**Donovan, Marim A.** Editor of the women's department of the *Post* (newspaper; Boston; 1831–1956). (*J*)

**Doolittle, Antoinette** Co-editor of the *Shaker and Shakeress*, later titled
*Manifesto* (official Shaker periodical; Shakers, N.Y., and East Canterbury,
N.H.; 1871–99). (*AWW*)

**Dugan, Elizabeth** Editor of *Rosa Pearle's Paper* (Sedalia, Mo.; 1894–1911).
("PWMP")

**Dumont, Julia Louisa** Editor of the *Chrystal and Ladies' Magazine* (Pittsburgh; 1828–?). Assistant editor of the *Cincinnati Mirror and Western Gazette of Literature and Science* (Cincinnati; 1831–36). (*ACAB;* "EWM")

**Duncan, Helen R.**  Editor of a temperance column in *Our Brother in Red* (mission paper; Muskogee, Creek Nation, McAlester, Choctaw Nation, Ardmore, Chickasaw Nation, and Oklahoma City; 1882–99). Editor of the educational department of the *Telephone*, later the *Weekly Capital* (Cherokee newspaper; Tahlequah, Cherokee Nation; 1887–96). (*AI*)

**Duniway, Abigail Scott**  Oregon editor, with EMILY PITTS STEVENS as editor, of the *Pioneer* (women's rights paper; San Francisco; 1869–73). Founder, publisher, and editor of the *New Northwest* (women's rights paper; Portland, Oreg.; 1871–87). Editor of the *Pacific Empire* (magazine supporting women's suffrage; Portland, Oreg.; 1895–98). (*AW; AWW; DAB; EFE; NAW*)

**Eaton, Mary**  Co-editor with EMMA CURTISS BASCOM and HELEN REMINGTON OLIN of the *Motor* (temperance paper; various locations in Wisconsin; 1886–1990). (*WPN*)

**Eaton, Rebecca**  Editor of the *Friend of Virtue*, later titled *Home Guardian* (reform journal; Boston; 1838–92). ("RP")

**Eddleman, Mary Daugherty**  Co-owner and later sole owner of the *Muskogee Evening Times*, later titled *Muskogee Times-Democrat* (Muskogee, Creek Nation [later Okla.]; 1896–1971). See also Eddleman's daughters, ORA VERALYN EDDLEMAN and MYRTA EDDLEMAN SAMS. (*AI*)

**Eddleman, Ora Veralyn**  City and society editor of the *Muskogee Evening Times*, later titled *Muskogee Times-Democrat* (Muskogee, Creek Nation [later Okla.]; 1896–1971). Editor of *Twin Territories: The Indian Magazine* (Muskogee, Creek Nation, Fort Gibson, Cherokee Nation, and Oklahoma City; 1898–1904). Editor of the Indian and history departments of *Sturm's Oklahoma Magazine* (Tulsa and Oklahoma City; 1905–11). See also her mother, MARY DAUGHERTY EDDLEMAN, her sister, MYRTA EDDLEMAN SAMS, and LURA A. ROWLAND. (*AI*)

**Eddy, Mary Baker**  Founder and then editor of the *Christian Science Journal* (Boston; 1883–current). Founder of the *Christian Science Weekly*, which soon became the *Christian Science Sentinel* (Boston; 1898–current). See also SARAH CROSSE, JULIA FIELD-KING, CAMILLA HANNA, and EMMA CURTIS HOPKINS. (*AWW; DAB; MBE-YA; MBE-YT; NAW*)

**Eddy, Sarah Hershey**  Editor of the *Musical Bulletin* (Chicago; 1879–83). (*AMP; AW*)

**Elan, Mrs. E. P.**  Editor of the *Family Christian Album* (Richmond, Va.; 1855–56). ("SML")

**Elder, Susan Blanchard** Member of the editorial staff of the *Morning Star* (Catholic magazine; New Orleans; 1868–1930). (*AWW; DAB*)

**Ellis, Anna M. B.** Editorial position with the *Boston Herald* (1846–current). Founder and editor of the *Boston Amusement Gazette*. (*J; WWA* 1).

**Embury, Emma Catherine** Member of editorial staff, probably nominally, of three magazines: *Graham's Magazine* (literary monthly; Philadelphia; 1826–58), Snowden's *Ladies' Companion* (New York; 1834–44), and *Godey's Lady's Book* (Philadelphia and New York; 1830–98). (*AWW; DAB; HAM* 1)

**Ensley, Elizabeth Piper** Department editor of JOSEPHINE ST. PIERRE RUFFIN's *Woman's Era* (African American women's club journal; Boston; 1894–1903). (*AAPP*)

**Evans, Marie** Editor of *Men and Matters* (literary monthly; New Orleans; 1894–1904). (*HAM* 4)

**Farley, Harriet** Editor and then co-editor with HARRIOT F. CURTIS (with the assistance of HARRIET LEES) of the *Lowell Offering* (factory magazine; Lowell, Mass.; 1840–45). Publisher and editor of the *New England Offering* (factory magazine; Lowell, Mass.; 1848–50). (*ALM; AWW; DAB;* "EFM"; *NAW*)

**Felton, Rebecca Ann Latimer** Co-editor and co-owner of the *Free-Press* (newspaper; Cartersville, Ga.; 1878–83) and the *Courant* (newspaper; Cartersville, Ga.; 1885–86). (*AW; AWW; DAB; NAW*)

**Ferris, Mary Lanman Douw** Editor of the *Bulletin of the Society of American Authors*, later titled *American Author* (Dobbs Ferry, N.Y.; 1899–1904). (*HAM* 4)

**Field, Kate** Editor of the dressmaking department of the *Continent* (general weekly; Philadelphia and New York; 1882–84). Founder and editor, with assistance from CAROLINE GRAY LINGLE and ELLA S. LEONARD, of *Kate Field's Washington* (weekly review; Washington, D.C., and Chicago; 1890–95). (*AW; AWW; DAB; HAM* 3–4; *NAW*)

**Field-King, Julia** Briefly editor of MARY BAKER EDDY's *Christian Science Journal* (Boston; 1883–current). (*MBE-YA*)

**Filkins, Carrie D.** Publisher of the *Western Olive Branch* (literary and temperance magazine; Bloomington, Ind., and Cincinnati; 1857–58). ("RP")

**Fillmore, Myrtle Page** Co-founder and co-editor of *Modern Thought*, eventually titled *Unity* (journal associated with the Unity School of Christianity; Kansas City and Unity Village, Mo.; 1889–current). Co-publisher and co-editor of *Wee Wisdom* (Unity children's paper; Kansas City and Unity Village, Mo.; 1893–1991). (*AWW; HAM* 4; *NAW*)

**Follen, Eliza Lee Cabot** Editor of the *Christian Teacher's Manual* (Boston; 1828–31). Editor of the *Child's Friend* (Boston; 1843–58). (*AWW; CP; DAB; NAW*)

**Foote, Helen R.** Co-editor with AMELIA STONE QUINTON of the *Indian's Friend* (missionary journal; Philadelphia, Lancaster, Pa., New Haven, Conn., and New York; 1888–1951). (*AI*)

**Ford, Sallie Rochester** Co-editor of *Ford's Christian Repository and Home Circle* (Louisville, Memphis, and St. Louis; 1852–1906). (*AWW; NCAB*)

**Forsythe, Piney W.** Editor of the *Advocate* (weekly newspaper; Liberty, Miss.; 1835–76). (*UFF*)

**Foute, Laura E.** Founder and editor of *Ladies' Messenger,* later titled *Gulf Messenger* (women's club periodical; Houston and San Antonio; 1888–98). (*HAM* 4)

**Fowler, Jessie Allen** Editor of the *Phrenological Journal and Science of Health* (Philadelphia and New York; 1838–1911). (*AP; NCAB*)

**Fowler, Lydia Folger** Member of the editorial staff, with her sister-in-law, CHARLOTTE FOWLER WELLS, of the *Phrenological Journal and Science of Health* (Philadelphia and New York; 1838–1911). (*DA; NAW*)

**Fox, Nettie Pease** Editor of the *Spiritual Offering* (spiritualist magazine; Springfield, Mo., and Rochester, N.Y.; 1877–79). ("NSW")

**Francis, Susan M.** Assistant editor of the *Atlantic Monthly* (literary magazine; Boston; 1857–current). (*HAM* 2)

**Frazer, Mrs. M. D.** Editor of *Home Life* (Boston). (*J*)

**French, Bella** Member of the editorial staff of the *Pioneer* (weekly newspaper; St. Paul; 1849–75). Editor of *Busy West* (western journal; St. Paul and Milwaukee; 1872–73). Editor of *Busy West Chronotype.* (*DA*)

**French, Florence** Editor of the *Musical Leader and Concert-Goer* (Chicago; 1895–1967). (*AMP*)

**French, Lucy Virginia Smith** Associate editor, literary editor, or editor of a number of southern periodicals, including the *Southern Ladies' Book* (New Orleans; 1852–53), the *Southern Homestead* (Nashville; 1858), *Rural Sun* (Atlanta), *Sunny South* (Atlanta; 1875–1907), *Georgia Literary and Temperance Crusader* (Washington, Penfield, and Atlanta, Ga.; 1834–61), *Ladies' Home Gazette* (Atlanta; 1866–72), and *Southern Literary Messenger* (Richmond, Va.; 1834–64). (*AWW; DAB; EGM;* "SML")

**Fry, Susanna Margaret Davidson** Editor of the *Union Signal* (temperance journal; Chicago and Evanston, Ill.; 1874–current). (*SEAP*)

**Fryatt, Frances Elizabeth** Assistant editor and art editor of the *Manhattan Magazine* (probably *Manhattan: An Illustrated Literary Magazine;* New York; 1883–84). Editor of the *Ladies' World* (New York; 1886–1918). (*AW; HAM* 4)

**Fuller, Margaret** Editor of the *Dial* (transcendental periodical; Boston; 1840–44). (*ALM; AWW; DAB; NAW*)

**Gage, Frances Dana Barker** Associate editor of the *Ohio Cultivator* (farming and family magazine; Columbus; 1845–66). Associate editor of *Field Notes* (farm weekly; Columbus; 1861–62). (*AW; AWW; DAB; DATB; NAW*)

**Gage, Matilda Joslyn** Publisher and editor of the *National Citizen and Ballot Box* (suffrage paper; Toledo, Ohio, and Syracuse, N.Y.; 1876–81). (*AW; DAB; HAM 3; NAW; WPN*)

**Galpin, Barbara N.** Assistant editor of the *Somerville Journal* (newspaper; Somerville, Mass.; 1870–current). (*J*)

**Gardener, Helen Hamilton (b. Alice Chenoweth)** Associate editor and briefly co-editor of the *Arena* (reform magazine; Boston, New York, and Trenton; 1889–1909). (*AW; AWW; DAB; HAM 4; NAW*)

**Gates, Susa Young** Co-editor of *Lanterns* (student literary magazine; University of Deseret, later University of Utah; Salt Lake City). Founder and editor of the *Young Woman's Journal* (Mormon women's journal; Salt Lake City; 1889–1929). Editor of the *Relief Society Magazine* (Mormon women's magazine; Salt Lake City; 1914–current). (*AWW; SS*)

**Gestefeld, Ursula Newell** Editor and publisher of *Exodus* (New Thought magazine; Pelham, N.Y., and Chicago; 1896–1904). (*AWW; HAM 4; NAW*)

**Gilder, Jeanette Leonard** Assistant editor of the *Newark Morning Register* (newspaper; Newark, N.J.; 1869–86). Literary editor of the *New York Herald* (newspaper; 1835–1924). Co-founder, co-editor, and then sole editor of the *Critic* (journal of literary criticism; New York; 1881–1906). Editor and publisher of the *Reader* (monthly magazine; New York and Indianapolis; 1902–8). Co-editor of *Putnam's Monthly* (literary magazine; New York; 1853–1910). Editor of a book review department for *McClure's Magazine* (general magazine; New York; 1893–1929). (*AW; DAB; HAM 2–4; NAW*)

**Gildersleeve, Mrs. C. H.** Assistant editor to HARRIET ELLEN GRANNIS AREY of both the *Youth's Casket* (Buffalo; 1852–57) and the *Home* (Buffalo and New York; 1856–60). (*HAM 2; CP*)

**Giles, Eva Bell** Editor and then co-editor with WINNIE LOUGHBOROUGH of *Youth's Instructor* (religious children's magazine; Rochester, N.Y., Battle Creek, Mich., and Washington, D.C.; 1852–1970). (*CP*)

**Gilman, Caroline Howard ("Clarissa Packard")** Founder and editor of the *Rose Bud* (children's and then family paper; Charleston, S.C.; 1832–39). (*AWW; CP; DAB; MAS; NAW*)

**Gilman, Charlotte Perkins** Editor of the *Pacific Monthly* (Los Angeles; 1889–91). Co-editor with HELEN STUART CAMPBELL of the *Impress* (women's reform paper; San Francisco; 1894–95). Contributing editor to the *American Fabian* (socialist magazine; Boston; 1895–1900). Editor and publisher of the *Forerunner* (reform magazine; New York; 1909–16). (*AWW*; *DAB*; *HAM* 4; *NAW*)

**Goddard, Abby A.** Co-editor, with LYDIA S. HALL, of the *Operatives' Magazine* (factory paper; Lowell, Mass.; 1841–42). ("EFM")

**Goodwin, Lavinia Stella** Associate editor of the *Watchman-Examiner* (Baptist paper; Worcester and Boston, Mass., and New York; 1819–1970). Editor of the *Journal of Education* (Boston; 1875–current). (*AW*; *J*; *WWA* 1)

**Gorman, Mrs. Henrie Clay Ligon** Editor of the *Bohemian* (literary quarterly; Fort Worth; 1899–1907). (*HAM* 4)

**Gougar, Helen Mar Jackson** Editor of *Our Herald* (women's suffrage journal; Lafayette, Ind.; 1879–84). (*AW*; *NAW*)

**Green, Frances Harriet Whipple (later McDougall)** Editor of the *Original* (Rhode Island local interest paper). Editor and publisher of the *Wampanoag and Operatives Journal* (factory journal; Fall River, R.I.; 1842–43). Assistant editor of the *Young People's Journal of Science, Literature, and Art* (New York and Boston; 1848). Co-editor of the *Spirit Messenger* (spiritualist paper; Springfield, Mass.; 1850–52). Co-editor of the *Spirit Messenger and Harmonial Guide* (spiritualist weekly; New York; 1852–53). Co-editor with ANNETTE BISHOP and others of the *Journal of Progress* (spiritualist weekly; New York; 1853–?). Editor, as Mrs. Frances H. McDougall, of *Golden Gate* (spiritualist weekly; Sacramento, Calif.; 1864). (*DAB*; "NSW")

**Green, Harriet N.** Co-editor or editor of four spiritualist papers published in Hopedale, Mass.: *Radical Spiritualist* (1858–60), *Spiritual Reformer* (1860–62), *Progressive Age* (1862), and *Modern Age* (1862–66). ("NSW")

**Gregory, Lillie** Editor of *Kings and Queens of the Range* (family literary paper; Denver, Colo., and Kansas City, Mo.; 1897–1902). ("PWMP")

**Grey, Lucy** Co-editor with ARIZONA JACKSON of the *Hallequah* (Seneca, Shawnee, and Wyandotte Industrial Boarding School paper; Quapaw Agency, Indian Territory; 1879–81). (*AI*)

**Griffin, Lulu** Local editor of *Griffin's Maryville Daily Review* (Missouri newspaper). See also PEARL GRIFFIN and ZOE GRIFFIN. ("PWMP")

**Griffin, Pearl** Editor of the *Skidmore Herald* (Missouri newspaper). Editor of *Griffin's Maryville Daily Review* (Missouri newspaper). See also LULU GRIFFIN and ZOE GRIFFIN. ("PWMP")

**Griffin, Sarah Lawrence** Editor of the *Family Companion and Ladies' Mirror* (Macon, Ga.; 1841–43). (*EGM*; "SML")

**Griffin, Zoe** Manager of *Griffin's Maryville Daily Review* (Missouri news-

paper). Editor of *Guilford Grit* (Missouri newspaper). See also LULU GRIF-
FIN and PEARL GRIFFIN. ("PWMP")

**Guernsey, Alice Margaret** Editor of the *Young Crusader* (temperance publication; Evanston, Ill.; 1887–current). Assistant editor of the *Silver Cross*
(International Order of the King's Daughters and Sons journal; New York;
1888–?). (*WWA* 1; *WWWA*)

**Guernsey, Lucy Ellen** Editor of the *Parish Visitor* (Episcopal paper; Rochester, N.Y.; 1880s–90s). (*AWW; WWA* 1)

**Haines, Helen E.** Managing editor of the *Library Journal* (New York; 1876–
current). (*HAM* 3)

**Hale, Sarah Josepha** Editor of the *Ladies' Magazine* (Boston; 1828–36). Editor of the *Juvenile Miscellany* (Boston; 1826–36). Editor of *Godey's Lady's
Book* (Philadelphia and New York; 1830–98). (*AWW; CP; DAB; NAW*)

**Hall, Lydia S.** Co-editor, with ABBY A. GODDARD, of the *Operatives' Magazine* (factory paper; Lowell, Mass.; 1841–42). ("EFM")

**Halloway, Laura C.** Literary editor of the *Brooklyn Daily Eagle* (newspaper;
Brooklyn; 1841–1964). (*J*)

**Hallowell, Mrs. R. C.** Editor of the *New Century for Women* (newspaper for
centennial exposition; Philadelphia; 1876). (*DA*)

**Hamilton, Fannie K.** Editor of the *Old Orchard Rambler* (Biddeford,
Maine). (*J*)

**Hanaford, Phebe Ann Coffin** Editor of the *Ladies' Repository* (Universal-
ist monthly; Boston; 1832–74). Editor of the *Myrtle* (Sunday school paper;
Boston; 1851–1900s). Editor of the children's department of the *Universalist*
(Boston; 1819–78). (*AW; AWW; DA; DAB; NAW*)

**Hanchett, Maria F.** Editor of the *Motor* (temperance paper; various locations
in Wisconsin; 1886–1990). (*WPN*)

**Hankins, Marie Louise** Publisher and editor of the *Family Newspaper*
(monthly; New York; 1855–56). (*HAM* 2)

**Hanna, Camilla** Assistant editor of MARY BAKER EDDY's *Christian Science
Journal* (Boston; 1883–current). (*MBE-YA*)

**Hanscom, Elizabeth Deering** Assistant editor of the *Golden Rule*, later titled
*Christian Endeavor World* (Boston; 1886–current). (*J; WNAA; WWWA*)

**Hansen, Ida** Editor of the women's section of *Fra Alle Lande* (From All
Lands) (Scandinavian monthly; Cedar Rapids, Iowa; 1883–86). Editor with
her sister, MINA JENSEN, of *Kvinden og Hjemmet* (The Woman and the
Home) (women's magazine published separately in Dano-Norwegian and in
Swedish as *Quinnan och hemmet;* Cedar Rapids, Iowa; 1888–1948). (*DLP*)

**Harbert, Elizabeth Boynton** Editor of the women's department of *Inter-*

*Ocean* (Chicago; 1876–92). Editor of the *New Era* (literary and suffrage magazine; Chicago; 1885). (*AW; WWWA*)

**Harman, Sara**  Editor of the *Gulf Messenger* (women's club periodical; Houston and San Antonio; 1888–98). (*HAM 4*)

**Harper, Ida A. Husted**  Editor of the women's department of the *Locomotive Firemen's Magazine*, later titled *Brotherhood of Locomotive Firemen and Enginemen's Magazine* (Cincinnati; 1873–1963). Editor of the *Terre Haute Daily News* (1880–91). Member of editorial staff of the *Indianapolis News* (1869–current). Editor of the women's department of the *Sun* (newspaper; New York; 1833–1950). Editor of the women's department of *Harper's Bazar* (women's magazine; New York; 1867–current). (*AW; AWW; DAB; NAW*)

**Harris, Carrie Jenkins**  Editor of the *South Atlantic* (monthly magazine; Wilmington, N.C., and Baltimore; 1877–82). (*HAM 3*)

**Hasbrouck, Lydia Sayer**  Editor of *Sibyl* (feminist journal; Middletown, N.Y.; 1856–64). Assistant editor of the *Whig Press* (newspaper; Middletown, N.Y.; 1851–1928). Co-editor and co-founder of the *Liberal Sentinel* (weekly reform paper; Middletown, N.Y.; 1881). (*AWW; DAB; HAM 2; NAW;* "RP")

**Haven, Alice Bradley Neal**  One of the editors of *Neal's Saturday Gazette and Ladies' Literary Museum* (Philadephia; 1836–53). (*AWW; DAB; HAM 2; NAW*)

**Haviland, Mrs. C. Augustus**  Co-editor of the *Western Soldiers' Friend* (Chicago; 1867–74). (*HAM 3*)

**Hawks, Annie C. Torrey**  Editor, with MARY DANA SHINDLER, of the *Voice of Truth* (spiritualist magazine; Memphis; 1878). ("NSW")

**Hawley, Maria**  Founder with MARY TOMLIN and editor with Tomlin, MRS. E. MACKWAY, and ODELIA BLINN of the *Balance* (women's paper; Chicago; 1871–75). (*DA*)

**Hawthorne, Alice**  Editor of the *Musical Journal* (Philadelphia; 1867). (*AMP*)

**Hawthorne, Elizabeth Manning**  Co-editor of the *American Magazine of Useful and Entertaining Knowledge* (Boston; 1834–37). (*AWW*)

**Heath, E. Addie**  Editor of the *Home Guest*. Editor of the *Boston Beacon* (society weekly; 1884–1904). Editor of the *Woman's Magazine*. Editor of *Babyland* (children's magazine; Boston; 1877–98). Editor of *Our Little Men and Women* (children's magazine; Boston; 1880–98). (*CP; J*)

**Henderson, Mattie L.**  Co-editor of the *Future State: A Monthly Journal of Negro Progress* (Kansas City, Mo.; 1891–98). (*AAPP;* "BWJ")

**Herrick, Christine Terhune**  Editor of the women's page of the *New York Recorder* (newspaper; 1891–96). (*AW; NAW*)

**Herrick, Maria** Editor of the *Mothers' and Young Ladies' Guide* (Ohio City; 1837–40). ("EWM")

**Herrick, Sophia Bledsoe** Associate editor and then editor of the *Southern Review* (literary and theological journal; Baltimore; 1867–79). Assistant editor of *Scribner's Monthly* (*Century Magazine*) (miscellany; New York; 1870–1930). (*DAB; HAM* 3; *WWWA*)

**Hewitt, Emma Churchman** Associate editor with Mrs. James H. Lambert of Louisa Knapp's *Ladies' Home Journal* (Philadelphia; 1883–current). Member of editorial staff of the *Home Magazine* (Washington, D.C., Minneapolis, and Indianapolis; 1888–1908). Associate editor of *Leisure Hours* (Philadelphia; 1885–1902). (*AW; WWWA*)

**Hicks, Mrs. R. B.** Editor of *Kaleidoscope* (women's magazine; Petersburg, Va.; 1856–57). (*HAM* 2)

**Higginson, Ella Rhoads** Editor of the women's department for the *West Shore* (literary magazine; Portland, Oreg., and Spokane; 1875–91). (*AW; AWW*)

**Hildenbrand, Ava H.** Editor of a *Gretna Courier*. (*J*)

**Hill, Agnes Leonard** Numerous editorial positions with the *Western Society* (Denver; 1888–?), *Society* (Denver), *Chaffee County Times* (Bueno Vista, Colo.; 1880–86), *Leadville Dispatch* (Leadville, Colo.; 1886–92), *Sorosis* (suffrage paper; Chicago; 1868–69), *Home and Society* (Chicago), *Elite News* (Chicago), *Chicago Tribune* (1847–current), *Chicago Times* (1854–95), and *Chicago News* (1876–?). (*AW; J; NCAB; WWA* 1)

**Hill, Eliza Trask** Editor of the *Woman's Voice and Public School Champion* (Boston; 1890–1907). (*AW*)

**Hillhouse, Sarah Porter** Publisher and editor of the *Monitor* (newspaper; Washington, Ga.; 1801–15). (*UFF*)

**Hiscox, Caroline O.** Editor of the *Mother's Journal and Family Visitant* (New York and Philadelphia; 1836–72). (*HAM* 2)

**Hodgkins, Louise Manning** Editor of the *Woman's Missionary Friend* (Boston; 1869–1940). (*AW; WPN; WWWA*)

**Hofer, Amalie** Co-editor with her sister Andrea Hofer Proudfoot of the *Child-Garden of Story, Song, and Play* (Chicago and Morgan Park, Ill.; 1892–1903). (*CP*)

**Holloway, Charlotte Molyneux** Editor of the *Telegraph* (newspaper; New London, Conn.; 1885–1921). (*J*)

**Hooker, Isabella Beecher** Contributing editor to the *Revolution* (suffrage journal; New York; 1868–72). See also Susan Brownell Anthony and Elizabeth Cady Stanton. (*AW; DAB; HAM* 3; *NAW*)

**Hooper, Lucy Hamilton Jones** Associate editor of *Lippincott's Magazine* (literary monthly; Philadelphia and New York; 1868–1916). (*AW; AWW; DAB; HAM* 3)

**Hopkins, Emma Curtis** Assistant editor and then acting editor of MARY BAKER EDDY's *Christian Science Journal* (Boston; 1883–current). Editor of the *Mental Science Magazine* (Chicago; 1884–89). Co-founder and co-editor with MARY PLUNKETT of *Truth* (Christian Science magazine; Chicago; 1887–88). Founder and editor of *Christian Metaphysician* (Chicago; 1887–97). (*MBE-YT; NAW*)

**Hopkins, Mary Sargent** Editor of *Wheelwoman* (women's bicycling magazine; Boston; 1895–1902). (*HAM* 4)

**Horne, Cornelia H.** Business manager, with LOUISA LULA GREENE RICHARDS as editor, of the *Woman's Exponent* (Mormon women's newspaper; Salt Lake City; 1872–1914). (*SS*)

**Horne, Minnie** Secretary of LOUISA LULA GREENE RICHARDS's executive committee for the *Woman's Exponent* (Mormon women's newspaper; Salt Lake City; 1872–1914). (*SS*)

**Horton, Agnes True** Editor of *Opera* (Chicago; 1894–95). (*AMP*)

**Hotchkiss, J. Elizabeth** Co-editor of *Metaphysical Magazine* (New York; 1895–1913). (*HAM* 4; *WWA* 5)

**Housh, Esther T.** Editor of the *Woman's Magazine* (Louisville, Ky., and Brattleboro, Vt.; 1877–90). Editor of *Our Home Guards* (Vermont temperance paper). Editor of the *Household* (Brattleboro, Vt., Boston, and New York; 1868–1903). Editor of the *New Idea Woman's Magazine* (Brattleboro, Vt., and New York; 1896–1920). (*AW; HAM* 3–4)

**Howe, Julia Ward** Assistant editor of *Commonwealth* (Free Soil journal; Boston; 1851–54). Editor of the *Listener* (weekly paper for friends and family; Boston; 1854–55). Editor of the *Northern Lights* (literary magazine; Boston; 1867). Editor of LUCY STONE's *Woman's Journal* (suffrage paper; Boston; 1870–1932). (*AW; AWW; DAB; HAM* 3; *NAW*)

**Howland, Marie** Editor of the *Credit Foncier of Sinaloa* (reform journal; Hammonton, N.J.; 1886–95). Editor of *Social Solutions* (reform journal). (*AWW*)

**Hudson, Norma E. Rasmus** Co-editor and co-publisher of the *Arrow-Telephone* (weekly newspaper; Tahlequah, Cherokee Nation; 1894). (*AI*)

**Huling, Caroline Augusta** Associate editor of the *Sentinel* (newspaper; Saratoga Springs, N.Y.; 1819–47). Editor of *Justitia: A Court for the Unrepresented* (Illinois suffrage paper; 1887–88). (*AW*)

**Humphrey, Frances A.** Editor of *Our Little Men and Women* (children's magazine; Boston; 1880–98). (*CP; HAM* 3)

**Humphrey, Marie E. Ives** Editor of the "Young People's Department" of the *Indian Bulletin* (Connecticut Indian Association journal; Hartford, Conn.; 1888–1901). Editor of the *Indian's Friend* (missionary journal; Philadelphia, Lancaster, Pa., New Haven, Conn., and New York; 1888–1951). See also KATHARINE BURBANK and MRS. FREDERICK C. JONES. (*AI; WWWA*)

**Hungerford, Mrs. M. C.** Editor of the *Housewife* (Greenfield, Mass., and New York; 1882–1917). Editor of *Good Cheer* (Greenfield, Mass.; 1882–88). (*J*)

**Hunt, Anna Sargent** Editor of the *Home Mission Echo* (Boston, Mass., and Augusta, Maine; 1885–96). (*J*)

**Irvine, Kate** Co-editor with MARIANNA BURGESS of the *Morning Star*, later titled *Red Man* (U.S. Indian Industrial School paper; Carlisle, Pa.; 1880–1904). (*AI*)

**Irving, Helen** Editor of the *Ladies' Wreath* (New York; 1846–55). (*HAM* 1)

**Jackson, Arizona** Associate editor with LULU WALKER (with IDA JOHNSON as editor) and later co-editor with LUCY GREY of the *Hallequah* (Seneca, Shawnee, and Wyandotte Industrial Boarding School paper; Quapaw Agency, Indian Territory; 1879–81). (*AI*)

**Jackson, Ida May** Co-editor with CAROLINE SANDERSON BERRY, LOUISE CUNNINGHAM BOWLES, and MARY ANTISDEL MARNER of the *Milwaukee Journal (Charity Edition)* (1895). (*WPN*)

**Jackson, Mary Anna Morrison** Editor of *Woman* (Richmond, Va.; 1894–97). (*HAM* 4; *WWWA*)

**Jensen, Mina** Editor with her sister, IDA HANSEN, of *Kvinden og Hjemmet* (The Woman and the Home) (women's magazine published separately in Dano-Norwegian and in Swedish as *Quinnan och hemmet*; Cedar Rapids, Iowa; 1888–1948). (*DLP*)

**Jewett, Susan W.** Editor of a *Youth's Visitor*, probably the *Youth's Monthly Visitor* (Cincinnati and Washington, D.C.; 1844–52). (*ACAB; PPW*)

**Johnson, Amelia E.** Editor of the *Ivy* (African American children's magazine; Baltimore; 1880s). Founder of *Joy* (literary magazine; 1887–?). ("BWJ"; *J*)

**Johnson, Mrs. Amos** Editor of the *Western Herald* (Keokuk, Iowa). (*J*)

**Johnson, Carrie Ashton** Editor of the women's department of *Farmer's Voice* (Chicago; 1887–1913). Editor of the women's page for the *Spectator* (family magazine; Rockford, Ill.). (*AW*)

**Johnson, Helen Kendrick** Editor, with MRS. R. VON HORRUM SCHRAMM as publisher, of the *Business Woman's Journal* (New York; 1889–96). (*DAB; HAM* 4)

**Johnson, Ida** Editor, with JULIA ROBITAILLE as associate editor, of the *Halaquah Times* (manuscript student magazine of the Wyandotte Mission School; Indian Territory; 1871–75). Editor, with assistance from LULU WALKER and ARIZONA JACKSON, of the *Hallequah* (Seneca, Shawnee, and Wyandotte Industrial Boarding School paper; Quapaw Agency, Indian Territory; 1879–81). (*AI*)

**Johnson, Mary Coffin** Publisher of the *Woman's Temperance Union*, later the *Union Signal* (temperance journal; Chicago and Evanston, Ill.; 1874–current). (*DA; SEAP*)

**Jones, Mrs. Frederick C.** Business manager for the *Indian Bulletin* (Connecticut Indian Association journal; Hartford, Conn.; 1888–1901). See also KATHARINE BURBANK and MARIE E. IVES HUMPHREY. (*AI*)

**Jones, Irma Theoda** Editor of the literary club department of *Mid-Continent* (monthly magazine; Lansing, Mich.). (*AW*)

**Jones, Jane Elizabeth Hitchcock** Co-editor of the *Anti-Slavery Bugle* (Salem, Ohio; 1845–61). (*NAW*)

**Jordan, Elizabeth Garver** Editor of the women's page of *Peck's Sun* (Milwaukee; 1874–94). Assistant editor of the *New York World* (newspaper; 1860–1931). Editor of *Harper's Bazar* (women's magazine; New York; 1867–current). (*AW; HAM* 3; *NAW; UFF*)

**Kearns, Lillian A.** Assistant editor of the *Old Providence Star and Press*, later titled *News* (newspaper; Providence). Possible editorial position with the *Pawtucket Evening Times* (Pawtucket, R.I.; 1886–90). Editor of the *Pawtucket Record*, later titled *Record Visitor* (newspaper; Pawtucket, R.I.; 1886–91). (*J*)

**Kellogg, Alice M.** Editor of *Treasure Trove* (children's magazine; New York; 1877–93). (*HAM* 3)

**Kellogg, Emily** Co-editor with CORA L. STOCKHAM and ALICE BUNKER STOCKHAM of the *Kindergarten Magazine* (Chicago; 1888–1933). (*HAM* 4; *J*)

**Kellogg, Eva D.** Editor of *Primary Education* (Boston; 1892–1929). (*HAM* 4)

**Kellogg, Mrs. F. Beulah** Co-editor of *Modern Priscilla* (craft and dress pattern magazine; Lynn, Mass., and Boston; 1887–1930). (*HAM* 4)

**Ketcham, Mrs. ("Annie")** Editor of the *Lotus* (magazine; Memphis; 1859). (*TWW*)

**Keyser, Harriette A.** Editor and publisher of *Hammer and Pen* (labor journal; New York; 1899–1909). (*HAM* 4; *WWWA*)

**Killey, Mrs. N. S.** Editor of the *Dutchess Farmer* (weekly; Poughkeepsie, N.Y.). (*Inland Monthly Magazine*, Dec. 1873)

**Kimball, Anna** Co-editor of *Gnostic* (spiritualist magazine; San Francisco; 1885–88). ("NSW")

**Kimball, Mrs. Lou H.** Publisher, with HANNAH F. M. BROWN as editor, of the *Lyceum Banner* (children's spiritualist paper; Chicago; 1867–72). ("NSW")

**Kirkland, Caroline Matilda Stansbury** Editor of the *Christian Inquirer* (Unitarian weekly; New York; 1846–77). Editor and later co-editor of *Sartain's Union Magazine of Literature and Art* (New York; 1847–52). (*AWW; DAB; HAM* 1; *NAW*)

**Kline, Mrs. Adolphus** Editor of the *Morning Star* (spiritualist paper; Van Wert, Ohio; 1873–74). ("NSW")

**Knapp, Louisa** Editor of the women's department of the *Tribune and Farmer* (Philadelphia; 1879–85). Editor, with assistance from EMMA CHURCHMAN HEWITT and MRS. JAMES H. LAMBERT, of the *Ladies' Home Journal* (Philadelphia; 1883–current). (*HAM* 3–4)

**Lamb, Ellen W.** Co-editor with EMMA J. CURTIS and HELEN REMINGTON OLIN of the *Motor* (temperance paper; various locations in Wisconsin; 1886–1990). (*WPN*)

**Lamb, Martha Joanna Reade Nash** Editor of the *Magazine of American History* (New York; 1877–1917). (*AW; AWW; DAB; HAM* 3; *NAW*)

**Lambert, Mrs. James H.** Associate editor with EMMA CHURCHMAN HEWITT of LOUISA KNAPP's *Ladies' Home Journal* (Philadelphia; 1883–current). (*HAM* 4)

**Lambert, Mary Tucker** Editor of *St. Matthews Lyceum Journal* (Detroit). (*AWP; J*)

**Lambert, Molly E.** Editor of the literary department of JULIA RINGWOOD COSTON's *Ringwood's Afro-American Journal of Fashion* (Cleveland; 1891–95). (*AAPP*)

**Lane, Gertrude Battles** Editor of a school literary magazine (Maine). Editor of the *Boston Beacon* (society weekly; 1884–1904). Household editor, managing editor, and then editor in chief of the *Woman's Home Companion* (Cleveland, Springfield, Ohio, and New York; 1874–1957). (*AWW; HAM* 4; *NAW*)

**Larcom, Lucy** Poetry editor of the *Congregationalist*, eventually known as the *Congregationalist and Herald of Gospel Liberty* (Boston; 1816–1934). Co-editor (for several years with MARY ABIGAIL DODGE) of *Our Young Folks* (children's magazine; Boston; 1865–73). (*AW; AWW; CP; DAB; NAW*)

**Larned, Augusta** Assistant editor with PHOEBE CARY to LAURA CURTIS

BULLARD and later associate editor of the *Revolution* (suffrage journal; New York; 1868–72). (*HAM* 3; *NCAB*; *WWA* 4)

**Layton, S. Willie** Department editor of JOSEPHINE ST. PIERRE RUFFIN's *Woman's Era* (African American women's club journal; Boston; 1894–1903). (*AAPP*)

**Lease, Mary Elizabeth Clyens** Editor of the *Union Labor Press* (Kansas). Editor of the *Colorado Workman* (labor paper; 1889–?). (*HAM* 4; *NAW*)

**Lee, Olive B.** Editor of the *Period* (literary miscellany; Dallas and Boston; 1893–1906). (*HAM* 4)

**Lees, Harriet** Assistant editor to HARRIOT F. CURTIS and HARRIET FARLEY of the *Lowell Offering* (factory magazine; Lowell, Mass.; 1840–45). (*AWW*, under Harriet Farley)

**Leonard, Ella S.** Business manager, with CAROLINE GRAY LINGLE as managing editor, of *Kate Field's Washington* (weekly review; Washington, D.C., and Chicago; 1890–95). (*HAM* 4)

**Leslie, Eliza** Editor of *Miss Leslie's Magazine* (women's magazine; Philadelphia; 1843). Assistant editor to SARAH JOSEPHA HALE of *Godey's Lady's Book* (Philadelphia and New York; 1830–98). (*AWW; DAB; HAM* 1; *NAW*)

**Leslie, Miriam Florence Squier** Editor and often also publisher of many of the Frank Leslie periodicals from New York, including *Frank Leslie's Lady's Magazine* (1857–82), *Frank Leslie's Chimney Corner* (1865–85), *Frank Leslie's Lady's Journal* (1871–81), *Frank Leslie's Illustrated Newspaper* (1855–1922), *Frank Leslie's Popular Monthly*, later titled *American Magazine* (1876–1956), and *Frank Leslie's Boy's and Girl's Weekly* (1866–84). (*AW; AWW; CP; HAM* 2–3; *DAB; NAW*)

**Lewis, Amelia** Editor of *Freund's Weekly* (music periodical; New York; 1883–92). (*AMP*)

**Lewis, Theresa Juan** Founder and editor (at times with SARA ANDREWS SPENCER) of *Woman's Words: An Original Review of What Women Are Doing* (Philadelphia and Washington, D.C.; 1877–81). (*HAM* 3; *HBA*, under "Juan" Lewis)

**Lindsay, Mrs. H. C.** Editor of the *Kentucky Garland* (women's magazine; Covington, Ky.; 1853). (*HAM* 2)

**Lingle, Caroline Gray** Managing editor, with ELLA S. LEONARD as business manager, of *Kate Field's Washington* (weekly review; Washington, D.C., and Chicago; 1890–95). (*HAM* 4)

**Lining, Ida Marshall** Editor of the *Keystone* (women's club journal; Charleston, S.C.; 1899–1913). (*WPN*)

**Lippincott, Sara Jane ("Grace Greenwood")** Editor of *Lady's Dollar Newspaper* (Philadelphia; 1848). Assistant editor to SARAH JOSEPHA HALE of *Godey's Lady's Book* (Philadelphia and New York; 1830–98). Editor of the *Little Pilgrim* (children's magazine; Philadelphia; 1853–68). (*AW; AWW; CP; DAB; HAM* 1; *NAW*)

**Livermore, Mary Ashton Rice** Associate editor of the *New Covenant* (Universalist paper; Chicago; 1848–83). Publisher and editor, with assistance from MARY L. WALKER, of the *Agitator* (suffrage paper; Chicago; 1869). Editor of LUCY STONE's *Woman's Journal* (suffrage paper; Boston; 1870–1932). (*AW; AWW; DAB; DATB; EFE; NAW; VTO*)

**Logan, Mary Simmerson Cunningham** Editor of the *Home Magazine* (Washington, D.C.; 1888–1908). (*AW; AWW; NAW*)

**Lombard, Mary** Editor of *Woman's Work for Woman* (Christian mission paper; Philadelphia; 1875–85). (*WPN*)

**Longenbaugh, May M.** Editor of the *Indian Advance* (Carson Indian School paper; Stewart, Nev.; 1899–1903). (*AI*)

**Longley, Margaret V.** Editor with MIRIAM M. COLE of the *Woman's Advocate* (Dayton, Ohio; 1869–70). (*DA*)

**Lord, Frances** Editor of *Woman's World* (Chicago and New York; 1884–1940). (*J*)

**Loud, Hulda Barker** Editor and later also owner and publisher of the *Independent* (weekly newspaper; Rockland, Mass.; 1884–1933). (*AW*)

**Loughborough, Mary Ann Webster** Founder and editor of the *Southern Ladies Journal* (Little Rock, Ark.; 1883–?). (*AWW*)

**Loughborough, Winnie** Co-editor with EVA BELL GILES and then editor of *Youth's Instructor* (religious children's magazine; Rochester, N.Y., Battle Creek, Mich., and Washington, D.C.; 1852–1970). (*CP*)

**Mackway, Mrs. E.** Co-editor with ODELIA BLINN, MARIA HAWLEY, and MARY TOMLIN of the *Balance* (women's paper; Chicago; 1871–75). (*DA*)

**Malkiel, Theresa Serber** Editor of the women's column in the *Jewish Daily News* (New York; 1885–1928). (*AWW*)

**Mallory, Lucy A.** Publisher and editor of the *World's Advance Thought and the Universal Republic* (spiritualist paper; Salem and Portland, Oreg.; 1876–1918). (*AW*; "NSW")

**Manford, Mrs. H. B.** Co-publisher and co-editor with her husband, Erasmus Manford, of *Manford's Magazine* (Universalist monthly; Chicago and St. Louis; 1856–96). (*HAM* 2)

**Manton, May (Mrs. George H. Bladworth)** Editor of *McCall's Magazine* (women's magazine; New York; 1873–current). Editor of the fashion department of the *Ladies' World* (New York; 1886–1918). (*HAM 4*)

**Maples, Sylvia Mann** Department editor of JOSEPHINE ST. PIERRE RUFFIN's *Woman's Era* (African American women's club journal; Boston; 1894–1903). (*AAPP*)

**Marcotte, Anna M.** Editor and publisher of the *Tatler of Society in Florida* (society paper; St. Augustine; 1892–1908). (*HAM 4*; *MAS*)

**Marner, Mary Antisdel** Co-editor with CAROLINE SANDERSON BERRY, LOUISE CUNNINGHAM BOWLES, and IDA MAY JACKSON of the *Milwaukee Journal (Charity Edition)* (1895). (*WPN*)

**Martyn, Sarah Towne Smith** Editor of the *Olive Plant and Ladies' Temperance Advocate* (New York; 1841–42). Editor of the *Advocate of Moral Reform* (New York; 1835–1941). Editor of the *True Advocate* (1840s). Editor of *White Banner* (1840s). Editor of the *Ladies' Wreath* (New York; 1846–55). (*AWW*; *DAB*; *HAM* 1; "RP")

**Matthews, Victoria Earle** Department editor of JOSEPHINE ST. PIERRE RUFFIN's *Woman's Era* (African American women's club journal; Boston; 1894–1903). (*AAPP*; "BWJ"; *NAW*)

**Mattison, Anna C.** Briefly co-editor with AMELIA JENKS BLOOMER of the *Lily* (women's rights journal; Seneca Falls, N.Y., Mount Vernon, Ohio, and Richmond, Ind.; 1849–56). (*HAM* 2)

**May, Emily H.** Editor of the women's department of *Peterson's Magazine* (Philadelphia and New York; 1842–98). Assistant editor of *Arthur's Home Magazine* (Philadelphia; 1852–98). (*HAM* 2)

**Mayo, Sarah Carter Edgarton** Associate editor of the *Ladies' Repository* (Universalist monthly; Boston; 1832–74). (*AWW*; *DAB*)

**McCabe, Harriet Calista Clark** Editor of the *Woman's Home Missions* (New York and Cincinnati; 1884–1940). (*AW*; *DATB*; *WWWA*)

**McCall, Mrs. James** Co-editor, possibly, and later president of *McCall's Magazine* (women's magazine; New York; 1873–current). (*HAM 4*)

**McCarty, Louise C.** Editor of the *Musical Bouquet* (New York; 1873–?). (*AMP*)

**McConnell, Martha A.** Editor, with assistance from HARRIET S. PRITCHARD, of a Pennsylvania *Journal*. (*J*)

**McCord, Wilhelmine** Editor of the *Southern Parlor Magazine* (Mobile and Memphis; 1851–56). (*TWW*)

**McCormick, Anne O'Hare** Associate editor of the *Catholic Universe Bulletin* (Cleveland; 1874–current). (*AWW*)

**McCrimmon, Mary A.** Editor of the *Educational Monthly* (Lumpkin, Ga.; 1860s). (*EGM*)

**McDowell, Anne Elizabeth** Editor, assisted by LYDIA J. PIERSON, of the *Woman's Advocate* (Philadelphia; 1855–60). Editor of the women's department of the *Sunday Dispatch* (Philadelphia; 1848–1920). Editor of the women's department of the *Sunday Republic* (Philadelphia; 1867–84). (*DA; EFE; NAW;* "PML"; "RP")

**McEwen, Alice E.** Assistant editor of the *Herald* (Montgomery, Ala.). Associate editor of the *Baptist Leader* (Birmingham, Ala.; 1883–?). ("BWJ"; *J*)

**McKane, Alice Woodby** Department editor of JOSEPHINE ST. PIERRE RUFFIN's *Woman's Era* (African American women's club journal; Boston; 1894–1903). (*AAPP*)

**McKay, Charlotte E.** Editor of *True Woman* (antisuffrage paper; Baltimore and Washington, D.C.; 1870–73). (*HAM* 3)

**McPherson, Lydia Starr** Assistant editor and later possibly editor in chief of the *Oklahoma Star*, later known as the *Star-Vindicator* (newspaper; Caddo and McAlester, Choctaw Nation, and Blanco, Tex.; 1874–79). Founder and editor of the *International News* (Caddo, Choctaw Nation). Founder and editor of the *Whitesboro Democrat* (newspaper; Whitesboro, Tex.; 1877–79). Founder and editor of the *Sherman Democrat* (Sherman, Tex.; 1879–current). (*AI; AW*)

**Meloney, Sarah Irwin** Founder of the *Kentucky Magazine* (Louisville; 1880–81). (*NAW*, under her daughter, Marie Mattingly Meloney)

**Melville, Velma Caldwell** Editor of the home and children's department of the *Practical Farmer* (Philadelphia). Editor of the health and home department of the *Wisconsin Farmer* (Madison). (*AW*)

**Meriwether, Elizabeth Avery** Publisher and editor of the *Tablet* (southern weekly newspaper; 1872). (*AWW*)

**Merriam, Jennie A.** Editor of *Youth's Instructor* (religious children's magazine; Rochester, N.Y., Battle Creek, Mich., and Washington, D.C.; 1852–1970). (*CP*)

**Merrill, Estelle M. H.** Member of the editorial staff of the *Journal of Education* (Boston; 1875–current). Co-founder and co-editor with ANNA BARROWS of the *New England Kitchen Magazine*, later titled *Everyday Housekeeping* (Boston; 1894–1908). (*HAM* 4; *J*)

**Michel, Nettie Leila** Business manager and then editor of the *Magazine of Poetry* (Buffalo; 1889–96). (*AW; HAM* 4)

**Miller, Anna Jenness** Editor of *Jenness Miller Magazine* (dress reform magazine; New York; 1887–98). Editor of the *Quarterly Journal* (1889–92). (*AW*; *HAM* 4)

**Miller, Emily Clark Huntington** Assistant editor and later editor of the *Little Corporal* (juvenile magazine; Chicago; 1865–75). Editor of the *Call* (temperance newsletter; 1874). Associate editor of the *Ladies' Home Journal* (Philadelphia; 1883–current). (*AW*; *AWW*; *CP*; *DAB*; *DATB*; *NAW*)

**Miller, Mary A.** Missionary editor of the women's department of the *Methodist Recorder* (Pittsburgh; 1839–1929). Editor and publisher of the *Woman's Missionary Record*, later titled *Missionary Record* (Methodist publication; Greensboro, N.C., and Baltimore; 1885–1940). (*AW*)

**Minor, Virginia Otey** Assistant editor of the *Southern Literary Messenger* (Richmond, Va.; 1834–64). (*HAM* 1)

**Mitchell, Sarah** Editor of the home department of JULIA RINGWOOD COS-TON's *Ringwood's Afro-American Journal of Fashion* (Cleveland; 1891–95). (*AAPP*)

**Mixter, Frances C.** Household editor of the *Chronicle* (newspaper; Athol, Mass.; 1866–1935). Household editor of a *Templeton Recorder*. Column editor of the *Woman's News* (Indianapolis). (*J*)

**Mize, Eva** Co-publisher and co-editor, with her sister FIDELIA MIZE, of the *Newton County News* (newspaper; Newtonia, Mo.; 1890–1906). ("PWMP")

**Mize, Fidelia** See EVA MIZE.

**Molloy, Emma** Co-editor of the *National Union*, later titled *South Bend Union* (newspaper; South Bend, Ind.; 1866–74). Co-owner and co-editor of the *Cortland Journal* (newspaper; Cortland, N.Y.; 1869–72). Co-owner and co-editor of the *Homer Herald* (newspaper; Cortland, N.Y.). Co-owner and co-editor of the *Daily Observer* (newspaper; Elkhart, Ind.). Editor of the political reform department of the *Advance Guard* (temperance paper; Elkhart, Ind.). (*DA*)

**Moore, Mrs. H. G.** Co-editor of *Moore's Western Lady's Book* (Cincinnati; 1849–56). See also ELIZABETH ALDRICH. (*BLC*; "EWM")

**Moore, Susanne Vandegrift** Editor and owner of *St. Louis Life* (weekly miscellany; St. Louis; 1889–97). (*AW*; *HAM* 4)

**Morgan, Emily Malbone** Assistant editor to MARIA BOWEN CHAPIN of *Far and Near* (journal focusing on women working outside the home; New York; 1890–94). Editor of *Mind* (perhaps the New Thought journal; New York; 1897–1906). Editor of church periodicals. (*HAM* 4; *WNAA*)

**Morgan, Sallie B.** Editor of the *Sunday Journal* (Nashville). (*J*)

**Morse, Amy Kellogg** Co-editor with EMMA J. CURTIS of the *Motor* (temperance paper; various locations in Wisconsin; 1886–1990). (*WPN*)

**Morse, Mrs. T. Vernette**  Editor of *Arts for America* (Chicago; 1892–1900). (*HAM* 4; *WWWA*)

**Mossell, Gertrude Bustill**  Assistant editor of the *Alumni Magazine* (African American magazine published at Lincoln University; Philadelphia; 1884–?). Editor of the women's pages of the *Freeman* (African American monthly; New York; 1908). Editor of the women's section of the *Philadelphia Echo*. (*AAPP;* "BWJ"; *J; UFF*)

**Moulton, Louise Chandler**  Editor of the society section of the *Continent* (general weekly; Philadelphia and New York; 1882–84). (*AW; AWW; DAB; HAM* 3; *NAW*)

**Mount, Mrs. P. W. (Ruth Ramay)**  Editor of *Current Topics for Leisure Hours* (literary monthly; New Orleans; 1890–95). (*HAM* 4)

**Murrow, Kathrina Lois Ellet**  Assistant editor of the *Indian Missionary* (various locations in the Creek, Choctaw, and Cherokee Nations and Oklahoma Territory; 1884–93). (*AI*)

**Muzzy, Harriet**  Department editor of the *Album and Ladies' Weekly Gazette* (Philadelphia; 1826–34). Assistant editor of the *Ladies' Literary Port Folio* (Philadelphia; 1828–29). ("EPM")

**Myers, Annie E.**  Editor of *American Housekeeper* (Chicago). (*J*)

**Nelson, Alice Ruth Moore Dunbar**  Department editor of JOSEPHINE ST. PIERRE RUFFIN's *Woman's Era* (African American women's club journal; Boston; 1894–1903). Associate editor of the *Wilmington Advocate* (weekly newspaper; Wilmington, Del.). Associate editor of the *A.M.E. Church Review* (Philadelphia and Nashville; 1884–current). (*AAPP; AWW; NAW*)

**Nesbitt, Earnestine Clark**  Editor of the "Mother's Corner" of JULIA RINGWOOD COSTON's *Ringwood's Afro-American Journal of Fashion* (Cleveland; 1891–95). (*AAPP*)

**Nichols, Clarina Irene Howard**  Editor of the *Windham County Democrat* (newspaper; Brattleboro, Vt.; 1836–53). (*DAB; NAW*)

**Nichols, Mary Sargeant Neal Gove**  Editor of the *Health Journal and Advocate of Physiological Reform* (Boston and Worcester, Mass.; 1840–42). Founder and editor of the *Health Journal and Independent Magazine* (Boston; 1843). Co-founder and co-editor of the *Nichols' Journal of Health, Water-Cure, and Human Progress* (New York; 1853–54). Co-founder and co-editor of the *Nichols' Monthly: A Magazine of Social Science and Progressive Literature* (Cincinnati; 1854–56). (*DAB; NAW;* "RP")

**Nichols, Rebecca S. Reed**  Co-editor of the *Pennant* (daily paper; St. Louis; 1839–40). Editor of the *Guest* (literary magazine; Cincinnati; 1846). Editor of the *Querist* (Cincinnati; 1844). (*ACAB; BLC; PPW*)

**Nicholson, Eliza Jane Poitevent Holbrook** Literary editor and later publisher of the *Daily Picayune* (newspaper; New Orleans; 1836–1914). (*AW; DAB; NAW*)

**Nirdlinger, Theresa A.** Editor of the *Casket* (undertakers' journal; Rochester, N.Y., and New York; 1876–1924). (*HAM 3*)

**Nolan, Mary** Co-editor with Charlotte Smith of the *Inland Monthly Magazine* (women's magazine; St. Louis; 1872–78). Publisher and editor, briefly with Mary Bowen, of the *Central Magazine* (women's magazine; St. Louis; 1872–75). (*HAM 3*; "PWMP")

**Northrup, Elizabeth C.** Co-editor of the *New England Conservatory Quarterly* (Boston; 1894–1904). (*AMP*)

**O'Hare, Teresa Beatrice** Editor of the women's page of the *Catholic Universe Bulletin* (Cleveland; 1874–current). (*AWW*, under her daughter, Anne O'Hare McCormick)

**Olin, Helen Remington** Co-editor with Mary Eaton and Emma Curtiss Bascom and later with Emma J. Curtis and Ellen W. Lamb of the *Motor* (temperance paper; various locations in Wisconsin; 1886–1990). (*WPN; WWWA*)

**O'Mahoney, Katharine A. O'Keeffe** Member of the editorial board of the *New England Catholic Herald* (Lawrence, Mass.; 1880–?). Owner and publisher of the *Catholic Register* (Sunday paper). (*AWW*)

**Orff, Annie L. Y.** Editor of the *Chaperone* (home and literary monthly; St. Louis; 1889–1911). (*AW; HAM 4*)

**Osgood, Frances Sargent Locke** Editor, probably nominally, of Snowden's *Ladies' Companion* (New York; 1834–44). (*AWW; DAB; NAW*)

**Otis, Elita Proctor** Editor of the *New York Saturday Review* (weekly miscellany; 1889–91). (*HAM 4*)

**Otis, Eliza Ann** Member of the editorial staff of the Los Angeles *Times* (1881–current). (*AW; NCAB*)

**Owen, Mattie P.** Co-editor of the *Golden Gate* (spiritualist magazine; San Francisco; 1885–90). Publisher with Rose L. Bushnell of the *Golden Way* (spiritualist paper; San Francisco; 1891). ("NSW")

**Ozha-guscoday-way-quay (Susan Johnston)** Possibly assistant editor of the *Muzzinyegun; or, Literary Voyager* (manuscript magazine devoted to Ojibwa culture; Sault Ste. Marie, Mich.; 1826–27). See also her daughter, Jane Johnston Schoolcraft. (*AI*)

**Pack, Emma D.** Editor of *Villa Range: Ladies Home Journal* (Topeka; 1880s). Editor of the *Farmer's Wife* (Topeka; 1891–94). (*VTO*)

**Palmer, Phoebe Worrall** Editor of the *Guide to Holiness* (Boston and New York; 1839–1901). (*AWW; NAW*)

**Parker, Mrs. J. M.** Editor of the *Woman's Council Magazine* (Minneapolis; 1894–96). (*WPN*)

**Parsons, Mary** Publisher of the *Comet* (newspaper; Union Star, Mo.; 1883–99). Editor of the *Bolckow Blade* (newspaper; Bolckow, Mo.). ("PWMP")

**Patten, Adelia P.** Editor of *Youth's Instructor* (religious children's magazine; Rochester, N.Y., Battle Creek, Mich., and Washington, D.C.; 1852–1970). (*CP*)

**Peabody, Elizabeth Palmer** Editor and publisher of the *Aesthetic Papers* (transcendental journal; Boston; 1849). (*AW; AWW; DAB; NAW*)

**Perkins, Sarah Maria Clinton** Editor of *A True Republic* (temperance and suffrage paper; Cleveland; 1891–1904). (*AW*)

**Peterson, Sarah Powell** Editor and business manager of *Peterson's Magazine* (Philadelphia and New York; 1842–98). (*HAM 2*)

**Peterson, Sarah Webb** Editor of the *Lady's Friend* (Philadelphia; 1864–73). (*ACAB; WPN*)

**Phelps, Almira Hart Lincoln** Publisher of the *Patapsco Young Ladies' Magazine* (student magazine; Ellicott's Mills, Md.; 1850). (*AWW; DAB; NAW*)

**Pierce, Katherine M.** Editor of the *Woman's Standard* (suffrage journal; Des Moines and Waterloo, Iowa; 1886–1911). (*WPN*)

**Pierson, Lydia J.** Assistant editor, with ANNE ELIZABETH MCDOWELL as editor, of the *Woman's Advocate* (Philadelphia; 1855–60). ("PML")

**Piggot, Margaret** Associate editor of the *Southern Lady's Magazine* (Baltimore; 1850). ("SML")

**Pilsbury, Caroline T.** Editor of *Boston Ideas* (city weekly and then spiritualist paper; Boston and elsewhere, as it became an itinerant publication; 1892–1929). (*HAM 4*)

**Plunkett, Mary** Co-founder and co-editor with EMMA CURTIS HOPKINS of *Truth* (Christian Science magazine; Chicago; 1887–88). Editor of the *International Magazine of Christian Science* (New York and Chicago; 1888–89). (*MBE-YT*)

**Pond, Hittie** Assistant to her daughter, MRS. A. B. COWELL, of the *Winthrop Visitor* (newspaper; Winthrop, Mass.; 1880–1905). (*J*)

**Porter, Charlotte Endymion** Editor of *Shakespeariana* (New York; 1883–93). Briefly, editor of *Ethical Record* (Philadelphia; 1888–90). Co-founder and co-editor with HELEN ARCHIBALD CLARKE of *Poet Lore* (literary magazine; Philadelphia and Boston; 1889–1953). (*NAW*)

**Porter, Ellen Jane Lorenz** Editor of the *Choir Leader* (Dayton, Ohio; 1894–?). (*AMP*)

**Post, Alice Thatcher** Assistant editor of the *New Church Messenger* (Swedenborgian weekly; Orange, N.J.; 1880s–90s). Assistant editor of the *New Earth* (Swedenborgian monthly; New York; 1889–1900). Assistant editor and then managing editor of the *Public* (weekly review; Chicago and New York, 1898–1918). (*HAM* 4; *WWWA*)

**Potts, Eugenia Dunlap** Editor of the *Illustrated Kentuckian* (literary monthly; Lexington; 1892–94). (*HAM* 4)

**Pratt, Eliza Anna Farman** Editor or co-editor of several children's magazines published in Boston, including *Wide Awake* (1875–93), *Babyland* (1877–98), *Our Little Men and Women* (1880–98), and *Little Folks* (1897–1926). (*AWW*; *CP*; *DAB*)

**Pritchard, Esther Tuttle** Editor and later also owner of the *Friend's Missionary Advocate* (Chicago; 1885–1976). (*AW*)

**Pritchard, Harriet S.** Member of editorial staff of the *Christian Nation* (New York; 1884–1928). Associate editor, with MARTHA A. McCONNELL as editor, of a Pennsylvania *Journal*. (*J*)

**Probosco, Mrs.** Publisher of *American Woman* (reform weekly; Philadelphia; 1845). ("PML"; "RP")

**Proudfoot, Andrea Hofer** Co-editor with her sister AMALIE HOFER and then sole editor of *Child-Garden of Story, Song, and Play* (Chicago and Morgan Park, Ill.; 1892–1903). (*CP*)

**Pugh, Esther** Publisher and editor of *Our Union*, later titled *Union Signal* (temperance journal; Chicago and Evanston, Ill.; 1874–current). (*AW*; *DATB*)

**Purinton, Julia M.** Founder and editor of the *St. Louis Ladies' Magazine* (1871–96). (*HAM* 3; "PWMP")

**Quinton, Amelia Stone** Co-editor with HELEN R. FOOTE and later editor with assistance from MISS C. M. ROCKWELL of the *Indian's Friend* (missionary journal; Philadelphia, Lancaster, Pa., New Haven, Conn., and New York; 1888–1951). (*AI*; *AW*; *NAW*)

**Rainsford, Mrs. M. L.** Editor of *Diana and Ladies' Spectator* (literary magazine; Boston; 1822). (*WPN*)

**Randall-Diehl, Anna** Editor of the *Fortnightly Shakespeare Magazine*, later titled *American Shakespeare Magazine* (New York; 1895–98). Editor of *Literary Life* (Cleveland, Chicago, and New York; 1884–1903). (*HAM* 4)

**Ransom, Emma S.** Editor of *Woman's Light and Love for Heathen Africa* (mission paper; Cleveland). (*Woman's Era*, July 1895)

**Rayne, Martha Louise** Editor of *Chicago Magazine of Fashion, Music and Home Reading* (1870–76). (*HAM* 3)

**Read, Elizabeth C. Bunnell** Editor of the *Mayflower* (literary, suffrage, and temperance journal; Peru, Ind.; 1861–?). Editor and publisher of the *Upper Des Moines* (weekly newspaper; Algona, Iowa; 1865–1902). Co-editor with CARRIE LANE CHAPMAN CATT and EVELYN M. RUSSELL of the *Woman's Standard* (suffrage journal; Des Moines and Waterloo, Iowa; 1886–1911). (*AW*)

**Redding, Josephine** Editor of *Vogue* (society and fashion magazine; New York; 1892–current). (*HAM* 4)

**Reed, Mrs. Gideon F. T.** Owner of the *Arena* (reform magazine; Boston, New York, and Trenton; 1889–1909). (*HAM* 4)

**Reid, Anna** Editor of *Passion Flower* (New York; 1835–36). (announcement in ANN SOPHIA WINTERBOTHAM STEPHENS's *Portland Magazine*, July 1835)

**Reifsnider, Anna Cyrene** Part owner and editor of the *Coming Age* (spiritualist magazine; Boston and St. Louis; 1899–1900). Associate editor of *Farm Machinery* (St. Louis; 1886–1945). (*HAM* 4; *NCAB*)

**Rhodes, Anne** Editor of the children's department of *Leslie's Weekly* (illustrated newspaper; New York; 1855–1922). (*HAM* 2)

**Richards, Louisa Lula Greene** Editor of the *Smithfield Sunday School Gazette* (manuscript paper; Smithfield, Utah; 1869–?). Founding editor of the *Woman's Exponent* (Mormon women's newspaper; Salt Lake City; 1872–1914). Department editor of the *Juvenile Instructor*, later titled *Instructor* (Mormon paper; Salt Lake City; 1866–1970). See also CORNELIA H. HORNE, MINNIE HORNE, and EMMELINE BLANCHE WOODWARD WELLS. (*AWW; SS; VTO*)

**Richmond, Cora L. V.** Medium/editor of *Ouina's Basket* (spiritualist paper; Chicago; 1878). Medium/editor of the *Spiritual Record* (spiritualist paper; Chicago; 1879–80). Medium/editor of the *Weekly Discourse* (spiritualist paper; Chicago; 1886–91). ("NSW")

**Ridley, Florida Ruffin** Co-editor and co-publisher with her mother, JOSEPHINE ST. PIERRE RUFFIN, of the *Woman's Era* (African American women's club journal; Boston; 1894–1903). (*AAPP*)

**Riley, Rebecca Haynes** Editor of the *Southern Literary Journal* (Oxford, Ga.; 1850). (*EGM*)

**Robertson, Ann Augusta** Co-editor of *Our Monthly* (school paper published in both Creek and English; Tullahassee Mission, Creek Nation; 1870–75). (*AI*)

**Robertson, Ann Eliza Worcester** Editor of the Muskogee section of the

*Indian Missionary* (various locations in the Creek, Choctaw, and Cherokee Nations and Oklahoma Territory; 1884–93). (*AI; NAW*)

**Robinson, Abbie C. B.** Assistant editor and then editor of the *Advocate* (newspaper; Green Bay, Wis.; 1846–1906). (*AW*)

**Robinson, Eliza Jane** Co-editor of the *Optimist and Kingdom of Heaven* (spiritualist paper; Anderson and Huntsville, Ind., Berlin Heights, Ohio, and Mammonton, N.J.; 1864–68). ("NSW")

**Robinson, Harriet Jane Hanson** Assistant editor of the *Lowell Courier* (newspaper; Lowell, Mass.; 1835–45). Assistant editor of the *Lowell American* (Free Soil newspaper; Lowell, Mass.; 1849–54). (*AW; AWW; DAB; NAW*)

**Robitaille, Julia** Associate editor, with IDA JOHNSON as editor, of the *Halaquah Times* (manuscript student magazine of the Wyandotte Mission School; Indian Territory; 1871–75). (*AI*)

**Rockwell, Miss C. M.** Assistant editor to AMELIA STONE QUINTON of the *Indian's Friend* (missionary journal; Philadelphia, Lancaster, Pa., New Haven, Conn., and New York; 1888–1951). (*AI*)

**Rockwood, Eleanor D.** Editor of unidentified publication. (*DA*)

**Romney, Caroline Wescott** Editor of the *Record* (Durango, Colo.). Editor of the *Review at Las Animas* (Republican paper; Colo.). (*J*)

**Rorer, Sarah Tyson Heston** Editor and owner of *Table Talk* (culinary magazine; Philadelphia; 1886–1920). Editor of *Household News* (Philadelphia; 1893–96). Domestic editor of *Ladies' Home Journal* (Philadelphia; 1883–current). Editor of the culinary department of *Good Housekeeping* (Holyoke and Springfield, Mass., and New York; 1885–current). (*HAM 3; NAW*)

**Rowland, Lura A.** Business manager and owner, with ORA VERALYN EDDLEMAN as editor, of *Twin Territories: The Indian Magazine* (Muskogee, Creek Nation, Fort Gibson, Cherokee Nation, and Oklahoma City; 1898–1904). (*AI*)

**Rowson, Susanna Haswell** Possibly editor of the *Boston Weekly Magazine* (miscellany aimed primarily at women; 1802–8). (*DAB; NAW*)

**Royall, Anne Newport** Founder and editor, with assistance from SARAH STACK, of *Paul Pry* (weekly newspaper; Washington, D.C.; 1831–36). Founder and editor of the *Huntress* (weekly newspaper; Washington, D.C.; 1836–54). (*AWW; DAB; NAW*)

**Ruffin, Josephine St. Pierre** Founder and co-editor with her daughter, FLORIDA RUFFIN RIDLEY, of the *Woman's Era* (African American women's club journal; Boston; 1894–1903). See also SADA J. ANDERSON, ROSA DIXON BOWSER, DORA J. COLE, ELIZABETH PIPER ENSLEY, S. WILLIE LAYTON, SYLVIA MANN MAPLES, VICTORIA EARLE MATTHEWS, ALICE

WOODBY MCKANE, ALICE RUTH MOORE DUNBAR NELSON, CORA L.
SMITH, MARY CHURCH TERRELL, FANNIE BARRIER WILLIAMS, and
JOSEPHINE SILONE YATES. (*AAPP; NAW*)

**Ruggles, Mrs. H. A.** Editor of the *Western Mirror and Ladies' Literary Gazette*
(St. Louis; 1837). ("EWM")

**Rumsey, Caroline** Co-editor with JENNY RUMSEY of the *Temperance Gem*
(Bath, N.Y.; 1854). ("RP")

**Rumsey, Jenny** See CAROLINE RUMSEY.

**Russell, Evelyn M.** Editor and then co-editor with ELIZABETH C. BUN-
NELL READ and CARRIE LANE CHAPMAN CATT of the *Woman's Standard*
(suffrage journal; Des Moines and Waterloo, Iowa; 1886–1911). (*WPN*)

**Sams, Myrta Eddleman** Business manager and later manager and owner of
the *Muskogee Evening Times*, later titled *Muskogee Times-Democrat* (Muskogee, Creek Nation [later Okla.]; 1896–1971). Co-editor and co-publisher
of *Twin Territories: The Indian Magazine* (Muskogee, Creek Nation, Fort
Gibson, Cherokee Nation, and Oklahoma City; 1898–1904). See also her
sister, ORA VERALYN EDDLEMAN, and her mother, MARY DAUGHERTY
EDDLEMAN. (*AI*)

**Sanford, Rebecca** Editor of the *True Kindred* (Akron, Ohio; 1848). ("RP")

**Sangster, Margaret Elizabeth Munson** Editor of the children's department and later assistant editor of *Hearth and Home* (New York; 1868–75).
Editor of *Christian at Work* (New York; 1866–1926). Editor of the family
page of the *Christian Intelligencer* (New York; 1829–1934). Department editor of *Harper's Young People* (New York; 1879–99). Editor of *Harper's Bazar*
(women's magazine; New York; 1867–current). Member of the editorial staff
of the *Woman's Home Companion* (Cleveland and Springfield, Ohio, and
New York; 1874–1957). (*AW; AWW; DAB; NAW*)

**Sawyer, Caroline Mehitable Fisher** Editor of the youth department of the
*Universalist Union* (New York; 1835–47). Editor of the *Ladies' Repository*
(Universalist monthly; Boston; 1832–74). (*NAW*)

**Schlesinger, Julia** Publisher and co-editor with ELIZABETH LOWE WAT-
SON of *Carrier Dove* (spiritualist journal; Oakland, Calif.; 1884–93). Editor
of *Pacific Coast Spiritualist* (San Francisco; 1893–95). Editor of *Liberator*
(spiritualist journal; San Francisco; 1898). ("NSW")

**Schoolcraft, Jane Johnston** An unofficial but likely assistant editor of the
*Muzzinyegun; or, Literary Voyager* (manuscript magazine devoted to Ojibwa
culture; Sault Ste. Marie, Mich.; 1826–27). See also Schoolcraft's mother,
OZHA-GUSCODAY-WAY-QUAY. (*AI*)

**Schramm, Mrs. R. von Horrum**  Publisher, with HELEN KENDRICK JOHN-SON as editor, of the *Business Woman's Journal* (New York; 1889–96). (*HAM* 4)

**Seavers, Fanny P.**  Editor of the *Nursery* (children's magazine; Boston; 1867–80). (*CP; HAM* 3)

**Severance, Mary Francis Harriman**  Co-editor of the *Literary Northwest* (St. Paul; 1892–93). (*HAM* 4; *WWWA*)

**Sewell, Elizabeth**  Editor of the *Mother's Journal and Family Visitant* (New York and Philadelphia; 1836–72). (*HAM* 2)

**Seymour, Mary Foot**  Founder and editor of the *Business Woman's Journal* (New York; 1889–96). (*AW;* HAW 4; *NAW*)

**Sheldon, Electra**  Editor of the *Western Literary Cabinet* (Detroit; 1853–54). ("EWM"; *HAM* 2)

**Shepard, Olivia F.**  Editor of the *World's Friend* (spiritualist paper; Dobbs Ferry, N.Y.; 1885). ("NSW")

**Sherwood, Emily Lee**  Assistant editor of the *Herald and Era* (Universalist journal; Madison, Ind., Louisville, and Indianapolis; 1850–63). (*AW; DA*)

**Sherwood, Katharine Margaret Brownlee**  Assistant editor and then editor and publisher of the *Williams County Gazette* (weekly newspaper; Bryan, Ohio; 1854–?). Assistant editor of the *Toledo Journal* (daily newspaper; Toledo). Editor of the women's department of the *National Tribune* (Grand Army of the Republic paper; Washington, D.C.; 1880s–90s). (*AW; DAB; NAW*)

**Shields, Sarah Annie Frost**  Editor of *Godey's Lady's Book* (Philadelphia and New York; 1830–98). (*HAM* 1)

**Shindler, Mary Dana**  Editor with ANNIE C. TORREY HAWKS of the *Voice of Truth* (spiritualist magazine; Memphis; 1878). (*AWW;* "NSW")

**Shinn, Milicent Washburn**  Member of the editorial staff of the *San Francisco Commercial Herald* (newspaper; 1867–1911). Managing editor of the *Californian and Overland Monthly* (San Francisco; 1880–82). Editor of the *Overland Monthly* (literary magazine; San Francisco; 1868–1935). (*HAM* 3; *NAW; WWWA*)

**Shipp, Ellis Reynolds**  Co-editor with MARGARET CURTIS SHIPP and their husband, Milford Shipp, of the *Salt Lake Sanitarian* (medical journal; Salt Lake City; 1888–91). (*SS*)

**Shipp, Margaret Curtis**  See ELLIS REYNOLDS SHIPP.

**Shorter, Susie I.**  Department editor of JULIA RINGWOOD COSTON's *Ringwood's Afro-American Journal of Fashion* (Cleveland; 1891–95). (*AAPP*)

**Sigourney, Lydia Howard Huntley**  Co-editor, probably nominally, of

Snowden's *Ladies' Companion* (New York; 1834–44). Editor, nominally, of *Godey's Lady's Book* (Philadelphia and New York; 1830–98). (*AW; AWW; DAB; NAW*)

**Sixkiller, Rachel** Co-editor of column with SUDIE CRABTREE for *Our Brother in Red* (mission paper; Muskogee, Creek Nation, McAlester, Choctaw Nation, Ardmore, Chickasaw Nation, and Oklahoma City; 1882–99). (*AI*)

**Skelton, Henrietta** Editor of *Der Bahnbrecher* (The Pioneer) (German temperance paper). (*AW; DATB*)

**Slocum, Amanda M.** Co-editor of *Common Sense* (spiritualist paper; San Francisco; 1874–75). ("NSW")

**Smiser, Norma E.** Associate editor, co-editor, and then editor of the *Indian Citizen* (Atoka, Choctaw Nation [later Okla.]; 1886–1993). (*AI*)

**Smith, Amanda Berry** Editor of the *Helper* (periodical associated with Smith's home for African American children; Harvey, Ill.; 1899–?). (*AAPP; AWW; NAW*)

**Smith, Annie** Assistant editor of *Youth's Instructor* (religious children's magazine; Rochester, N.Y., Battle Creek, Mich., and Washington, D.C.; 1852–1970). (*CP*)

**Smith, Charlotte** Co-editor with MARY NOLAN and then editor of the *Inland Monthly Magazine* (women's magazine; St. Louis; 1872–78). Editor of *Working Woman* (Washington, D.C.; 1887–91). (*HAM 3; WPN*)

**Smith, Cora L.** Department editor of JOSEPHINE ST. PIERRE RUFFIN'S *Woman's Era* (African American women's club journal; Boston; 1894–1903). (*AAPP*)

**Smith, Elizabeth J.** Editor and publisher of the *Home Guard* (temperance paper; Providence; 1880s–90s). (*AW*)

**Smith, Elizabeth Oakes** Co-editor of the *Great Republic Monthly* (literary monthly; New York; 1859). (*AWW; DAB; HAM 2; NAW*)

**Smith, Helen Morton** Local editor and then managing editor of the *Record* (weekly newspaper; Bar Harbor, Maine; 1887–1917). (*AW*)

**Smith, Lucy Wilmot** Editor of the women's work department of *Our Women and Children* (African American magazine; Louisville; 1888–90). (*AAPP;* "BWJ")

**Smith, Lura Eugenia Brown** Editor of *Arkansas Life*. Department editor of the *Sunday Telegraph* (newspaper; Milwaukee; 1878–99). (*AW*)

**Smith, Mrs. Sydney** Editor of the *Round Table* (literary miscellany; Dallas; 1889–93). (*HAM 4*)

**Snelson, Waterloo B.** Co-editor of the *Negro Educational Journal* (Cartersville and Athens, Ga.; 1894–95). (*AAPP*)

**Sonneschein, Rosa** Editor of the *American Jewess* (New York; 1895–99). (Only known source is the magazine itself.)

**Soper, Grace W.** Member of the editorial staff of the *Boston Journal* (1833–1917). (*J*)

**Soule, Caroline Augusta White** Assistant editor of the *Connecticut Odd Fellow* (Hartford). Western editor of the *Ladies' Repository* (Universalist monthly; Boston; 1852–74). Founder and editor of the *Guiding Star* (Sunday school paper; New York; 1868–70s). Editor of the children's department and briefly editor of the *Christian Leader* (Universalist paper). (*AWW; DA; NAW*)

**Span, Eleanor** Editor of the *Texian Monthly Magazine* (Galveston; 1858). (*HAM* 2)

**Sparhawk, Frances Campbell** Co-editor with MARIANNA BURGESS of the *Red Man* (U.S. Indian Industrial School paper; Carlisle, Pa.; 1880–1904). (*AI; WWA* 4)

**Spaulding, Mrs. H. B.** Editor of a temperance column in *Our Brother in Red* (mission paper; Muskogee, Creek Nation, McAlester, Choctaw Nation, Ardmore, Chickasaw Nation, and Oklahoma City; 1882–99). (*AI*)

**Spencer, Almira** Editor of the *Young Ladies' Journal of Literature and Science* (Baltimore, Md., and Hartford, Conn.; 1830–31). ("SML")

**Spencer, Anna W.** Editor of *Pioneer and Woman's Advocate* (Providence; 1852–?). (*HAM* 2; "RP")

**Spencer, Bella Zilfa** Co-owner and co-editor of the *Saturday Evening Post* (weekly miscellany; Philadelphia; 1821–current). (*HAM* 4)

**Spencer, Martha** Co-editor of *Theocrat* (spiritualist journal; Harmony Springs, Ark.; 1860). ("NSW")

**Spencer, Sara Andrews** Co-editor with THERESA JUAN LEWIS of *Woman's Words: An Original Review of What Women Are Doing* (Philadelphia and Washington, D.C.; 1877–81). (*HBA*, under "Juan" Lewis; *WWA* 1)

**Stack, Sarah** Assistant editor to ANNE NEWPORT ROYALL of *Paul Pry* (weekly newspaper; Washington, D.C.; 1831–36). (*DAB; NAW*, both under Anne Newport Royall)

**Stackhouse, Elnora** Editor of the *Peoria Call*, probably the *Saturday Evening Call and Mirror* (newspaper; Peoria, Ill.; 1877–99). (*J*)

**Stanton, Elizabeth Cady** Co-editor and then editor, with SUSAN BROWNELL ANTHONY as publisher, of the *Revolution* (suffrage journal; New York; 1868–72). Associate editor of the *Ballot Box*, later titled *National Citizen and Ballot Box* (suffrage paper; Toledo, Ohio, and Syracuse, N.Y.; 1876–81). (*AW; AWW; DAB; HAM* 3; *NAW; VTO*)

**Starr, Adella S.** Co-editor with MARY STARR of the *Cooking Club* (Goshen, Ind.; 1895–1917). (*HAM* 4)

**Starr, Ella** Editor of the women's department of *Leslie's Weekly* (illustrated newspaper; New York; 1855–1922). (*HAM* 2; *J*)

**Starr, Laura B.** Editor of *Dorcas Magazine of Woman's Handi-Work* (New York; 1884–85). (*WPN*)

**Starr, Mary** See ADELLA S. STARR.

**Starrett, Helen Elkin** Editor of the *Western Magazine* (Omaha and Chicago; 1876–84). (*HAM* 3; *WWWA*)

**Steinmetz, Lessie Goodell** Co-editor of *Champion of Humanity* (spiritualist paper; New York; 1874). ("NSW")

**Stephens, Ann Sophia Winterbotham** Editor of the *Portland Magazine* (literary monthly; Portland, Maine; 1834–36). Associate editor of Snowden's *Ladies' Companion* (New York; 1834–44). Co-editor of *Graham's Magazine* (literary monthly; Philadelphia; 1826–58). Co-editor of *Peterson's Magazine* (Philadelphia and New York; 1842–98). Editor of *Frank Leslie's Ladies' Gazette of Fashion and Fancy Needlework* (New York; 1854–57). Editor of *Mrs. Stephens' Illustrated New Monthly* (New York; 1856–58). (*AWW; DAB; HAM* 1–2; *NAW*)

**Stevens, Emily Pitts** Editor of the *Pioneer* (women's rights paper; San Francisco; 1869–73). (*AW; EFE*)

**Stevens, Lillian Marion Norton Ames** Editor of the *Union Signal* (temperance journal; Chicago and Evanston, Ill.; 1874–current). (*AW; DATB; NAW*)

**Stevenson, Katharine Adelia Lent** Associate editor of the *Union Signal* (temperance journal; Chicago and Evanston, Ill.; 1874–current). (*DATB*)

**Stewart, Jennie A.** Co-editor with MARGARET ASHMORE SUDDUTH and later sole editor of *Oak and Ivy Leaf* (temperance paper; Chicago; 1887–94). (*SEAP*, under Woman's Christian Temperance Union)

**Stinson, Lizzie** Co-editor of the *Children's Play Ground* (weekly newspaper published by the Cherokee Orphan Asylum; Cherokee Nation; 1881–?). (*AI*)

**Stockham, Alice Bunker** Co-founder and co-editor with CORA L. STOCKHAM of the *Kindergarten Magazine* (Chicago; 1888–1933). See also EMILY KELLOGG. (*AW; HAM* 4)

**Stockham, Cora L.** See ALICE BUNKER STOCKHAM.

**Stockton, Louise** Literary and musical editor of the *Morning Post* (daily newspaper; Philadelphia; 1867–78). Editor of the *New Century for Women* (newspaper for centennial exposition; Philadelphia; 1876). (*DA; NCAB*)

**Stoddard, Anna Elizabeth** Publisher and editor of *Home Light* (women's magazine opposed to secret societies; Boston). (*AW; WWWA*)

**Stone, Ellen Maria** Associate editor of the *Congregationalist*, eventually known as the *Congregationalist and Herald of Gospel Liberty* (Boston; 1816–1934). (*DAB; WWWA*)

**Stone, Emma** Owner and editor of the *Telephone*, later the *Weekly Capital* (Cherokee newspaper; Tahlequah, Cherokee Nation; 1887–96). (*AI*)

**Stone, Lucy** Co-founder and co-editor of the *Woman's Journal* (suffrage paper; Boston; 1870–1932). See also Stone's daughter, ALICE STONE BLACKWELL, JULIA WARD HOWE, MARY ASHTON RICE LIVERMORE, and SUSIE C. VOGL. (*AW; DAB; EFE; NAW; VTO*)

**Stow, Marietta Lois** Editor of the *Woman's Herald of Industry & Social Science Cooperator* (San Francisco; 1881–84). (*WPN*)

**Stowe, Harriet Beecher** Co-editor, with MARY ELIZABETH MAPES DODGE as associate editor, of *Hearth and Home* (New York; 1868–75). Contributing editor to the *Revolution* (suffrage journal; New York; 1868–72). See also SUSAN BROWNELL ANTHONY and ELIZABETH CADY STANTON. (*AW; AWW; DAB; HAM 3; NAW*)

**Stowell, Louise Reed** Co-founder and editor of the *Microscope* (medical journal; Ann Arbor and Detroit, Mich., and Washington, D.C.; 1881–97). (*AW; HAM 3; WWWA*)

**Stuart, Ruth McEnery** Substitute editor of *Harper's Bazar* (women's magazine; New York; 1867–current). (*DAB; NAW*)

**Sudduth, Margaret Ashmore** Editor of the *Union Signal* (temperance journal; Chicago and Evanston, Ill.; 1874–current). Co-editor with JENNIE A. STEWART of *Oak and Ivy Leaf* (temperance paper; Chicago; 1887–94). (*SEAP*)

**Swart, Annie L. Y.** Editor of the *Chaperone* (home and literary monthly; St. Louis; 1889–1911). (*HAM 4*)

**Swenson, Carrie** Editor of *Skandinaviske Spiritulisten* (The Scandinavian Spiritualist) (Minneapolis; 1897). ("NSW")

**Swett, Sophia Mariam** Associate editor of *Wide Awake* (children's magazine; Boston; 1875–93). (*AWW*)

**Swisshelm, Jane Grey Cannon** Editor and publisher of the *Pittsburgh Saturday Visiter* (political and literary weekly; 1848–57). Editor and publisher of the *St. Cloud Visiter* (weekly newspaper; St. Cloud, Minn.; 1857–58). Editor and publisher of the *St. Cloud Democrat* (weekly newspaper; St. Cloud, Minn.; 1858–66). Editor and publisher of the *Reconstructionist* (Republican paper; Washington, D.C.; 1865–66). (*AWW; DAB; NAW;* "RP")

**Tarbell, Ida Minerva** Member of editorial staff of *McClure's Magazine* (general magazine; New York; 1893–1929). Member of the editorial staff of the *Chautauquan* (Meadville, Pa., Cleveland, Springfield, Ohio, and Chautauqua, N.Y.; 1880–1914). Member of the editorial staff of the *American Magazine* (family and journalistic magazine; New York; 1876–1956). (*AWW; HAM* 4; *NAW*)

**Terhune, Mary Virginia Hawes ("Marion Harland")** Department editor of *Wide Awake* (children's magazine; Boston; 1875–93). Department editor of *St. Nicholas* (children's magazine; New York, Columbus, Ohio, and Darien, Conn.; 1873–1943). Editor of *Babyhood* (New York; 1884–1909). Founder and editor of *Home-Maker* (New York; 1888–93). Editor of *Housekeeper's Weekly* (Philadelphia; 1890–93). Department editor for the *Chicago Tribune* (1847–current). (*AW; AWW; DAB; NAW*)

**Terrell, Mary Church** Department editor of JULIA RINGWOOD COSTON's *Ringwood's Afro-American Journal of Fashion* (Cleveland; 1891–95). Department editor of JOSEPHINE ST. PIERRE RUFFIN's *Woman's Era* (African American women's club journal; Boston; 1894–1903). (*AAPP; NCAB; WWA* 3)

**Thomas, Mary Ann** Editor and publisher of the *Record* (newspaper; Springfield, Tenn.; 1869–1919). (*AW*)

**Thomas, Mary Frame Myers** Editor of AMELIA BLOOMER's *Lily* (women's rights journal; Seneca Falls, N.Y., Mount Vernon, Ohio, and Richmond, Ind.; 1849–56). Associate editor of the *Mayflower* (literary, suffrage, and temperance journal; Peru, Ind.; 1861–?). (*NAW*)

**Thompson, Eva Griffith** Owner and editor of the *News* (Indiana, Pa.). (*AW*)

**Thompson, Miss J. C.** Editor of *Woman's Work for Woman* (Christian mission paper; Philadelphia; 1875–85). (*WPN*)

**Tilghman, Amelia L.** Editor, with assistance from LUCINDA BRAGG ADAMS, of the *Musical Messenger* (African American magazine of music; Montgomery, Ala., and Washington, D.C.; 1886–89). (*AAPP*; "BWJ")

**Tingley, Katherine Augusta Westcott** Founder and editor of several theosophical periodicals published from Point Loma, Calif., including *New Century* (New York and Point Loma; 1897–1911), the *Râja Yoga Messenger* (1904–29), the *Theosophical Path* (1911–35), *El Sendero Teosofico* (a Spanish edition of *Theosophical Path;* 1911–17), and the *New Way* (1911–29). (*DAB; NAW; WWWA*)

**Todd, Marion Marsh** Editor of the *Express* (national reform weekly; Chicago; 1890s). (*AW; AWW*)

**Tomlin, Mary** Founder with MARIA HAWLEY and editor with Hawley, MRS. E. MACKWAY, and ODELIA BLINN of the *Balance* (women's paper; Chicago; 1871–75). (*DA*)

**Tompkins, Juliet Wilbor** Editor of the *Puritan* (women's magazine; New York; 1897–1901). (*HAM* 4)

**Toomer, Adele** Editor of *Over the Tea Cups* (society paper; Springfield, Mo.). ("PWMP")

**Tourgée, Emma Lodoiska** Assistant editor of the *Continent* (general weekly; Philadelphia and New York; 1882–84). (*ALM; HAM* 3)

**Towne, Belle Kellogg** Editor of *Young People's Weekly* (Elgin, Ill.; 1887–?). Managing editor of *Girls' Companion* (Elgin, Ill.; 1902–49). (*AW; CP*)

**Towne, Elizabeth Lois Struble** Editor of *Nautilus Magazine of New Thought* (Portland, Oreg., Sioux Falls, S. Dak., and Holyoke, Mass.; 1898–1951). (*HAM* 4; *NCAB*)

**Townsend, Virginia Frances** Assistant editor and then co-editor of *Arthur's Home Magazine* (Philadelphia; 1852–98). (*ACAB; HAM* 2; *NCAB*)

**Trembley, Jennie R.** Editor of *Youth's Instructor* (religious children's magazine; Rochester, N.Y., Battle Creek, Mich., and Washington, D.C.; 1852–1970). (*CP*)

**Tretbar, Helen D.** Editor of *Musical Items* (New York; 1883–87). (*AMP*)

**Trott, Novella Jewell** Editor of *Practical Housekeeper* (Portland, Maine; 1886–94). Editor of *Daughters of America* (Augusta, Maine; 1886–94). (*AW*)

**Tupper, Ellen Smith** Editor of the *Bee-Keepers' Journal*. (*AW; DA*)

**Twing, Mrs. A. T.** Editor of *Church Work* (New York; 1885–89). (*WPN*)

**Tyson, Miss W. C.** Editor of *Youth's Friend* (Augusta, Ga.; 1850). (*EGM*)

**Underhill, Sarah E.** Editor, with assistance from AMANDA M. WAY, of the *Woman's Tribune* (newspaper; Indianapolis). (*NAW*, under Amanda M. Way)

**Underwood, Sara A.** Associate editor of *Open Court* (Chicago; 1887–1936). Editor of women's department for the *Religio-Philosophical Journal*, later titled *Philosophical Journal* (Chicago and San Francisco; 1865–1905). (*J; WWA* 1)

**Van Duyne, Miss** Editor of *Harper's Young People* (New York; 1879–99). (*CP*)

**Vaughan, Mary C.** Editor of the *Woman's Temperance Paper* (New York; 1854). ("RP")

**Victor, Metta Victoria Fuller** Co-editor and then editor of the *Cosmopolitan Art Journal* (New York; 1856–61). Assistant editor of the *United States Journal* (New York; 1858–60). Editor of the *Home* (Buffalo and New York; 1856–60). (*AW; AWW; NAW*)

**Vogl, Susie C.** Business manager of LUCY STONE's *Woman's Journal* (suffrage paper; Boston; 1870–1932). (*J*)

**Waite, Catherine Van Valkenburg** Editor and publisher of the *Chicago Law Times* (1886–89). (*AW; NAW*)

**Wakeman, Antoinette Van Hoesen** Editor and publisher of the *Journal of Industrial Education* (Chicago; 1886–94). Editor of unidentified fashion magazine in New York. Editor of *American Housekeeping*. Member of editorial staff responsible for women's issues in the *Chicago Evening Post* (1890–1932). (*AW; WWWA*)

**Walker, Lulu** Associate editor with ARIZONA JACKSON (with IDA JOHNSON as editor) of the *Hallequah* (Seneca, Shawnee, and Wyandotte Industrial Boarding School paper; Quapaw Agency, Indian Territory; 1879–81). (*AI*)

**Walker, Mary L.** Editor of *Sorosis* (suffrage paper; Chicago; 1868–69). Associate editor, with MARY ASHTON RICE LIVERMORE as publisher and editor, of the *Agitator* (suffrage paper; Chicago; 1869). (*HAM 3*)

**Walker, Rose Kershaw** Owner and editor of *Fashion and Fancy* (fashion and society magazine; St. Louis; 1889–91). (*AW*)

**Walter, Cornelia Wells** Editor of the *Boston Transcript* (newspaper; 1830–1941). (*NAW*)

**Ward, Susan Hayes** Literary editor of the *Independent* (religious and literary weekly; New York and Boston; 1848–1928). (*HAM 2; WWWA*)

**Ware, Katherine Augusta** Editor of the *Bower of Taste* (women's magazine; Boston; 1828–30). ("BG")

**Warner, Anna Bartlett** Editor, with sister SUSAN BOGERT WARNER, of the *Little American* (children's magazine; West Point, N.Y.; 1862–64). (*AWW; NAW*)

**Warner, Susan Bogert** See ANNA BARTLETT WARNER.

**Warren, Harriet Cornelia Merrick** Editor of the *Heathen Woman's Friend*, later titled *Woman's Missionary Friend* (Boston; 1869–1940). Editor of *Der Heidenfrauen Freund* (The Heathen Women's Friend). (*DAB*, under her husband, William Fairfield Warren)

**Washington, Margaret Murray** Editor of the *National Association Notes* (newsletter of the National Association of Colored Women; Tuskegee; 1897–current). Department editor of JOSEPHINE ST. PIERRE RUFFIN's *Woman's Era* (African American women's club journal; Boston; 1894–1903). (*AAPP*)

**Watson, Elizabeth Lowe** Co-editor with JULIA SCHLESINGER of *Carrier Dove* (spiritualist journal; Oakland, Calif.; 1884–93). (*AW; HAM 3*; "NSW")

**Way, Amanda M.** Assistant editor to SARAH E. UNDERHILL of the *Woman's Tribune* (newspaper; Indianapolis). (*DATB; NAW*)

**Webb, Laura** Co-editor and co-publisher with MARY BOWEN of *South St. Louis* (weekly). ("PWMP")

**Wells, Charlotte Fowler** Editor and publisher of the *Phrenological Journal and Science of Health* (Philadelphia and New York; 1838–1911). (*AW; NAW*)

**Wells, Emmeline Blanche Woodward** Associate editor and then editor and publisher of LOUISA LULA GREENE RICHARDS's *Woman's Exponent* (Mormon women's newspaper; Salt Lake City; 1872–1914). (*AWW; NAW; SS; VTO*)

**Wentworth, Ella [pseud.]** Co-editor with MRS. E. K. BANKS of the *Literary Journal* (Cincinnati; 1854). (*BLC;* "EWM")

**West, Mary Allen** Editor of *Our Home Monthly* (Philadelphia; 1870–74). Assistant editor, with MARY BANNISTER WILLARD as editor, of the *Signal* (temperance journal; Chicago; 1880–82). Editor, with assistance from ELIZABETH W. ANDREW, of the *Union Signal* (temperance journal; Chicago and Evanston, Ill.; 1874–current). (*AW; SEAP*)

**Wheeler, Cora Stuart** Editor of the *Yankee Blade* (general magazine; Waterville and Gardiner, Maine, and Boston; 1841–94). (*AW; HAM 2; J*)

**Whitaker, Alice E.** Co-editor of the *Southbridge Journal* (newspaper; Southbridge, Mass.; 1861–1900). Co-editor of the *New England Farmer* (Boston; 1822–46 and 1865–1913). Co-editor of *Our Grange Homes* (Boston; 1887–94). (*HAM 3; J; WWWA*)

**Whitaker, Mary S.** Co-editor of *Whitaker's Magazine: The Rights of the South* (Charleston, S.C.; 1850–51). (Only known source is the magazine itself.)

**White, Adina E.** Art editor of JULIA RINGWOOD COSTON's *Ringwood's Afro-American Journal of Fashion* (Cleveland; 1891–95). (*AAPP*)

**White, Anna** Editor of *Youth's Instructor* (religious children's magazine; Rochester, N.Y., Battle Creek, Mich., and Washington, D.C.; 1852–1970). (*CP*)

**White, Mary K.** Co-editor of *Youth's Instructor* (religious children's magazine; Rochester, N.Y., Battle Creek, Mich., and Washington, D.C.; 1852–1970). (*CP*)

**Whiting, Lilian** Art and literary editor of the *Boston Evening Traveler* (newspaper; Boston; 1845–89). Editor of *Boston Budget* (weekly home journal; 1879–1918). (*AW; AWW; NAW*)

**Whiting, Lucretia Calista Clement** Assistant editor of the *Bureau County Republican* (weekly newspaper; Princeton, Ill.; 1858–current). (*AW; AWW*, both under her daughter, Lilian Whiting)

**Whitney, Mary Traffarn** Editor of *Familyculture* (Boston; 1896–97). (*AW; WPN*)

**Whitney, Sarah Ware** Editor of the *Woman's Standard* (suffrage journal; Des Moines and Waterloo, Iowa; 1886–1911). (*WPN*)

**Whittelsey, Abigail Goodrich** Editor of the *Mother's Magazine* (Utica, N.Y., and New York; 1833–88). Founder and editor of *Mrs. Whittelsey's Magazine for Mothers* (New York; 1850–52). (*DAB; NAW*)

**Willard, Frances Elizabeth Caroline** One of the founders and also editor of *Our Union*, later titled *Union Signal* (temperance journal; Chicago and Evanston, Ill.; 1874–current). Assistant editor to her sister-in-law, MARY BANNISTER WILLARD, of *Post and Mail* (daily paper; Chicago; 1865–78). One of the founders of the *Signal* (temperance journal; Chicago; 1880–82). Associate editor of *Our Day* (reform monthly; Boston, Chicago, Dansville, N.Y., and Dayton, Ohio; 1888–1913). (*AW; AWW; DAB; NAW*)

**Willard, Mary Bannister** Editor, with assistance from her sister-in-law, FRANCES ELIZABETH CAROLINE WILLARD, of *Post and Mail* (daily paper; Chicago; 1865–78). Editor of the *Signal* (temperance journal; Chicago; 1880–82). Editor of the *Union Signal* (temperance journal; Chicago and Evanston, Ill.; 1874–current). (*AW; HAM 3; WT*)

**Williams, Fannie Barrier** Department editor of JOSEPHINE ST. PIERRE RUFFIN's *Woman's Era* (African American women's club journal; Boston; 1894–1903). (*AWW; NAW; AAPP*)

**Williams, Florence B.** Editor of the *Eagle* (weekly county newspaper; Statesboro, Ga.; 1884–94). Founder and editor of the *Telescope* (news and literary paper; Valdosta, Ga.; 1892–?). (*AW*)

**Williams, Mrs. M. E.** Publisher and editor of *Beacon Light* (spiritualist paper; New York; 1885–87). ("NSW")

**Williams, Sarah Langdon** Editor of the women's department of the *Toledo Blade* (newspaper; 1835–current). Editor of the *Ballot Box*, later titled *National Citizen and Ballot Box* (suffrage paper; Toledo, Ohio, and Syracuse, N.Y.; 1876–81). (*DA; HAM 3*)

**Willing, Jennie Fowler** First editor of *Our Union*, later titled *Union Signal* (temperance journal; Chicago and Evanston, Ill.; 1874–current). (*AW; HAM 3; NAW*)

**Wilson, Miss A. V.** Editor of the women's department of *Our Brother in Red* (mission paper; Muskogee, Creek Nation, McAlester, Choctaw Nation, Ardmore, Chickasaw Nation, and Oklahoma City; 1882–99). (*AI*)

**Wilson, Mrs. Augustus** Founder and editor of the *Journal* (newspaper; Wilsonton, Kans.; 1888–1908). (*AW*)

**Winchester, Mrs. A. S.** Co-publisher of *Light for All* (spiritualist paper; San Francisco; 1880–83). ("NSW")

**Winkler, Angelina Virginia** Editor of *Texas Prairie Flower* (literary magazine; Corsicana, Tex.; 1882–85). Associate editor and business manager of the *Round Table* (literary miscellany; Dallas; 1889–93). (*AW*)

**Winslow, Helen Maria**  Drama editor of the *Boston Beacon* (society weekly; 1884–1904). Assistant editor of the *Woman's Cycle* (club journal; New York; 1889–96). Editor and publisher of the *Club Woman* (Boston; 1897–1904). Founder and editor of "Woman's Club Column" in the *Boston Transcript* (newspaper; 1830–1941). Editor of the women's club department of the *Delineator* (fashion and literary monthly; New York; 1873–1937). (*AW; AWW; WWWA*)

**Winslow, Margaret Elizabeth**  Editor of *Our Union*, later titled *Union Signal* (temperance journal; Chicago and Evanston, Ill.; 1874–current). (*WT*)

**Wittenmyer, Annie Turner**  Editor and publisher of the *Christian Woman* (Philadelphia; 1871–80s). One of the founders and publisher of *Our Union*, later titled *Union Signal* (temperance journal; Chicago and Evanston, Ill.; 1874–current). Associate editor of *Home and Country* (New York; 1885–97). Column editor for the *Weekly Tribune* (newspaper; New York; 1841–1906). Founder and editor of the *Christian Child*. (*AW; DA; DATB; NAW; SEAP*)

**Wood, Ione E.**  Temperance editor of *Our Women and Children* (African American magazine; Louisville; 1888–90). (*AAPP;* "BWJ"; *J*)

**Wood, Julia Amanda Sargent**  Editor of the *New Era*, formerly the *Sauk Rapids Frontiersman* (newspaper; Sauk Rapids, Minn.; 1855–63). Co-editor of the *Free Press* (weekly newspaper; Sauk Rapids, Minn.; 1885–1903). (*AW; NAW*)

**Wood, Mary Camilla Foster**  Co-founder and co-editor of the *Index* (newspaper; Santa Barbara, Calif.; 1872–77). Co-founder and editor of the *Daily Independent* (newspaper; Santa Barbara, Calif.; 1883–?). (*AW*)

**Wood-Allen, Mary**  Editor of *Mothers' Friend*, later titled *American Motherhood* (Ann Arbor, Mich., and Cooperstown, N.Y.; 1895–1919). (*HAM* 4; *WWA* 1)

**Woodbridge, Mary A. Brayton**  Editor of the *Amendment Herald* (weekly temperance paper). (*AW*)

**Woodhull, Victoria Claflin**  Co-editor and co-publisher, with her sister, TENNESSEE CELESTE CLAFLIN, of *Woodhull & Claflin's Weekly* (magazine advocating women's suffrage, free love, and workers' rights; New York; 1870–76). (*AWW; DAB; HAM* 3; *NAW*)

**Woods, Roma Wheeler**  Editor of the *Woman's Standard* (suffrage journal; Des Moines and Waterloo, Iowa; 1886–1911). (*WPN; WWWA*)

**Worden, Harriet M.**  Editor of the *Oneida Circular* (journal of perfectionist communities; Brooklyn and Oneida, N.Y., and Wallingford, Conn.; 1851–76). (*AP*)

**Wright, Frances**  Co-editor and co-publisher of the *New-Harmony Gazette*, later titled *Free Enquirer* (socialist journal; New Harmony, Ind.; 1825–35). Editor of the *Sentinel*, later titled *New York Sentinel and Working Man's Advocate* and then *Young America* (reform paper; New York; 1829–49). (*AWW; DAB; HAM* 1; *NAW; UFF*)

**Wright, Laura** Likely co-editor of *Ne Jaguhnigŏageśgwathah* (The Mental Elevator) (mission paper; Buffalo Creek and Cattaraugus Reservations; 1841–50). (*AI; NAW*).

**Wylie, Lollie Bell** Society editor of the *Atlanta Journal* (newspaper; 1883–current). Founder and editor of *Society* (Atlanta; 1890–92). (*AW*)

**Wyly, Captola** Editor of the women's department of the *Telephone*, later the *Weekly Capital* (Cherokee newspaper; Tahlequah, Cherokee Nation; 1887–96). (*AI*)

**Yates, Josephine Silone** Department editor of JOSEPHINE ST. PIERRE RUFFIN's *Woman's Era* (African American women's club journal; Boston; 1894–1903). Editor of the education department of the *Colored American Magazine* (Boston and New York; 1900–1909). Associate editor of the *Negro Educational Review* (Vincennes, Ind.; 1904–7). (*AAPP*)

**Young, Carrie** Editor of the *Pacific Journal* (monthly; San Francisco; 1879–72). (*DA*)

# NOTES

## Introduction

1. The most complete bibliography of Hale's work is in Jacob Blanck, comp., *Bibliography of American Literature*, 9 vols. (New Haven, Conn.: Yale University Press, 1955–91). The many collections in which Hale's work appears include John S. Hart, *The Female Prose Writers of America* (Philadelphia: E. H. Butler, 1852); Rufus Wilmot Griswold, *The Poets and Poetry of America* (Philadelphia: Carey and Hart, 1842); idem, *The Female Poets of America* (Philadelphia: Carey and Hart, 1849); Caroline May, *The American Female Poets* (Philadelphia: Lindsay and Blakiston, 1848); and Evert A. Duyckinck and George L. Duyckinck, *Cyclopaedia of American Literature*, 2 vols. (New York: Scribner, 1855).

2. More has been written about Hale's authorship of "Mary's Lamb" than any other facet of her career. See E. A. Warren, "The True Story of Mary and Her Little Lamb," *National Magazine*, June 1897, 251–55; Richard Walden Hale, " 'Mary Had a Little Lamb' and Its Author," *Century Magazine*, March 1904, 738–42; George Bancroft Griffith, "Author of 'Mary's Little Lamb,' " *Granite State Magazine*, May 1906, 210–14; and "The True Story of Mary's Little Lamb," *Dearborn Independent*, 26 March 1927, 12–13, 20–22. The author of a short book, *The Story of Mary and Her Little Lamb, as Told by Mary and Her Neighbors and Friends* (Dearborn, Mich.: Mr. and Mrs. Henry Ford, 1928), claims that John Roulstone—not Hale—originally wrote the poem, arguing in considerable detail that Hale could not have written the first twelve lines and that she simply expanded and popularized Roulstone's poem. Interest in the poem has hardly abated over time. See, for example, Joseph Kastner, "The Tale Behind Mary's Little Lamb," *New York Times Magazine*, 13 April 1980, 116–19.

3. Algernon Tassin, *The Magazine in America* (New York: Dodd, Mead, 1916), 103; William R. Taylor, *Cavalier and Yankee: The Old South and American National Character* (New York: George Braziller, 1961), 116; John Tebbel, *The American Magazine: A Compact History* (New York: Hawthorn Books, 1969), 50.

4. Frank Luther Mott, *A History of American Magazines*, 5 vols. (Cambridge, Mass.: Harvard University Press, 1938–68), 1: 349, 587; Elizabeth H. Davis, "*Godey's Lady's Book*, 1830–1898," *Kansas State Agricultural College Bulletin* 14 (Dec. 1930): 4.

For more on how modernist writers and critics relied on binary and ultimately gendered oppositions such as "modernism" versus "sentimentalism" and "literary" versus "popular," see Suzanne Clark, *Sentimental Modernism: Women Writers and the Revolution of the Word* (Bloomington: Indiana University Press, 1991).

5. Ruth E. Finley, *The Lady of Godey's: Sarah Josepha Hale* (Philadelphia: J. B. Lippincott, 1931).

6. Isabelle Webb Entrikin, *Sarah Josepha Hale and "Godey's Lady's Book"* (Lancaster, Pa.: Lancaster Press, 1946), v, 5.

7. Olive Burt, *First Woman Editor: Sarah J. Hale* (New York: Messner, 1960); Norma R. Fryatt, *Sarah Josepha Hale: The Life and Times of a Nineteenth-Century Career Woman* (New York: Hawthorn Books, 1975); Sherbrooke Rogers, *Sarah Josepha Hale: A New England Pioneer, 1788–1879* (Grantham, N.H.: Tompson and Rutter, 1985).

8. Nicole Tonkovich Hoffman, "*Legacy* Profile: Sarah Josepha Hale," *Legacy* 7 (Fall 1990): 47–55; Barbara Bardes and Suzanne Gossett, *Declarations of Independence: Women and Political Power in Nineteenth-Century American Fiction* (New Brunswick, N.J.: Rutgers University Press, 1990); Nina Baym, "Onward Christian Women: Sarah J. Hale's History of the World," *New England Quarterly* 63 (1990): 249–70; idem, *Feminism and American Literary History: Essays* (New Brunswick, N.J.: Rutgers University Press, 1992), 167–82.

## 1. Women Periodical Editors
### in the Nineteenth-Century United States

1. Marion Tuttle Marzolf, *Up from the Footnote: A History of Women Journalists* (New York: Hastings House, 1977), 1–8.

2. Ibid., 10–11.

3. Numerous scholars have suggested that Rowson did edit the *Boston Weekly*. For an account of the questions associated with these claims, see Dorothy Weil, *In Defense of Women: Susanna Rowson, 1762–1824* (University Park: Pennsylvania State University Press, 1976), 170–71 n. 16. Here and elsewhere, I have relied on the following sources by Bertha Monica Stearns for information about early American magazines for women: "Before *Godey's*," *American Literature* 2 (1930): 248–55; "Early New England Magazines for Ladies," *New England Quarterly* 2 (1929): 420–57; "Early Philadelphia Magazines for Ladies," *Pennsylvania Magazine of History and Biography* 64 (1940): 479–91; "Early Western Magazines for Ladies," *Mississippi Valley Historical Review* 18 (1931): 319–30; and "Southern Magazines for Ladies, 1819–1860," *South Atlantic Quarterly* 31 (1932): 70–87.

4. On the expansion of magazines in the United States after 1825, see Mott, *History of American Magazines* 1: 340–43.

5. Bradwell's work with the *Legal News* suggests that periodicals may have provided professional opportunities for women that were otherwise denied them. Although in 1869 she was refused admission to the Illinois bar on the basis of her sex, Bradwell achieved a long professional law career through her *Legal News*, which she edited until her death in 1894. Bradwell's paper continued until 1925 under the editorship first of her husband, James Bolesworth Bradwell, and then of their daughter, Bessie Bradwell Helmer, a graduate of Union College of Law (later Northwestern University Law School).

6. For an overview, see Bertha Monica Stearns, "Reform Periodicals and Female Reformers, 1830–1860," *American Historical Review* 37 (1932): 678–99.

7. See Ann Braude, "News from the Spirit World: A Checklist of American Spiritualist Periodicals, 1847–1900," *Proceedings of the American Antiquarian Society* 99 (1989): 399–462. A good place to begin a study of other religious periodicals is Charles H. Lippy, ed., *Religious Periodicals of the United States: Academic and Scholarly Journals*, Historical Guides to the World's Periodicals and Newspapers (New York: Greenwood Press, 1986). Mott also discusses religious periodicals in *History of American Magazines*.

8. For example, as Daniel F. Littlefield Jr. and James W. Parins suggest, Cora and Thomas Bland's *Council Fire* opposed military action against the Indians but also advocated assimilation, including off-reservation schools, as the solution to the "Indian problem." As the paper itself declared, the *Council Fire* was "devoted" not only to the "rights of the American Indian" but also to their "civilization." More religious periodicals like Elizabeth Keller Shaule Crannell's *Indian Advocate*, which promoted both the "civilization" and the

"evangelization" of the American Indian population, were even stronger in their ethnocentrism. See Daniel F. Littlefield Jr. and James W. Parins, *American Indian and Alaska Native Newspapers and Periodicals, 1826–1924*, Historical Guides to the World's Periodicals and Newspapers (Westport, Conn.: Greenwood Press, 1984), 116–21, 167–68.

9. In describing the *Hallequah*, I have relied on Littlefield and Parins, *American Indian and Alaska Native Newspapers and Periodicals* 144–45. Littlefield and Parins describe another periodical that apparently supported tribal identity to some extent. Published from the Tullahassee Manual Labor School in Creek Nation, *Our Monthly* was edited by the Reverend William S. Robertson and his daughter, Ann Augusta Robertson, yet most of the contributions came from the Creek students, much of the contents was written in Creek, and the paper did not shy away from criticizing U.S. policies that threatened the Creek Nation. One letter in *Our Monthly*, for example, attacked the Treaty of 1866, which favored the railroad industry in land disputes. Perhaps because of these efforts, the editors received considerable financial support from the Creek Nation: the Creek National Council donated funds to purchase a printing press and type and later subsidized printing costs so that the paper could be distributed free within the Creek Nation. See Littlefield and Parins, 293–96.

10. For example, Charles H. Parrish and William J. Simmons enlisted women to serve as department editors for their African American magazine, *Our Women and Children*. Among those serving in this capacity were Mary Virginia Cook, Ione E. Wood, Lucy Wilmot Smith, and Ida B. Wells Barnett.

11. On African American women's contributions to nineteenth-century periodicals, see J. William Snorgrass, "Black Women and Journalism, 1800–1950," *Western Journal of Black Studies* 6 (1982): 150–58; and Penelope L. Bullock, *The Afro-American Periodical Press, 1838–1909* (Baton Rouge: Louisiana State University Press, 1981). Also helpful is Lucy Wilmot Smith's contemporary account, "Some Female Writers of the Negro Race," *Journalist*, 26 Jan. 1889.

12. For circulation figures related to the *Dial*, see Mott, *History of American Magazines* 1: 702–10. For information on the *Hallequah*, see Littlefield and Parins, *American Indian and Alaska Native Newspapers and Periodicals* 144–45. On *Kvinden og Hjemmet*, see Marion Tuttle Marzolf, *The Danish-Language Press in America* (New York: Arno Press, 1979), 105. Subscription rates for *Godey's Lady's Book* come from the magazine itself (July 1860, 83).

13. On the idea of "separate spheres" as a constantly shifting and negotiated metaphor used by people, including historians, to explain both liberating and oppressive relations among people, see Linda K. Kerber, "Separate Spheres,

Female Worlds, Woman's Place: The Rhetoric of Women's History," *Journal of American History* 75 (1988): 9–39. Other significant sources treating this idea include Barbara Welter, "The Cult of True Womanhood, 1820–1860," *American Quarterly* 18 (1966): 151–74; Aileen S. Kraditor, ed., *Up from the Pedestal: Selected Writings in the History of American Feminism* (Chicago: Quadrangle Books, 1968); Gerda Lerner, "The Lady and the Mill Girl: Changes in the Status of Women in the Age of Jackson," *Midcontinent American Studies Journal* 10 (1969): 5–15; Carroll Smith-Rosenberg, "The Female World of Love and Ritual: Relations Between Women in Nineteenth-Century America," *Signs: Journal of Women in Culture and Society* 1 (1975): 1–29; and Nancy F. Cott, *The Bonds of Womanhood: "Woman's Sphere" in New England, 1780–1835* (New Haven, Conn.: Yale University Press, 1977).

14. During the Civil War, Louis Godey commended the Union soldiers for reading his magazine (*Godey's Lady's Book*, March 1865, 284).

15. The relationship between popular constructions of "woman" and women's editing possibilities is further suggested by the number of women who edited periodicals for children. Though the association of women with children hardly originated in the nineteenth century, women editing periodicals for children fit well with the Victorian construction of woman as moral and maternal.

16. Jane Swisshelm, *Half a Century* (Chicago: J. G. Swisshelm, 1880), 113–14.

17. Sandra A. Zagarell, introduction to *A New Home, Who'll Follow?; or, Glimpses of Western Life*, by Caroline M. Kirkland, ed. Sandra A. Zagarell, American Women Writers Series (New Brunswick, N.J.: Rutgers University Press, 1990), xxi.

18. See, for instance, the *Portland Magazine*, Nov. 1834, 63; March 1836, 192.

19. Estelle Freedman, "Separatism as Strategy: Female Institution Building and American Feminism, 1870–1930," *Feminist Studies* 5 (1979): 512–29. Although the Woman's Temple was completed, it proved to be a severe financial liability and was sold in 1898.

20. On Abigail Scott Duniway's debt to Emily Pitts Stevens, see Patricia Smith Butcher, *Education for Equality: Women's Rights Periodicals and Women's Higher Education, 1849–1920*, Contributions in Women's Studies, no. 111 (New York: Greenwood Press, 1989), 6.

21. Caroline Kirkland responded in a slightly different fashion to suggest the importance of community among women editors. When the publishers of *Sartain's Union Magazine of Literature and Art*, which Kirkland was then editing, objected to a piece published in *Godey's Lady's Book*, Kirkland wrote that she

was "much troubled at the idea of being implicated in any unfriendly rivalry with the *Lady's Book*—Mrs. Hale's being considered both by Mrs. Howitt and . myself as a friend would make it particularly painful to be arrayed against her" (in Zagarell, introduction to *A New Home, Who'll Follow?* xxii).

22. The sense of community must have been particularly strong among the women who joined sisters or mothers in becoming editors. Editors who either followed in the footsteps of mothers or sisters or worked with female relatives included the sisters Victoria Claflin Woodhull and Tennessee Claflin; Lucretia Whiting and her daughter, Lilian Whiting; Sarah Irwin Meloney and her daughter, Marie Mattingly Meloney; Ann Eliza Robertson and her daughter, Ann Augusta Robertson; Teresa Beatrice O'Hare and her daughter, Anne O'Hare McCormick; Mary Daugherty Eddleman and her two daughters, Myrta Eddleman Sams and Ora Eddleman; Mrs. A. B. Cowell and her mother, Hittie Pond; and Ellis Reynolds Shipp and Margaret Curtis Shipp, Mormon physicians and "sister-wives" who, together with their husband, Milford Shipp, edited a Salt Lake City medical journal.

23. Kathryn Shevelow, "Fathers and Daughters: Women as Readers of the *Tatler*," in *Gender and Reading: Essays on Readers, Texts, and Contexts*, ed. Elizabeth A. Flynn and Patrocinio P. Schweickart (Baltimore: Johns Hopkins University Press, 1986), 121; Smith-Rosenberg, "Female World of Love and Ritual" 2.

24. See, for example, Louisa Knapp's references to readers as "our friends," "old friends," and "sisters" (*Ladies' Home Journal*, Sept. 1884, 4).

25. In subsequent citations of *Godey's Lady's Book*, I will use the abbreviation *GLB*.

26. Many scholars have asserted that nineteenth-century American women writers struggled with the tension between authorial position and womanhood. Ann Douglas, for instance, has portrayed nineteenth-century women writers as "professionals masquerading as amateurs." Sandra M. Gilbert and Susan Gubar have argued that women writers responded to social definitions of literary creation as a masculine act by assuming self-effacing stances that produced what these two scholars have called the anxiety of authorship. Mary Kelley, likewise, asserts that "literary domestics" experienced a "continuing crisis of identity" between their roles as public writers and private women. However disparate their arguments, these scholars all suggest that women had trouble presenting professional images of themselves. See Ann Douglas, *The Feminization of American Culture* (New York: Alfred A. Knopf, 1977), 85; Sandra M. Gilbert and Susan Gubar, *The Madwoman in the Attic: The Woman Writer and the Nineteenth-Century Literary Imagination* (New Haven, Conn.: Yale Univer-

sity Press, 1979), 3–7, 45–53; and Mary Kelley, *Private Woman, Public Stage: Literary Domesticity in Nineteenth-Century America* (New York: Oxford University Press, 1984), 111. For studies by scholars that see less tension between constructions of public authorship and womanhood, see Nina Baym, *Woman's Fiction: A Guide to Novels by and about Women in America, 1820–1870*, 2d ed. (Urbana: University of Illinois Press, 1993); and Judith Fetterley, ed., *Provisions: A Reader from 19th-Century American Women* (Bloomington: Indiana University Press, 1985).

27. Quoted in Phebe A. Hanaford, *Daughters of America; or, Women of the Century* (Augusta, Maine: True and Co., 1883), 674–75, 206.

28. Frances E. Willard and Mary A. Livermore, eds., *American Women*, 2 vols. (1897; rpt., Detroit: Gale Research, 1973), 2: 474.

29. For my sketch of Miriam Squier Leslie, I have relied on Madeleine B. Stern, *Purple Passage: The Life of Mrs. Frank Leslie* (Norman: University of Oklahoma Press, 1953). Leslie is one of the many women editors of the nineteenth century who deserve more scholarly attention.

30. Jacqueline Van Voris, *Carrie Chapman Catt: A Public Life* (New York: Feminist Press, 1987), 143–45, 250.

31. For a fine analysis of quilting as a metaphor for women's writing, see Elaine Showalter, *Sister's Choice: Tradition and Change in American Women's Writing* (Oxford: Clarendon Press, 1991), 145–75.

32. Such is clearly the case with Poe's "Cask of Amontillado." Appearing in the month following his series "Literati of New York City," in which Poe attacked his critics, "Cask" has been read as Poe's comments on his literary feud with Hiram Fuller and Thomas Dunn English. See, for example, Francis B. Dedmond, " 'The Cask of Amontillado' and the War of the Literati," *Modern Language Quarterly* 15 (1954): 137–46; and Kenneth Silverman, *Edgar A. Poe: Mournful and Never-Ending Remembrance* (New York: HarperCollins, 1991), 316–17.

## 2. From Intellectual Equality to Moral Difference

1. Thomas Laqueur, *Making Sex: Body and Gender from the Greeks to Freud* (Cambridge, Mass.: Harvard University Press, 1990), 5–6; Baym, *Feminism and American Literary History* 105–20. See also Joan B. Landes, *Women and the Public Sphere in the Age of the French Revolution* (Ithaca, N.Y.: Cornell University Press, 1988); and Londa Schiebinger, *The Mind Has No Sex?: Women in the Origins of Modern Science* (Cambridge, Mass.: Harvard University Press,

1989), esp. chaps. 6–8. For an analysis of the shift away from what Laqueur calls the two-sex model in the late nineteenth and early twentieth centuries, see Rosalind Rosenberg, *Beyond Separate Spheres: Intellectual Roots of Modern Feminism* (New Haven, Conn.: Yale University Press, 1982).

2. For biographical information here and elsewhere, I have relied on the following sources: Entrikin, *Sarah Josepha Hale;* Finley, *Lady of Godey's;* Rogers, *Sarah Josepha Hale;* and Edmund Wheeler, *The History of Newport, New Hampshire, from 1766 to 1878* (Concord, N.H.: Republican Press Association, 1879). For a short sketch of Hale's life and career, see Hoffman, "*Legacy* Profile" 47–55.

3. On republican motherhood, see Linda K. Kerber, *Women of the Republic: Intellect and Ideology in Revolutionary America* (Chapel Hill: University of North Carolina Press, 1980); and Mary Beth Norton, *Liberty's Daughters: The Revolutionary Experience of American Women, 1750–1800* (Boston: Little, Brown, 1980). On the impact of republican motherhood on women writers, see Baym, *Feminism and American Literary History* 105–20.

4. For a good but brief discussion of women's education in the late eighteenth century, see Cott, *Bonds of Womanhood* 110–12.

5. Sarah Josepha Hale, *The Ladies' Wreath: A Selection from the Female Poetic Writers of England and America* (Boston: Marsh, Capen and Lyon, 1837), 384.

6. Sarah Josepha Hale, *Woman's Record; or, Sketches of All Distinguished Women from 'The Beginning' till A.D. 1850* (New York: Harper and Brothers, 1853), 686.

7. Quoted in Wheeler, *History of Newport* 126–27.

8. Hale, *Ladies' Wreath* 385.

9. For a history of women's opportunities in teaching, see Nancy Hoffman, *Woman's "True" Profession: Voices from the History of Teaching* (Old Westbury, N.Y.: Feminist Press, 1981).

10. Finley, *Lady of Godey's* 30.

11. Hale, *Ladies' Wreath* 385–86.

12. Ibid. 385–88. While Hale probably did experience considerable economic hardship on her husband's death, her insistence that she was "left poor" was probably exaggerated. After the publication of her first volume of poems, Hale's literary efforts appeared primarily in periodicals. Since magazines did not yet pay contributors, such efforts could hardly have supported a family of six.

13. For a brief discussion of the novel's treatment of such traits as connected

with the republic's prosperity, see Baym, *Feminism and American Literary History* 168–71.

14. Sarah Josepha Hale, *Northwood: A Tale of New England*, 2 vols. (Boston: Bowles and Dearborn, 1827), 1: 23, 6, 129.

15. In this section I have relied on Blanck, *Bibliography of American Literature;* and Entrikin, *Sarah Josepha Hale.*

16. Hale and subsequent scholars have exaggerated the popular and critical success of *Northwood* and its impact on Hale's being offered the editorship of the *Ladies' Magazine.* The only known source indicating actual sales figures— the 28 April 1827 issue of the *Boston Spectator*—did report that *Northwood* was outselling comparable works published in Boston during the past several years, but it gave neither information about sales outside Boston nor any exact figures. Furthermore, the timing of this announcement—it appeared during the same month as the novel's publication—suggests that rather than providing information about actual sales, the *Spectator* announcement may have been intended as an advertisement for Hale, one of the magazine's frequent contributors.

Information about the critical success of *Northwood* has also been exaggerated, as the novel received limited and somewhat mixed reviews. The *Boston Lyceum*, for instance, commended *Northwood*'s "many beauties of an unusual kind" and predicted "deserved popularity," but it also examined its "faults," specifically the need for "more boldness in the development of intellectual capacity, more vividness in descriptive scenery, and more actual skill and power exerted in laying open the inmost recesses of the human heart" (*Boston Lyceum*, 15 April 1827, 219). The only truly positive reviews of the novel, moreover, can hardly be considered disinterested critical evaluations. One appeared in the *United States Review and Literary Gazette*, a magazine published by the same company that issued Hale's novel. Another appeared in 1833, six years after the novel's publication. By this time Hale had already achieved considerable fame as both an editor and an author. This late review therefore represents an attempt to add authority to Hale's already established literary reputation rather than an examination of a beginning writer's abilities (*American Monthly Review*, Sept. 1833, 239).

Hale was indeed offered the editing position at the *Ladies' Magazine* shortly after the novel's publication, but she probably received that offer not because of the novel's success but because friends of her husband came to her aid. According to Isabelle Webb Entrikin, the magazine's publisher was probably associated with Hale's husband's Masonic order, which had also published

her first volume of poetry (*Sarah Josepha Hale* 17). This claim is substanti-
ated by Elizabeth Oakes Smith's recollection that the Masons had "rallied to
Mrs. Hale's assistance" and started the magazine themselves in order to make
her editor. See Smith, *Selections from the Autobiography of Elizabeth Oakes
Smith,* ed. Mary Alice Wyman (Lewiston, Maine: Lewiston, 1924), 97.

17. Like many nineteenth-century periodicals, Hale's *Ladies' Magazine* used
several different titles, including *The Ladies' Magazine, The Ladies' Magazine
and Literary Gazette,* and *American Ladies' Magazine.* Like most studies, this
one will refer to the periodical by the title *Ladies' Magazine,* regardless of the
title on a particular issue under consideration. The abbreviation *LM* will be
used within parenthetical citations.

18. For overviews of early American magazines for women, see Lawrence
Martin, "The Genesis of *Godey's Lady's Book,*" *New England Quarterly* 1
(1928): 41–70; and Stearns, "Before *Godey's*" 248–55.

19. Douglas, *Feminization of American Culture* 85.

20. On appeals to moral criticism, see Nina Baym, *Novels, Readers, and
Reviewers: Responses to Fiction in Antebellum America* (Ithaca, N.Y.: Cornell
University Press, 1984), 173–95.

21. Fashion plates continued as regular features through 1833, though often
with Hale's denouncement of the interest of American women in foreign fashions. During the last three years of the publication of the *Ladies' Magazine,*
however, no fashion drawings appeared, despite their increased frequency in
other magazines. Entrikin reports that Hale dropped the engravings and fashion plates after becoming part owner of the magazine (*Sarah Josepha Hale* 53).

22. An unsigned essay titled "Education," published in the *Ladies' Magazine,* assumed that "females" had "an equality of intellect" and then argued
for the importance of mothers' educating their sons. Women may obtain an
"influence in society, that will be paramount to authority . . . if they are careful
to train their young sons to industry, and teach them knowledge, and inspire
them with the spirit of enterprize and the love of excellence" (*LM,* Sept. 1828,
422–23).

23. Hale's motives in accepting Godey's offer are not certain, but the *Ladies'
Magazine* apparently faced financial difficulties. Several appeals to delinquent
subscribers appeared in 1836, and in the announcement of her new position,
Hale said that more than one thousand dollars was due the *Ladies' Magazine*
(*LM,* July 1836, 424; Nov. 1836, 664). Hale may also have accepted the new
position because Godey agreed to let her remain in Boston, since her youngest
son attended Harvard. She did not move to Philadelphia until 1841, when her
son graduated.

The *Lady's Book* also used the titles *Godey's Lady's Book and Ladies' American Magazine, Godey's Magazine and Lady's Book, Godey's Lady's Book and Magazine,* and *Godey's Magazine.*

24. At various times other people were listed as editors, though their duties varied considerably. From 1842 until 1846, for example, Morton McMichael (later mayor of Philadelphia) was identified as one of the editors. His role, like Louis Godey's, is probably best understood as that of a publisher.

25. In one column, for instance, Godey wrote: "Mrs. Hale is not the fashion editor. How often will it be necessary for us to repeat this? Address Fashion Editor, care of L. A. Godey" (*GLB*, April 1859, 378).

26. Hale boasted: "Our writers in this department are among the most accomplished in the country. Mrs. Sedgwick, Mrs. Embury, Mrs. Gilman, Mrs. Smith, Miss Leslie, Mrs. Lee Hentz, Mrs. Stephens, Miss Gooch, Mrs. Woodhull, and many others will grace our 'Conversaziónes.'" She also promised essays by Emma Willard and her sister, Almira Phelps (*GLB*, Jan. 1837, 4–5).

27. For a brief but good overview of *Sketches of American Character* and *Traits of American Life*, see Baym, *Feminism and American Literary History* 171–72.

28. Sarah Josepha Hale, *Sketches of American Character* (Boston: Putnam and Hunt, 1829), 8.

29. For a good overview of Hale's contributions to children's literature, see M. Sarah Smedman, "Sarah Josepha Hale," in *American Writers for Children Before 1900*, ed. Glenn E. Estes, Dictionary of Literary Biography, no. 42 (Detroit: Gale Research, 1985), 207–17.

30. Hale, *Ladies' Wreath* 4.

31. Hale's advice books on housekeeping and cooking include *The Good Housekeeper; or, The Way to Live Well and to Be Well While We Live* (1839), *The Ladies' New Book of Cookery: A Practical System* (1852), *The New Household Receipt-Book* (1853), which was expanded as *Mrs. Hale's Receipts for the Million* (1857), and *Manners; or, Happy Homes and Good Society All the Year Round* (1867). *Keeping House and Housekeeping* (1845) and *Boarding Out: A Tale of Domestic Life* (1846) are both novels of domestic life. Hale edited *The White Veil: A Bridal Gift* in 1854. *The Letters of Madame de Sévigné, to Her Daughter and Friends* and *The Letters of Lady Mary Wortley Montagu* were both published in 1856. For a complete bibliography of Hale's work, see Entrikin, *Sarah Josepha Hale* 137–55; and Blanck, *Bibliography of American Literature.*

32. On Hale's *Woman's Record*, see Baym, "Onward Christian Women" 249–70. Portions of that essay appear in Baym, *Feminism and American Literary History.*

33. William Charvat, *Literary Publishing in America, 1790–1850* (Philadelphia: University of Pennsylvania Press, 1959), 8–9, 25–27.

34. Sarah Josepha Hale, *Northwood; or, Life North and South, Showing the Character of Both,* 1852, rpt., with an introduction by Rita K. Gollin (New York: Johnson Reprint, 1970), iii.

35. For figures on the average number of subscribers and circulation of the *North American Review,* the *Southern Literary Messenger,* and *Peterson's,* see Mott, *History of American Magazines* 1: 514, 645; 2: 309.

36. Frank Luther Mott, *Golden Multitudes: The Story of Best Sellers in the United States* (New York: Macmillan, 1947), 317; Smedman, "Sarah Josepha Hale," 214.

37. Quoted in Finley, *Lady of Godey's* 307.


## 3. Essentialism and Empowerment

1. For descriptions of Hale as an antifeminist, see Jill K. Conway, *The Female Experience in Eighteenth- and Nineteenth-Century America: A Guide to the History of American Women* (New York: Garland, 1982), 206; and Caroline Bird, *Enterprising Women* (New York: Norton, 1976), 13–14. Others have described Hale as one who hypocritically gained personal political power by exploiting the idea of women's subordination. See, for example, Douglas, *Feminization of American Culture* 45. For less common characterizations of Hale as a feminist, even a "fanatical" and "militant" one, see Helen Beal Woodward, *The Bold Women* (New York: Farrar, Straus and Young, 1953), 182; and James Playsted Wood, *Magazines in the United States,* 3d ed. (New York: Ronald Press, 1971), 54.

2. Diana Fuss, *Essentially Speaking: Feminism, Nature, and Difference* (New York: Routledge, 1989), xi.

3. Barbara J. Berg, for example, includes "freedom from sex-determined roles" in her definition of feminism. See Berg, *The Remembered Gate: Origins of American Feminism; The Woman and the City, 1800–1860* (New York: Oxford University Press, 1978), 5.

4. In *Mrs. Hale's Receipts for the Million* (Philadelphia: T. B. Peterson, 1857), Hale portrayed women's domestic work as equally complex and diverse, and she provided instructions for such tasks as cooking, beekeeping, quilting, and managing a dairy.

5. Sarah Josepha Hale, *The Ladies' New Book of Cookery: A Practical System,* (New York: H. Long and Brother, 1852), iii. As historians have noted, domestic

work was generally valued more highly in the nineteenth century than it had been previously. Hale's campaign here, then, is part of a larger reevaluation of domestic work. See Norton, *Liberty's Daughters* 155–70.

6. Isabelle Lehuu, "Sentimental Figures: Reading *Godey's Lady's Book* in Antebellum America," in *The Culture of Sentiment: Race, Gender, and Sentimentality in Nineteenth-Century America*, ed. Shirley Samuels (New York: Oxford University Press, 1992), 79.

7. In addition to praising the sewing machine, Hale enthusiastically supported the washing machine. In 1853 she surveyed the available models and concluded that "a thoroughly serviceable and cheap washing-machine is a thing not yet invented." She then asked her readers to "contrive some suitable apparatus" and to submit the plans to the *Lady's Book* (*GLB*, Jan. 1853, 31–32). For a historical analysis of the effect of the sewing machine on women's work, see Susan Strasser, *Never Done: A History of American Housework* (New York: Pantheon Books, 1982), 125–44.

8. On how the idea of women's moral superiority could be used to confine women to the home and also to extend women's sphere, see Glenda Gates Riley, "The Subtle Subversion: Changes in the Traditionalist Images of the American Woman," *Historian* 32 (1970): 210–27.

9. For a discussion of the political action of women as consumers in the American Revolution, see Norton, *Liberty's Daughters* 163–70.

10. Berg, *Remembered Gate* 174. See also Mary P. Ryan, *Womanhood in America: From Colonial Times to the Present* (New York: New Viewpoints, 1975), 128–29.

11. For details about the women's fair, I have relied on Finley, *Lady of Godey's* 64–73.

12. For a good overview of the Seaman's Aid Society, see Finley, *Lady of Godey's* 73–80. Additional material is available in Entrikin, *Sarah Josepha Hale* 40–41.

13. Sarah Josepha Hale, *Sixth Annual Report of the Seaman's Aid Society of the City of Boston* (Boston: James B. Dow, 1839), 4.

14. Ibid.

15. Nancy Woloch, *Women and the American Experience* (New York: Alfred A. Knopf, 1984), 123.

16. For information on nineteenth-century midwifery, see Alice Kessler-Harris, *Out to Work: A History of Wage-Earning Women in the United States* (New York: Oxford University Press, 1982), 57; and Woloch, *Women and the American Experience* 123.

17. Hale was clearly not the only woman magazine editor to invoke domestic

metaphors when discussing literary activities. Ann Stephens once compared writing novels to making broth: "You clap it on the fire cold, and let it gradually warm, hotter and hotter, until the boiling point is reached, then whisk it off—your novel is cooked" (*Mrs. Stephens' Illustrated New Monthly*, Sept. 1856, 147).

18. Kessler-Harris, *Out to Work* 48.

19. Like many scholars, Entrikin claims that the *Lady's Book* remained "completely oblivious to the approach of the Civil War, the actual conflict and the tragic years of reconstruction" (*Sarah Josepha Hale* 102). For a good but brief discussion of Hale's engagement with political issues, including the Civil War, see Hoffman, "*Legacy* Profile" 50–51.

20. Because this one editorial is most often used to define Hale's position against women's suffrage, I provide it here in its entirety: "HOW AMERICAN WOMEN SHOULD VOTE.—'I control seven votes; why should I desire to cast one myself?' said a lady who, if women went to the polls, would be acknowledged as a leader. This lady is a devoted, beloved wife, a faithful, tender mother; she has six sons. She *knows* her influence is paramount over the minds she has carefully trained. She *feels* her interests are safe confided to those her affection has made happy. She *trusts* her country will be nobly served by those whom her example has taught to believe in goodness, therefore she is proud to vote by her proxies. This is the way American women should vote, namely, by influencing rightly the votes of men" (*GLB*, April 1852, 293).

21. Paula Baker, "The Domestication of Politics: Women and American Political Society, 1780–1920," *American Historical Review* 89 (1984): 627–28.

22. Hale was not the only woman editor to equate politics with competitive partisanship. An editorial in *Mrs. Stephens' Illustrated New Monthly*, for example, portrayed politics as full of "confusion" (Sept. 1856, 146). Similarly, Anne Royall said that her weekly newspaper about congressional news, published from 1836 to 1854, would abstain from party politics: the *Huntress*, she wrote, "will advocate no party in politics, nor no sect in religion; but will expose corruption, hypocrisy and usurpation, without favor or affection, in All" (*Huntress*, 2 Dec. 1836, 4).

23. Hale, *Northwood; or, Life North and South* 407.

24. Sarah Josepha Hale, *Liberia; or, Mr. Peyton's Experiments* (1853; rpt., Upper Saddle River, N.J.: Gregg Press, 1968), 145.

## 4. The Professionalization of Authorship

1. Oliver Wendell Holmes quoted in Ida M. Tarbell, "The American Woman: Those Who Did Not Fight," *American Magazine*, March 1910, 668; Charles Dickens, *The Letters of Charles Dickens*, ed. Madeline House, Graham Storey, and Kathleen Tillotson, vol. 3 (Oxford: Clarendon Press, 1974), 115; Smith, *Selections from the Autobiography* 97–98. According to Smith, young writers "were apt to outgrow their kind mentor," but Hale "was generous to [them], paid them somewhat liberally, and kept a sharp eye upon their doings."

2. William Charvat, *The Profession of Authorship in America, 1800–1870: The Papers of William Charvat*, ed. Matthew J. Bruccoli (Columbus: Ohio State University Press, 1968), 3.

3. Ibid. 6–7. For other analyses of the nonprofessional status of authorship in the early nineteenth century, see Lewis P. Simpson, *The Man of Letters in New England and the South: Essays on the History of the Literary Vocation in America* (Baton Rouge: Louisiana State University Press, 1973); and Lawrence Buell, *New England Literary Culture: From Revolution Through Renaissance* (Cambridge: Cambridge University Press, 1986).

4. Charvat, *Literary Publishing in America* 41–43, 17–21, 30.

5. Mott, *History of American Magazines* 1: 119–20, 200. On the early nineteenth-century magazine industry, see also Tassin, *Magazine in America* 28–130; Tebbel, *American Magazine* 15–43; Wood, *Magazines in the United States* 27–44; and John Tebbel and Mary Ellen Zuckerman, *The Magazine in America, 1741–1990* (New York: Oxford University Press, 1991), 8–13.

6. Gordon S. Haight, *Mrs. Sigourney, the Sweet Singer of Hartford* (New Haven, Conn.: Yale University Press, 1930), 34–36.

7. R. Jackson Wilson, *Figures of Speech: American Writers and the Literary Marketplace, from Benjamin Franklin to Emily Dickinson* (New York: Alfred A. Knopf, 1989), 19.

8. The shift from reprints to original material actually began shortly before Hale began editing the *Lady's Book*. Louis Godey may have modeled his magazine after the *Ladies' Magazine* in hope of convincing Hale to accept his offer.

9. Allison Bulsterbaum, *"Godey's Lady's Book,"* in *American Literary Magazines: The Eighteenth and Nineteenth Centuries*, ed. Edward E. Chielens, Historical Guides to the World's Periodicals and Newspapers (New York: Greenwood Press, 1986), 146.

10. The *Lady's Book* published at least one of the newspaper responses. The

*Baltimore Visiter* faulted Louis Godey for resorting "to the narrowly selfish course of taking out a *copyright* for his book. He will rue it bitterly" (*GLB*, May 1845, 240).

11. Cathy N. Davidson, *Revolution and the Word: The Rise of the Novel in America* (New York: Oxford University Press, 1986), 35; Edward Hazen, *Popular Technology; or, Professions and Trades*, 2 vols. (New York: Harper, 1843), 2: 60.

12. In the *New Mirror*, Nathaniel Parker Willis described Louis Godey and George R. Graham as the "most liberal paymasters" (23 Dec. 1843, 192). Similarly, in his *Southern and Western Monthly Magazine and Review*, William Gilmore Simms acknowledged that although payment for authors was extremely discouraging, "Godey's and Graham's Magazines, have been among the most liberal, having paid certain of their contributors for their articles, at rates which would not discredit the reported liberality of the British publishers" (Nov. 1845, 356).

13. Mott, *History of American Magazines* 1: 504–10; Entrikin, *Sarah Josepha Hale* 61.

14. *Al Aaraaf* received little critical attention and even less favorable treatment. Hale's notice reads: "It is very difficult to speak of these poems as they deserve. A part are exceedingly boyish, feeble, and altogether deficient in the common characteristics of poetry; but then we have parts, and parts too of considerable length, which remind us of no less poet than Shelly [*sic*]. The author, who appears to be very young, is evidently a fine genius; but he wants judgment, experience, tact" (*LM*, Jan. 1830, 47).

15. Hervey Allen, *Israfel: The Life and Times of Edgar Allan Poe* (New York: Farrar and Rinehart, 1934), 547; Entrikin, *Sarah Josepha Hale* 78–79, 60; Edgar Allan Poe, *The Letters of Edgar Allan Poe*, ed. John Ward Ostrom, 2 vols. (Cambridge, Mass.: Harvard University Press, 1948), 1: 255. It is not clear why Poe was satisfied with the rate of fifty cents per page for the *Opal*. One explanation is that Poe wanted to reach the gift annual's audience. Another possibility is that Poe welcomed the opportunity to work with Hale, knowing that the *Lady's Book* could prove to be a financially rewarding outlet, even if the *Opal* was not.

16. Charvat, *Literary Publishing in America* 8–9, 55. For another overview of book publishing during this period, see John Tebbel, *A History of Book Publishing in the United States*, vol. 1, *The Creation of an Industry, 1630–1865* (New York: R. R. Bowker, 1972).

17. For biographical information on Lydia Sigourney, I have relied on

Gordon S. Haight's dated, though still useful, *Mrs. Sigourney* (1930). For a more recent overview of Sigourney's life and career, see Mary G. De Jong, "*Legacy* Profile: Lydia Howard Huntley Sigourney," *Legacy* 5 (Spring 1988): 35–43.

18. Although specific rates are not known, Hale probably paid Sigourney at least as well as other editors did, and by 1833 (if not before) Sigourney was earning enough to support herself and her family. In a letter written in 1834, Sigourney explained her financial situation: "As my husband has not recently been prosperous in his business, I have felt it my duty to aid him, by pursuing more as a trade, what had previously been only a recreation or solace. It is now considerably more than a year, since I have supplied all my expenses of clothing, charity, literature &c, beside paying the wages of a woman, who relieves me a part of the day from household care." Like Hale, Sigourney demonstrated no anguish about her professionalism; indeed, she insisted that it gave her "great pleasure" to support her family with her writing (quoted in Haight, *Mrs. Sigourney* 36).

19. According to Bradford A. Booth's analysis of American annuals and gift books, Sigourney's contributions far outnumbered those of any other writer. Sigourney published 225 items in the annuals and gift books, and the next most prolific writer, Hannah F. Gould, contributed 153 pieces. See Booth, "Taste in the Annuals," *American Literature* 14 (1942): 301.

20. Although scholars continue to suggest that the *Lady's Book* held exclusive rights to Sigourney's work, she did publish elsewhere throughout her tenure as editor. Sigourney's writing appeared occasionally, for example, in William W. Snowden's *Ladies' Companion*, published in New York, during this three-year period. Sigourney's arrangement with the *Lady's Book* apparently ended, however, when the *Ladies' Companion* featured Sigourney as one of its editors. By April 1843 Sigourney's work was again appearing in the *Lady's Book*.

21. Sigourney recalled in her autobiography, "I think now with amazement, and almost incredulity, of the number of articles I was induced by the urgency of editors to furnish. Before I ceased to keep a regular catalogue, they had amounted to more than two thousand. . . . They were divided among nearly three hundred different publications." Lydia Huntley Sigourney, *Letters of Life* (New York: D. Appleton, 1866), 366.

22. Like many literary scholars, Charvat credits Longfellow with popularizing American poetry (*Literary Publishing in America* 66–67). For an overview of the historical development of popular poetry in America that includes

Sigourney, see Janice Radway and Perry Frank, "Verse and Popular Poetry," in *Handbook of American Popular Literature*, ed. M. Thomas Inge (New York: Greenwood Press, 1988), 299–322.

23. Buell, *New England Literary Culture* 33–34.

24. John R. Adams, *Harriet Beecher Stowe*, updated ed. (Boston: Twayne, 1989), 14, 16–18. Like other critics, Adams has little regard for Stowe's early magazine work, describing a "complete analysis of Stowe's commercial writing preceding *Uncle Tom's Cabin*" as "more wearisome than profitable" (20).

In addition to the *Western Monthly Magazine* and the *Chronicle*, Stowe also wrote for another Cincinnati periodical, the *Journal and Western Luminary*, which was edited in 1836 by Stowe's brother, Henry Ward Beecher. Stowe's actual contributions to this Presbyterian weekly are unknown, as none of her work there is signed (Adams, 18).

25. Quoted in Jeanne Boydston, Mary Kelley, and Anne Margolis, *The Limits of Sisterhood: The Beecher Sisters on Women's Rights and Woman's Sphere* (Chapel Hill: University of North Carolina Press, 1988), 67.

26. Adams, *Harriet Beecher Stowe* 19–37. Further evidence of Stowe's national reputation comes from Hale herself. In 1850, well before serial publication of *Uncle Tom's Cabin* began in June 1851, Hale wrote to Stowe, asking for a biographical sketch to include in her *Woman's Record* (Boydston, Kelley, and Margolis, *Limits of Sisterhood* 46).

27. The titles and dates of Stowe's *Lady's Book* pieces are as follows: "Trials of a Housekeeper" (Jan. 1839), "The Only Daughter" (March 1839), "Olympiana" (June 1839), "Art and Nature" (Dec. 1839), "Eliza" (Jan. 1840), "Sketches from the Note Book of an Old Gentleman. No. I.—The Old Meeting-House" (Aug. 1840), "Mark Meriden" (June 1841), a translation of a Goethe ballad titled "The Fisherman Caught" (July 1841), "The Canal Boat" (Oct. 1841), and "The Tea Rose" (March 1842).

28. Quoted in Boydston, Kelley, and Margolis, *Limits of Sisterhood* 69; Noel B. Gerson, *Harriet Beecher Stowe: A Biography* (New York: Praeger, 1976), 49–50.

29. Constance Buel Burnett, *Happily Ever After: A Portrait of Frances Hodgson Burnett* (New York: Vanguard Press, n.d.), 69–71.

30. For a historical account of similar relations among nineteenth-century mothers and daughters in the United States, see Smith-Rosenberg, "Female World of Love and Ritual" 16.

31. Nathaniel Hawthorne, *The Letters, 1853–1856*, ed. Thomas Woodson, James A. Rubino, L. Neal Smith, and Norman Holmes Pearson, vol. 17 of *The*

*Centenary Edition of the Works of Nathaniel Hawthorne* (Columbus: Ohio State University Press, 1987), 304.

32. For a sense of Hale's parody of *Pierre*, consider its concluding sentence: "We have listened to its outbreathing of sweet-swarming sounds, and their melodious, mournful, wonderful, and unintelligible melodiousness has 'dropped like pendulous, glittering icicles,' with soft-ringing silveriness, upon our never-to-be-delighted-sufficiently organs of hearing; and, in the insignificant significancies of that deftly-stealing and wonderfully-serpentining melodiousness, we have found an infinite, unbounded, inexpressible mysteriousness of nothingness" (*GLB*, Oct. 1852, 390).

33. Kelley, *Private Woman, Public Stage;* letter from Sarah Josepha Hale to Kennedy Furlong, 17 Feb. 1855, Yale Collection of American Literature, Beinecke Rare Book and Manuscript Library, Yale University, New Haven, Conn.; Entrikin, *Sarah Josepha Hale* 125.

34. Letter from Sarah Josepha Hale to Harpers, 24 July 1850, Pierpont Morgan Library, New York, MA 1950. For more on relationships between women writers and publishers, see Susan Coultrap-McQuin, *Doing Literary Business: American Women Writers in the Nineteenth Century* (Chapel Hill: University of North Carolina Press, 1990).

35. Alice B. Neal presents a similar view of female authorship in a story titled "'Flora Farleigh's' Manuscript. An Attack of Authorship, and How It Was Cured." Published in the *Lady's Book* in 1856, this story features a young woman who naively decides to become an authoress, thinking it will make her rich. Unaware of the difficulties of writing and publishing, Lizzie meets a successful woman writer, who tells of her own apprenticeship: "I have written steadily and industriously fifteen years, and I have always lived very plainly" (*GLB*, Nov. 1856, 428).

36. Baym, *Novels, Readers, and Reviewers* 249–58.

37. Hale, *Woman's Record* 597–98, 624.

38. Baym, *Novels, Readers, and Reviewers* 254.

39. In her review of *Tales of the Grotesque and Arabesque*, Hale portrayed Poe as "a writer of rare and various abilities" with a "mind of unusual grasp— a vigorous power of analysis, and an acuteness of perception" (*GLB*, Jan. 1840, 46). Hale admired Thoreau's *Cape Cod* for treating the "barren subject" with "most undreamed-of interest," and she explained that "the roar of the ocean becomes a grand anthem in his ears" (*GLB*, June 1865, 556).

40. Hale, *Woman's Record* 719.

41. Ibid. 597, 615, 624.

42. For a general discussion of belittling behaviors, see Joanna Russ, *How to Suppress Women's Writing* (Austin: University of Texas Press, 1983).

## 5. Women's Reading

1. Lee Soltow and Edward Stevens, *The Rise of Literacy and the Common School in the United States: A Socioeconomic Analysis to 1870* (Chicago: University of Chicago Press, 1981), 39, 155; Tebbel, *History of Book Publishing* 207. As Soltow and Stevens have demonstrated, rates of illiteracy were based especially on geographic location, wealth, occupation, race, and gender. The rate of illiteracy at the beginning of the nineteenth century was 25 percent in the North but between 40 and 50 percent in the South. Similarly, records of merchant seamen demonstrate the gap between literacy rates for whites and nonwhites. While roughly 30 percent of Philadelphia's white seamen in 1798 were illiterate, the rate for nonwhite seamen reached more than 70 percent (Soltow and Stevens, 153, 50–51).

For discussions of the problems and issues in defining literacy and the methodological challenges in estimating rates, see Soltow and Stevens, 1–27; Davidson, *Revolution and the Word* 55–61; and E. Jennifer Monaghan, "Literacy Instruction and Gender in Colonial New England," in *Reading in America: Literature and Social History*, ed. Cathy N. Davidson (Baltimore: Johns Hopkins University Press, 1989), 53–80.

Production and sales figures of nineteenth-century book publishers indicate the potential financial benefits of appealing to this new mass audience. In the 1830s U.S. publishers produced approximately one hundred books annually; by 1855 that number had risen to more than one thousand. Profits grew as well. U.S. book publishing was worth 2.5 million dollars in 1820 and 12.5 million in 1850 (Tebbel, *History of Book Publishing* 221).

2. Kenneth A. Lockridge, *Literacy in Colonial New England: An Enquiry into the Social Context of Literacy in the Early Modern West* (New York: Norton, 1974), 13, 38; Soltow and Stevens, *Rise of Literacy* 156. As Lockridge explains, the discrepancies between men's and women's literacy cannot be dismissed by related factors such as wealth: "Women were discriminated against because they were women, not because they were poor: men who had as little wealth as the women in the sample were 80% literate while their female companions in poverty were only 45% literate. In its deliberate discrimination against women New England proclaimed its allegiance to tradition" (42).

3. Nathaniel P. Willis, quoted in Douglas, *Feminization of American Culture* 103.

4. Mary Lynn Stevens Heininger, *At Home with a Book: Reading in America, 1840–1940* (Rochester: Strong Museum, 1986), 28–30.

5. Annette Kolodny, "Reply to Commentaries: Women Writers, Literary Historians, and Martian Readers," *New Literary History* 11 (1980): 588. Judith Fetterley's influential book *The Resisting Reader: A Feminist Approach to American Fiction* (Bloomington: Indiana University Press, 1978), presents the woman reader as one who has self-consciously rejected androcentric reading strategies. For Fetterley, the way to become a woman reader is to "become a resisting rather than an assenting reader and, by this refusal to assent, to begin the process of exorcizing the male mind that has been implanted in us" (xxii). Similarly, in *On Deconstruction: Theory and Criticism After Structuralism* (Ithaca, N.Y.: Cornell University Press, 1982), Jonathan Culler has offered this definition of the woman reader: "Though it is difficult to work out in positive, independent terms what it might mean to read as a woman, one may confidently propose a purely differential definition: to read as a woman is to avoid reading as a man, to identify the specific defenses and distortions of male readings and provide correctives" (54). This image of the resisting woman reader has proved influential. Several of the essays in Elizabeth A. Flynn and Patrocinio P. Schweickart, eds., *Gender and Reading: Essays on Readers, Texts, and Contexts* (Baltimore: Johns Hopkins University Press, 1986), for example, adopt a similar paradigm.

6. The actual experiences of women readers have always differed from public descriptions of their experiences. On the way that eighteenth-century American women ignored public prescriptions of their reading, for example, see Kerber, *Women of the Republic* 235–64.

7. Heininger, *At Home with a Book* 15–17. Though reading and book ownership could function as distinguishing markers of class, neither was confined to the wealthy in antebellum America, as is suggested by the sale of cheap editions. In 1831 the Boston Society for the Diffusion of Knowledge began to publish inexpensive books for the general public for the first time in the United States. Other attempts soon followed, and by the early 1840s cheap editions flooded the market. Novels appeared in newspaper print for as little as twenty-five cents, while book publishers sold the same novels for one or two dollars. The emerging price war brought book prices as low as six cents (Tebbel, *History of Book Publishing* 241–44). By 1848 inexpensive reading material was so common that the *Lady's Book* declared: "Verily, reading is cheap" (*GLB*, Feb. 1848, 132).

8. Susan Warner, *The Wide, Wide World*, 1850, rpt., with a foreword by Jane Tompkins (New York: Feminist Press, 1987), 164, 181–82. Ellen's purchase of a Bible early in the novel also demonstrates how Christian utilitarian explanations of women's reading blend with notions of gentility. When she and her mother go on a "shopping project," Ellen must choose among the "various kinds and sizes" of Bibles. Overwhelmed by their splendor, Ellen "pore[s] in ecstasy over their varieties of type and binding" and eventually decides upon a red Bible (31). Although Ellen never denies the religious value of the purchase, the book signifies economic, rather than religious, standing. As Ann Douglas has suggested, Ellen's shopping trip in search of a Bible identifies her as a consumer: "The truth is that luxuries are by definition her needs" (*Feminization of American Culture* 64).

9. "The Lazy Novel Reader," in Heininger, *At Home with a Book* 8. On similar concerns about novel reading, see Baym, *Novels, Readers, and Reviewers*. Such fears about the incompatibility of novel reading by young women and learning proper domestic life appear even within the novels themselves. In *The Wide, Wide World*, for example, young Ellen reads no novels. In choosing from the library of the older Alice, Ellen must avoid those few "books that would do her mischief" (Warner, *Wide, Wide World* 335). Novels are not explicitly named here, but they are the implied offenders. Ellen's guardian (and eventual husband), after all, specifically instructs her to avoid reading novels. Alice, presumably, can indulge in novel reading because she has achieved the status of a genteel lady; that is, she has learned to check her own pursuit of pleasure for the benefit of her family. Ellen must abstain because she is only in the process of becoming a lady. Fearful that novel reading may lead Ellen to abandon her familial duties and thus make her a domestic idler, her guardians teach her to control her desire for individualistic pleasure.

10. Fanny Fern, "A Practical Blue Stocking," in *"Ruth Hall" and Other Writings*, ed. Joyce W. Warren, American Women Writers Series (New Brunswick, N.J.: Rutgers University Press, 1986), 232.

11. Similarly, in *Mrs. Hale's Receipts for the Million*, Hale argued the benefits of reading: "Never keep house without books. Life is not life to any great purpose where books are not" (383).

12. History assumed a special importance, for Hale named four historical texts that "should be accessible to every family in the Union": Bancroft's *History of the United States*, Sparkes's *American Biographies*, Lippincott's *Cabinet Histories of the States*, and Elizabeth Ellet's *Women of the Revolution* (*Mrs. Hale's Receipts* 383).

13. According to Kerber, the association between newspapers and men began

in the eighteenth century (*Women of the Republic* 235), and it continued, I would argue, throughout the 1800s. Nineteenth-century portraits frequently show men reading newspapers but women reading novels or magazines. An 1882 portrait of President James A. Garfield and his family portrays him reading a newspaper, while the grandmother in the portrait reads a devotional book. See Heininger, *At Home with a Book* 16.

14. Hale, *Mrs. Hale's Receipts* 383.

15. Heininger, *At Home with a Book* 31. On the association of reading with sexual pleasure, see also Baym, *Novels, Readers, and Reviewers* 54–62.

16. Smith-Rosenberg, "Female World of Love and Ritual" 14.


## 6. Hale's Aesthetics of Poetry and Fiction

1. Bulsterbaum, "*Godey's Lady's Book*," 147. For similar comments, see Mott, *History of American Magazines* 1: 578–88; Cheryl Walker, *The Nightingale's Burden: Women Poets and American Culture Before 1900* (Bloomington: Indiana University Press, 1982), 57; and Joseph N. Satterwhite, "The Tremulous Formula: Form and Technique in *Godey's* Fiction," *American Quarterly* 8 (1956): 99–113.

2. For similar sketches, see also "An Editor's Troubles" (*GLB*, June 1861, 512–16), and "How We Filled the Columns" (*GLB*, March 1865, 232–37).

3. On constraints on the poetess, see Emily Stipes Watts, *The Poetry of American Women from 1632 to 1945* (Austin: University of Texas Press, 1977), 63–82; Alicia Suskin Ostriker, *Stealing the Language: The Emergence of Women's Poetry in America* (Boston: Beacon Press, 1986), 28–37; and Walker, *Nightingale's Burden* 21–58.

4. Joanne Dobson, *Dickinson and the Strategies of Reticence: The Woman Writer in Nineteenth-Century America* (Bloomington: Indiana University Press, 1989), 61.

5. A shorter version of this essay, dated November 1836, originally appeared as the preface to Hale's anthology of women poets, *The Ladies' Wreath*.

6. Hale's confidence in this distinction between men and women poets increased over time. Although in this essay she explained that she would not use the term *poetess* because a reviewer had objected to her use of that expression in an earlier work, Hale soon reinstated *poetess*, using it to emphasize the difference between men's and women's verse. In reviews of individual writers, Hale repeatedly returned to this belief that men's poetry focused on passions and pride and women's focused on truth and faith. In one review, for instance,

she contrasted the abilities of two women poets. Though acknowledging the achievements of one who wrote "passionately (or egotistically) as men write," Hale expressed her preference for Elizabeth Barrett, a "learned and gifted, and loving-minded" poet with "high-souled devotion to humanity" (*GLB*, Sept. 1847, 154).

7. See Watts, *Poetry of American Women*; De Jong, "*Legacy* Profile" 35–43; Annie Finch, "The Sentimental Poetess in the World: Metaphor and Subjectivity in Lydia Sigourney's Nature Poetry," *Legacy* 5 (Fall 1988): 3–18; and Baym, *Feminism and American Literary History* 151–66.

8. Quoted in Walker, *Nightingale's Burden* 57.

9. Sigourney's decision not to focus on women's tears also appears to have been motivated by Christian teaching, which would suggest that the true believer has little reason to grieve when a fellow Christian has died. Given the belief that the dead loved one is in heaven, excessive mourning could be interpreted as a lack of faith.

10. If Sigourney were making a political point with this poem, her strategy would fit Joanne Dobson's discussion of nineteenth-century American women's poetry. As Dobson explains, women poets relied on techniques of indirection to express what otherwise could not be mentioned. See Dobson, *Dickinson and the Strategies of Reticence*, esp. chap. 5.

11. Sigourney's fusion of private sentiments with public power is hardly unique. Much of the sentimental literature of the nineteenth century is based on a similar assumption. Harriet Beecher Stowe's *Uncle Tom's Cabin* and Frances Ellen Watkins Harper's "The Slave Mother" are just two examples of mid-nineteenth-century texts that tried to inspire political action by appealing to private sentiments.

12. A dated, though still influential, essay by Joseph N. Satterwhite faulted the magazine's fiction for its "interminable moralizing," its "preposterous" endings that favored "the horrific and the horrendous," its stock characters, and its emphasis on suffering and melancholy. He concluded that from "the point of view of technique *Godey's* fiction might be taken as the epitome of the sentimental spirit—the triumph of matter over form, emotion over good sense, and license over restraint" ("Tremulous Formula" 109, 105, 112).

Another criticism has been that the fiction preached a doctrine similar to Barbara Welter's "cult of true womanhood," based on piety, purity, submissiveness, and domesticity. In her fine analysis of women characters in the *Lady's Book*, Laura McCall has offered an important challenge to this criticism. Having found the women characters in the *Lady's Book* to be intelligent, independent, and physically strong, McCall concludes: "The women in *Godey's* fiction were not passive, purity did not connote asexuality, piety was under-stated, and home was not the only sphere to which women aspired. None of the stereotypical traits were pervasive." See Welter, "Cult of True Woman-hood" 151–74; and Laura McCall, " 'The Reign of Brute Force Is Now Over': A Content Analysis of *Godey's Lady's Book*, 1830–1860," *Journal of the Early Republic* 9 (1989): 236.

13. On reviewers' attitudes toward "moral tendency," see Baym, *Novels, Readers, and Reviewers* 173–95. For a good analysis of a similar aesthetic described as sentimental, see Fred Kaplan, *Sacred Tears: Sentimentality in Victorian Literature* (Princeton, N.J.: Princeton University Press, 1987).

14. Kaplan, *Sacred Tears* 3.

15. On the general use of realistic rhetoric among reviewers of fiction, see Baym, *Novels, Readers, and Reviewers*, esp. 38–39. Hale's attacks on sensa-tional novels were particularly strong. One sketch in the *Lady's Book* parodied sensational fiction by describing a story that had seventeen possible titles, in-cluding "The Terrors of a Stricken Conscience; or, The Revenge of the Red Pirate," "The Maniac Mother; or, The Raving Rover of the Black Forest," and "The Midday Murder; or, The Bloody Sword of the Gay Brigand" (*GLB*, Sept. 1860, 242).

16. For a similar discussion of historical fiction, see Baym, *Feminism and American Literary History* 122–23.

17. Baym, *Woman's Fiction* 22–50.

18. Sentimental literature sometimes rewards moral characters by sending them to heaven, as in this case. *Uncle Tom's Cabin* also adopts this variation. In most sentimental literature, however, the rewards occur in this life.

# WORKS CITED

## Works by Sarah Josepha Hale

*The Ladies' New Book of Cookery: A Practical System.* New York: H. Long and Brother, 1852.

*The Ladies' Wreath: A Selection from the Female Poetic Writers of England and America.* Boston: Marsh, Capen and Lyon, 1837.

Letter to Harpers. 24 July 1850. Pierpont Morgan Library, New York. MA 1950.

Letter to Kennedy Furlong. 17 Feb. 1855. Yale Collection of American Literature. Beinecke Rare Book and Manuscript Library, Yale University, New Haven, Conn.

*Liberia; or, Mr. Peyton's Experiments.* 1853. Rpt., Upper Saddle River, N.J.: Gregg Press, 1968.

*Mrs. Hale's Receipts for the Million.* Philadelphia: T. B. Peterson, 1857.

*Northwood: A Tale of New England.* 2 vols. Boston: Bowles and Dearborn, 1827.

*Northwood; or, Life North and South, Showing the Character of Both.* 1852. Rpt., with an introduction by Rita K. Gollin. New York: Johnson Reprint, 1970.

*Sixth Annual Report of the Seaman's Aid Society of the City of Boston.* Boston: James B. Dow, 1839.

*Sketches of American Character.* Boston: Putnam and Hunt, 1829.

*Woman's Record; or, Sketches of All Distinguished Women from 'The Beginning' till A.D. 1850.* New York: Harper and Brothers, 1853.

## Nineteenth-Century Periodicals

*Agitator*, Chicago
*Akron Offering*, Akron, Ohio
*American Jewess*, New York
*American Monthly Review*, Cambridge and Boston, Mass.
*Boston Lyceum*, Boston
*Boston Spectator*, Boston
*Central Magazine*, St. Louis
*Child's Friend*, Boston
*Far and Near*, New York
*Frank Leslie's Chimney Corner*, New York
*Frank Leslie's Illustrated Newspaper*, New York
*Frank Leslie's Lady's Journal*, New York
*Godey's Lady's Book*, Philadelphia and New York
*Huntress*, Washington, D.C.
*Inland Monthly Magazine*, St. Louis
*Journalist*, New York
*Ladies' Home Journal*, Philadelphia
*Ladies' Magazine*, Boston
*Mahogany Tree*, Boston
*Michigan Farmer*, Lansing and Detroit
*Mrs. Stephens' Illustrated New Monthly*, New York
*New Mirror*, New York
*North American Review*, Boston and New York
*Philadelphia Evening Bulletin*, Philadelphia
*Portland Magazine*, Portland, Maine
*Southern and Western Monthly Magazine and Review*, Charleston, S.C.
*Whitaker's Magazine: The Rights of the South*, Charleston, S.C.
*Woman's Era*, Boston
*Woman's Exponent*, Salt Lake City
*Woman's Journal*, Boston
*Yankee and Boston Literary Gazette*, Portland, Maine

Secondary Sources

Adams, John R. *Harriet Beecher Stowe*. Updated ed. Boston: Twayne, 1989.

Allen, Hervey. *Israfel: The Life and Times of Edgar Allan Poe*. New York: Farrar and Rinehart, 1934.

*American Periodicals, 1741–1900: An Index to the Microfilm Collections*. Edited by Jean Hoornstra and Trudy Heath. Ann Arbor, Mich.: University Microfilms International, 1979.

*American Women Writers: A Critical Reference Guide from Colonial Times to the Present*. Edited by Lina Mainiero. 4 vols. New York: Frederick Ungar, 1979–82.

*Appleton's Cyclopaedia of American Biography*. Edited by James Grant Wilson and John Fiske. 6 vols. New York: D. Appleton, 1886–89.

Baker, Paula. "The Domestication of Politics: Women and American Political Society, 1780–1920." *American Historical Review* 89 (1984): 620–47.

Bardes, Barbara, and Suzanne Gossett. *Declarations of Independence: Women and Political Power in Nineteenth-Century American Fiction*. New Brunswick, N.J.: Rutgers University Press, 1990.

Baym, Nina. *Feminism and American Literary History: Essays*. New Brunswick, N.J.: Rutgers University Press, 1992.

——. *Novels, Readers, and Reviewers: Responses to Fiction in Antebellum America*. Ithaca, N.Y.: Cornell University Press, 1984.

——. "Onward Christian Women: Sarah J. Hale's History of the World." *New England Quarterly* 63 (1990): 249–70.

——. *Woman's Fiction: A Guide to Novels by and about Women in America, 1820–1870*. 2d ed. Urbana: University of Illinois Press, 1993.

Berg, Barbara J. *The Remembered Gate: Origins of American Feminism; The Woman and the City, 1800–1860*. New York: Oxford University Press, 1978.

*Biographical Dictionary of American Educators*. Edited by John F. Ohles. 3 vols. Westport, Conn.: Greenwood Press, 1978.

*Biographical Dictionary of Southern Authors*. Compiled by Lucian Lamar Knight. 1929. Rpt., Detroit: Gale Research, 1978.

Bird, Caroline. *Enterprising Women*. New York: Norton, 1976.

Blanck, Jacob, comp. *Bibliography of American Literature*. 9 vols. New Haven, Conn.: Yale University Press, 1955–91.

Booth, Bradford A. "Taste in the Annuals." *American Literature* 14 (1942): 299–302.

Boydston, Jeanne, Mary Kelley, and Anne Margolis. *The Limits of Sisterhood:*

*The Beecher Sisters on Women's Rights and Woman's Sphere.* Chapel Hill: University of North Carolina Press, 1988.

Braude, Ann. "News from the Spirit World: A Checklist of American Spiritualist Periodicals, 1847–1900." *Proceedings of the American Antiquarian Society* 99 (1989): 399–462.

Buell, Lawrence. *New England Literary Culture: From Revolution Through Renaissance.* Cambridge: Cambridge University Press, 1986.

Bullock, Penelope L. *The Afro-American Periodical Press, 1838–1909.* Baton Rouge: Louisiana State University Press, 1981.

Bulsterbaum, Allison. "*Godey's Lady's Book.*" In *American Literary Magazines: The Eighteenth and Nineteenth Centuries,* edited by Edward E. Chielens, 144–50. Historical Guides to the World's Periodicals and Newspapers. New York: Greenwood Press, 1986.

Burgess-Olson, Vicky, ed. *Sister Saints.* Studies in Mormon History, vol. 5. Provo, Utah: Brigham Young University Press, 1978.

Burnett, Constance Buel. *Happily Ever After: A Portrait of Frances Hodgson Burnett.* New York: Vanguard Press, n.d.

Burt, Olive. *First Woman Editor: Sarah J. Hale.* New York: Messner, 1960.

Butcher, Patricia Smith. *Education for Equality: Women's Rights Periodicals and Women's Higher Education, 1849–1920.* Contributions in Women's Studies, no. 111. New York: Greenwood Press, 1989.

Charvat, William. *Literary Publishing in America, 1790–1850.* Philadelphia: University of Pennsylvania Press, 1959.

———. *The Profession of Authorship in America, 1800–1870: The Papers of William Charvat.* Edited by Matthew J. Bruccoli. Columbus: Ohio State University Press, 1968.

Chielens, Edward E., ed. *American Literary Magazines: The Eighteenth and Nineteenth Centuries.* Historical Guides to the World's Periodicals and Newspapers. New York: Greenwood Press, 1986.

Clark, Suzanne. *Sentimental Modernism: Women Writers and the Revolution of the Word.* Bloomington: Indiana University Press, 1991.

Coggeshall, William T. *The Poets and Poetry of the West.* New York: Follett, Foster, 1864.

Conway, Jill K. *The Female Experience in Eighteenth- and Nineteenth-Century America: A Guide to the History of American Women.* New York: Garland, 1982.

Cott, Nancy F. *The Bonds of Womanhood: "Woman's Sphere" in New England, 1780–1835.* New Haven, Conn.: Yale University Press, 1977.

Coultrap-McQuin, Susan. *Doing Literary Business: American Women Writers in the Nineteenth Century.* Chapel Hill: University of North Carolina Press, 1990.

Culler, Jonathan. *On Deconstruction: Theory and Criticism After Structuralism.* Ithaca, N.Y.: Cornell University Press, 1982.

Davidson, Cathy N. *Revolution and the Word: The Rise of the Novel in America.* New York: Oxford University Press, 1986.

Davis, Elizabeth H. "*Godey's Lady's Book, 1830–1898.*" *Kansas State Agricultural College Bulletin* 14 (Dec. 1930): 3–29.

Dedmond, Francis B. " 'The Cask of Amontillado' and the War of the Literati." *Modern Language Quarterly* 15 (1954): 137–46.

De Jong, Mary G. "*Legacy* Profile: Lydia Howard Huntley Sigourney." *Legacy* 5 (Spring 1988): 35–43.

Dickens, Charles. *The Letters of Charles Dickens.* Edited by Madeline House, Graham Storey, and Kathleen Tillotson. Vol. 3. Oxford: Clarendon Press, 1974.

*Dictionary of American Biography.* 10 vols. and 8 supplementary vols. New York: Charles Scribner's Sons, 1946–88.

*Dictionary of American Temperance Biography: From Temperance Reform to Alcohol Research, the 1600s to the 1980s.* Edited by Mark Edward Lender. Westport, Conn.: Greenwood Press, 1984.

Dobson, Joanne. *Dickinson and the Strategies of Reticence: The Woman Writer in Nineteenth-Century America.* Bloomington: Indiana University Press, 1989.

Douglas, Ann. *The Feminization of American Culture.* New York: Alfred A. Knopf, 1977.

Duyckinck, Evert A., and George L. Duyckinck. *Cyclopaedia of American Literature.* 2 vols. New York: Scribner, 1855.

Entrikin, Isabelle Webb. *Sarah Josepha Hale and "Godey's Lady's Book."* Lancaster, Pa.: Lancaster Press, 1946.

Fern, Fanny. "A Practical Blue Stocking." In *"Ruth Hall" and Other Writings,* edited by Joyce W. Warren, 232–35. American Women Writers Series. New Brunswick, N.J.: Rutgers University Press, 1986.

Fetterley, Judith. *The Resisting Reader: A Feminist Approach to American Fiction.* Bloomington: Indiana University Press, 1978.

———, ed. *Provisions: A Reader from 19th-Century American Women.* Bloomington: Indiana University Press, 1985.

Finch, Annie. "The Sentimental Poetess in the World: Metaphor and Subjectivity in Lydia Sigourney's Nature Poetry." *Legacy* 5 (Fall 1988): 3–18.

Finley, Ruth E. *The Lady of Godey's: Sarah Josepha Hale*. Philadelphia: J. B. Lippincott, 1931.

Flanders, Bertram Holland. *Early Georgia Magazines: Literary Periodicals to 1865*. Athens: University of Georgia Press, 1944.

Flynn, Elizabeth A., and Patrocinio P. Schweickart, eds. *Gender and Reading: Essays on Readers, Texts, and Contexts*. Baltimore: Johns Hopkins University Press, 1986.

Freedman, Estelle. "Separatism as Strategy: Female Institution Building and American Feminism, 1870–1930." *Feminist Studies* 5 (1979): 512–29.

Fryatt, Norma R. *Sarah Josepha Hale: The Life and Times of a Nineteenth-Century Career Woman*. New York: Hawthorn Books, 1975.

Fuss, Diana. *Essentially Speaking: Feminism, Nature, and Difference*. New York: Routledge, 1989.

Gerson, Noel B. *Harriet Beecher Stowe: A Biography*. New York: Praeger, 1976.

Gilbert, Sandra M., and Susan Gubar. *The Madwoman in the Attic: The Woman Writer and the Nineteenth-Century Literary Imagination*. New Haven, Conn.: Yale University Press, 1979.

Griffith, George Bancroft. "Author of 'Mary's Little Lamb.'" *Granite State Magazine*, May 1906, 210–14.

Griswold, Rufus Wilmot. *The Female Poets of America*. Philadelphia: Carey and Hart, 1849.

——. *The Poets and Poetry of America*. Philadelphia: Carey and Hart, 1842.

Haight, Gordon S. *Mrs. Sigourney, the Sweet Singer of Hartford*. New Haven, Conn.: Yale University Press, 1930.

Hale, Richard Walden. "'Mary Had a Little Lamb' and Its Author." *Century Magazine*, March 1904, 738–42.

Hanaford, Phebe A. *Daughters of America; or, Women of the Century*. Augusta, Maine: True and Co., 1883.

Hart, John S. *The Female Prose Writers of America*. Philadelphia: E. H. Butler, 1852.

Hawthorne, Nathaniel. *The Letters, 1853–1856*. Edited by Thomas Woodson, James A. Rubino, L. Neal Smith, and Norman Holmes Pearson. Vol. 17 of *The Centenary Edition of the Works of Nathaniel Hawthorne*. Columbus: Ohio State University Press, 1987.

Hazen, Edward. *Popular Technology; or, Professions and Trades*. 2 vols. New York: Harper, 1843.

Heininger, Mary Lynn Stevens. *At Home with a Book: Reading in America, 1840–1940*. Rochester: Strong Museum, 1986.

Hoffman, Nancy. *Woman's "True" Profession: Voices from the History of Teaching.* Old Westbury, N.Y.: Feminist Press, 1981.

Hoffman, Nicole Tonkovich. *"Legacy* Profile: Sarah Josepha Hale." *Legacy* 7 (Fall 1990): 47–55.

Johannsen, Albert. *The House of Beadle and Adams and Its Dime and Nickel Novels: The Story of a Vanished Literature.* 2 vols. Norman: University of Oklahoma Press, 1950.

Kaplan, Fred. *Sacred Tears: Sentimentality in Victorian Literature.* Princeton, N.J.: Princeton University Press, 1987.

Kastner, Joseph. "The Tale Behind Mary's Little Lamb." *New York Times Magazine,* 13 April 1980, 116–19.

Kelley, Mary. *Private Woman, Public Stage: Literary Domesticity in Nineteenth-Century America.* New York: Oxford University Press, 1984.

Kelly, R. Gordon. *Children's Periodicals of the United States.* Historical Guides to the World's Periodicals and Newspapers. Westport, Conn.: Greenwood Press, 1984.

Kerber, Linda K. "Separate Spheres, Female Worlds, Woman's Place: The Rhetoric of Women's History." *Journal of American History* 75 (1988): 9–39.

———. *Women of the Republic: Intellect and Ideology in Revolutionary America.* Chapel Hill: University of North Carolina Press, 1980.

Kessler-Harris, Alice. *Out to Work: A History of Wage-Earning Women in the United States.* New York: Oxford University Press, 1982.

Kolodny, Annette. "Reply to Commentaries: Women Writers, Literary Historians, and Martian Readers." *New Literary History* 11 (1980): 587–92.

Kraditor, Aileen S., ed. *Up from the Pedestal: Selected Writings in the History of American Feminism.* Chicago: Quadrangle Books, 1968.

Landes, Joan B. *Women and the Public Sphere in the Age of the French Revolution.* Ithaca, N.Y.: Cornell University Press, 1988.

Laqueur, Thomas. *Making Sex: Body and Gender from the Greeks to Freud.* Cambridge, Mass.: Harvard University Press, 1990.

Lehuu, Isabelle. "Sentimental Figures: Reading *Godey's Lady's Book* in Antebellum America." In *The Culture of Sentiment: Race, Gender, and Sentimentality in Nineteenth-Century America,* edited by Shirley Samuels, 73–91. New York: Oxford University Press, 1992.

Lerner, Gerda. "The Lady and the Mill Girl: Changes in the Status of Women in the Age of Jackson." *Midcontinent American Studies Journal* 10 (1969): 5–15.

Lippy, Charles H., ed. *Religious Periodicals of the United States: Academic and Scholarly Journals*. Historical Guides to the World's Periodicals and Newspapers. New York: Greenwood Press, 1986.

Littlefield, Daniel F., Jr., and James W. Parins. *American Indian and Alaska Native Newspapers and Periodicals, 1826–1924*. Historical Guides to the World's Periodicals and Newspapers. Westport, Conn.: Greenwood Press, 1984.

Lockridge, Kenneth A. *Literacy in Colonial New England: An Enquiry into the Social Context of Literacy in the Early Modern West*. New York: Norton, 1974.

Martin, Lawrence. "The Genesis of *Godey's Lady's Book*." *New England Quarterly* 1 (1928): 41–70.

Marzolf, Marion Tuttle. *The Danish-Language Press in America*. New York: Arno Press, 1979.

———. *Up from the Footnote: A History of Women Journalists*. New York: Hastings House, 1977.

Mason, Philip P., ed. *The Literary Voyager; or, Muzzeniegun*, by Henry Rowe Schoolcraft. East Lansing: Michigan State University Press, 1962.

May, Caroline. *The American Female Poets*. Philadelphia: Lindsay and Blakiston, 1848.

McCall, Laura. " 'The Reign of Brute Force Is Now Over': A Content Analysis of *Godey's Lady's Book*, 1830–1860." *Journal of the Early Republic* 9 (1989): 217–36.

Monaghan, E. Jennifer. "Literacy Instruction and Gender in Colonial New England." In *Reading in America: Literature and Social History*, edited by Cathy N. Davidson, 53–80. Baltimore: Johns Hopkins University Press, 1989.

Mott, Frank Luther. *Golden Multitudes: The Story of Best Sellers in the United States*. New York: Macmillan, 1947.

———. *A History of American Magazines*. 5 vols. Cambridge, Mass.: Harvard University Press, 1938–68.

*The National Cyclopaedia of American Biography*. 63 vols. New York: James T. White, 1892–1984.

Norton, Mary Beth. *Liberty's Daughters: The Revolutionary Experience of American Women, 1750–1800*. Boston: Little, Brown, 1980.

*Notable American Women, 1607–1950: A Biographical Dictionary*. Edited by Edward T. James. 3 vols. Cambridge, Mass.: Belknap Press of Harvard University Press, 1971.

Ostriker, Alicia Suskin. *Stealing the Language: The Emergence of Women's Poetry in America*. Boston: Beacon Press, 1986.

Peel, Robert. *Mary Baker Eddy: The Years of Authority*. New York: Holt, Rinehart and Winston, 1977.

———. *Mary Baker Eddy: The Years of Trial.* New York: Holt, Rinehart and Winston, 1971.

Poe, Edgar Allan. *The Letters of Edgar Allan Poe.* Edited by John Ward Ostrom. 2 vols. Cambridge, Mass.: Harvard University Press, 1948.

Radway, Janice, and Perry Frank. "Verse and Popular Poetry." In *Handbook of American Popular Literature,* edited by M. Thomas Inge, 299–322. New York: Greenwood Press, 1988.

Read, Thomas Buchanan. *The Female Poets of America.* Philadelphia: E. H. Butler, 1849.

Riley, Glenda Gates. "The Subtle Subversion: Changes in the Traditionalist Image of the American Woman." *Historian* 32 (1970): 210–27.

Riley, Sam G. *Magazines of the American South.* Historical Guides to the World's Periodicals and Newspapers. New York: Greenwood Press, 1986.

Rogers, Sherbrooke. *Sarah Josepha Hale: A New England Pioneer, 1788–1879.* Grantham, N.H.: Tompson and Rutter, 1985.

Rosenberg, Rosalind. *Beyond Separate Spheres: Intellectual Roots of Modern Feminism.* New Haven, Conn.: Yale University Press, 1982.

Russ, Joanna. *How to Suppress Women's Writing.* Austin: University of Texas Press, 1983.

Ryan, Mary P. *Womanhood in America: From Colonial Times to the Present.* New York: New Viewpoints, 1975.

Satterwhite, Joseph N. "The Tremulous Formula: Form and Technique in *Godey's* Fiction." *American Quarterly* 8 (1956): 99–113.

Schiebinger, Londa. *The Mind Has No Sex?: Women in the Origins of Modern Science.* Cambridge, Mass.: Harvard University Press, 1989.

Shevelow, Kathryn. "Fathers and Daughters: Women as Readers of the *Tatler.*" In *Gender and Reading: Essays on Readers, Texts, and Contexts,* edited by Elizabeth A. Flynn and Patrocinio P. Schweickart, 107–23. Baltimore: Johns Hopkins University Press, 1986.

Showalter, Elaine. *Sister's Choice: Tradition and Change in American Women's Writing.* Oxford: Clarendon Press, 1991.

Sigourney, Lydia Huntley. *Letters of Life.* New York: D. Appleton, 1866.

Silverman, Kenneth. *Edgar A. Poe: Mournful and Never-Ending Remembrance.* New York: HarperCollins, 1991.

Simpson, Lewis P. *The Man of Letters in New England and the South: Essays on the History of the Literary Vocation in America.* Baton Rouge: Louisiana State University Press, 1973.

Smedman, M. Sarah. "Sarah Josepha Hale." In *American Writers for Chil-*

*dren Before 1900*, edited by Glenn E. Estes, 207–17. Dictionary of Literary Biography, no. 42. Detroit: Gale Research, 1985.

Smith, Elizabeth Oakes. *Selections from the Autobiography of Elizabeth Oakes Smith*. Edited by Mary Alice Wyman. Lewiston, Maine: Lewiston, 1924.

Smith-Rosenberg, Carroll. "The Female World of Love and Ritual: Relations Between Women in Nineteenth-Century America." *Signs: Journal of Women in Culture and Society* 1 (1975): 1–29.

Snorgrass, J. William. "Black Women and Journalism, 1800–1950." *Western Journal of Black Studies* 6 (1982): 150–58.

Solomon, Martha M., ed. *A Voice of Their Own: The Woman Suffrage Press, 1840–1910*. Tuscaloosa: University of Alabama Press, 1991.

Soltow, Lee, and Edward Stevens. *The Rise of Literacy and the Common School in the United States: A Socioeconomic Analysis to 1870*. Chicago: University of Chicago Press, 1981.

*Standard Encyclopedia of the Alcohol Problem*. Edited by Ernest Hurst Cherrington. 6 vols. Westerville, Ohio: American Issue Publishing, 1925–30.

Stearns, Bertha Monica. "Before *Godey's*." *American Literature* 2 (1930): 248–55.

———. "Early Factory Magazines in New England: The Lowell Offering and Its Contemporaries." *Journal of Economic and Business History* 2 (1930): 685–705.

———. "Early New England Magazines for Ladies." *New England Quarterly* 2 (1929): 420–57.

———. "Early Philadelphia Magazines for Ladies." *Pennsylvania Magazine of History and Biography* 64 (1940): 479–91.

———. "Early Western Magazines for Ladies." *Mississippi Valley Historical Review* 18 (1931): 319–30.

———. "Philadelphia Magazines for Ladies, 1830–1860." *Pennsylvania Magazine of History and Biography* 69 (1945): 207–19.

———. "Reform Periodicals and Female Reformers, 1830–1860." *American Historical Review* 37 (1932): 678–99.

———. "Southern Magazines for Ladies, 1819–1860." *South Atlantic Quarterly* 31 (1932): 70–87.

*The Story of Mary and Her Little Lamb, as Told by Mary and Her Neighbors and Friends*. Dearborn, Mich.: Mr. and Mrs. Henry Ford, 1928.

Stern, Madeleine B. *Purple Passage: The Life of Mrs. Frank Leslie*. Norman: University of Oklahoma Press, 1953.

Strasser, Susan. *Never Done: A History of American Housework*. New York: Pantheon Books, 1982.

Swisshelm, Jane. *Half a Century*. Chicago: J. G. Swisshelm, 1880.

Tarbell, Ida M. "The American Woman: Those Who Did Not Fight." *American Magazine*, March 1910, 656–69.

Tassin, Algernon. *The Magazine in America*. New York: Dodd, Mead, 1916.

Taylor, William R. *Cavalier and Yankee: The Old South and American National Character*. New York: George Braziller, 1961.

Tebbel, John. *The American Magazine: A Compact History*. New York: Hawthorn Books, 1969.

———. *A History of Book Publishing in the United States*. Vol. 1, *The Creation of an Industry, 1630–1865*. New York: R. R. Bowker, 1972.

Tebbel, John, and Mary Ellen Zuckerman. *The Magazine in America, 1741–1990*. New York: Oxford University Press, 1991.

"The True Story of Mary's Little Lamb." *Dearborn Independent*, 26 March 1927, 12–13, 20–22.

Van Voris, Jacqueline. *Carrie Chapman Catt: A Public Life*. New York: Feminist Press, 1987.

Vaughan, Alma F. "Pioneer Women of the Missouri Press." *Missouri Historical Review* 64 (1970): 289–305.

Venable, W. H. *Beginnings of Literary Culture in the Ohio Valley*. Cincinnati: Robert Clarke, 1891.

Walker, Cheryl. *The Nightingale's Burden: Women Poets and American Culture Before 1900*. Bloomington: Indiana University Press, 1982.

———, ed. *American Women Poets of the Nineteenth Century: An Anthology*. American Women Writers Series. New Brunswick, N.J.: Rutgers University Press, 1992.

Warner, Susan. *The Wide, Wide World*. 1850. Rpt., with a foreword by Jane Tompkins. New York: Feminist Press, 1987.

Warren, E. A. "The True Story of Mary and Her Little Lamb." *National Magazine*, June 1897, 251–55.

Watts, Emily Stipes. *The Poetry of American Women from 1632 to 1945*. Austin: University of Texas Press, 1977.

Weichlein, William J. *A Checklist of American Music Periodicals, 1850–1900*. Detroit Studies in Music Bibliography, no. 16. Detroit: Information Coordinators, 1970.

Weil, Dorothy. *In Defense of Women: Susanna Rowson, 1762–1824*. University Park: Pennsylvania State University Press, 1976.

Welter, Barbara. "The Cult of True Womanhood, 1820–1860." *American Quarterly* 18 (1966): 151–74.

Wheeler, Edmund. *The History of Newport, New Hampshire, from 1766 to 1878.* Concord, N.H.: Republican Press Association, 1879.

Whitton, Mary Ormsbee. *These Were the Women, U.S.A., 1776–1860.* New York: Hastings House, 1954.

*Who Was Who Among North American Authors.* 2 vols. Gale Composite Biographical Dictionary Series, no. 1. Detroit: Gale Research, 1976.

*Who Was Who in America.* 10 vols. to date. Chicago: A. N. Marquis, 1943–.

Willard, Frances E. *Woman and Temperance; or, The Work and Workers of the Woman's Christian Temperance Union.* 3d ed. Hartford, Conn.: Park Publishing, 1883.

Willard, Frances E., and Mary A. Livermore, eds. *American Women.* 2 vols. 1897. Rpt., Detroit: Gale Research, 1973.

Wilson, R. Jackson. *Figures of Speech: American Writers and the Literary Marketplace, from Benjamin Franklin to Emily Dickinson.* New York: Alfred A. Knopf, 1989.

Woloch, Nancy. *Women and the American Experience.* New York: Alfred A. Knopf, 1984.

*Woman's Who's Who of America: A Biographical Dictionary of Contemporary Women of the United States and Canada.* Edited by John William Leonard. New York: American Commonwealth, 1914.

*Women's Periodicals and Newspapers from the 18th Century to 1981: A Union List of the Holdings of Madison, Wisconsin, Libraries.* Edited by James P. Danky, compiled by Maureen E. Hady, Barry Christopher Noonan, and Neil E. Strache. Boston: G. K. Hall, 1982.

Wood, James Playsted. *Magazines in the United States.* 3d ed. New York: Ronald Press, 1971.

Woodward, Helen Beal. *The Bold Women.* New York: Farrar, Straus and Young, 1953.

Zagarell, Sandra A. Introduction to *A New Home, Who'll Follow?; or, Glimpses of Western Life,* by Caroline M. Kirkland. Edited by Sandra A. Zagarell. American Women Writers Series. New Brunswick, N.J.: Rutgers University Press, 1990.

# INDEX